Nanotechnology

ENVIRONMENTAL LAW, POLICY, AND BUSINESS CONSIDERATIONS

Lynn L. Bergeson, Editor

ABA
AMERICAN BAR ASSOCIATION
Section of Environment, Energy, and Resources

Cover design by ABA Publishing.

Printed in the United States of America
14 13 12 11 10 5 4 3 2 1

Library of Congress Cataloging-in-Publication Data

Nanotechnology : environmental law, policy, and business considerations / edited by Lynn L. Bergeson.
    p. cm.
Includes bibliographical references and index.
ISBN-13: 978-1-60442-582-6
    1. Nanostructured materials industry—Law and legislation—United States. 2. Environmental law—United States. 3. Nanostructured materials industry—Environmental aspects—United States. I. Bergeson, Lynn L., 1953–

KF1890.H53 U15 2009
343.73'0786205—dc22

                                                                                    2009043610

CONTENTS

CHAPTER 5
Nanotechnology and the Endangered Species Act 117

CHAPTER 6
RCRA and Nanotechnology 131

GLOSSARY

PREFACE AND ACKNOWLEDGMENTS

Nanotechnology is one of the most intriguing industrial phenomena of the early twenty-first century. Consumer products derived from the application of engineered nanotechnologies now number in the many hundreds, and new products are entering the market at a fast clip.

As the universe of applied nanotechnology is burgeoning, so also are the questions raised about the potential impacts of exposure to nanoscale materials on human health and the environment. The properties of these materials are still not well understood in all cases, and many challenges must be overcome to understand more completely the possible health and environmental effects, risks, and benefits of nanoscale materials and nano-enabled products.

The commercialization of nanotechnology poses challenges for environmental regulators and policy-makers, as well as for the many government scientists, engineers, and lawyers who are now focusing on the implications and applications of nanotechnology. The core United States environmental statutes with which legal practitioners are very familiar are products of twentieth-century end-of-pipe treatment and control thinking, and are being applied in new and creative ways to address the challenges and promote the benefits of emerging nanotechnologies. Whether and how federal agencies deploy the broad statutory authority granted under these laws to adequately address concerns that have been raised with respect to the implications of nanotechnology remains to be seen, as do questions going to health and environmental effects, exposure pathway, and persistence. Unique properties of nanoparticles, such as their large surface area relative to particle size, lend complexity to the task of regulation.

This book is intended to assist legal practitioners, regulatory professionals, consultants, in-house counsel, product managers, and others in understanding the application of the core United States environmental statutes to nanotechnologies. Collectively, the contributors to this volume have sought to identify regulatory, governance, and business issues of ongoing—and evolving—importance in an area that is as fascinating as it is challenging. Necessarily there is a moving target aspect to writing usefully about nanotechnology, whether from the perspective of science, business, law, policy, or government. Still, the contributors have endeavored, and we believe have succeeded, in producing a treatise that will remain relevant for the foreseeable future even as commercialized technology, and those charged with regulating it, are moving forward.

* * *

A book is a result of the effort of many, and this book is no exception. Thanks to all who have contributed. Special thanks to Bethami Auerbach for her scholarship and enduring commitment to excellent writing, and Allison MacDougall Davidson for her research, editing, and tireless efforts in preparing this book for publication. Finally, thanks to the many, many nano stakeholders around the world who are committed to the responsible development of nanotechnologies.

ABOUT THE EDITOR

Lynn L. Bergeson is managing director of Bergeson & Campbell, P.C. (B&C), a law firm based in Washington, D.C., that concentrates on conventional and engineered nanoscale chemical, pesticide, and other specialty chemical product approval, regulation, litigation, and associated business issues. Ms. Bergeson is also president of the Acta Group, L.L.C., and the Acta Group EU, Ltd, B&C's consulting affiliates, with offices in Washington, D.C., and Manchester, U.K., respectively. Ms. Bergeson counsels clients on a wide range of issues pertaining to chemical hazard, exposure and risk assessment, risk communication, and related legal and regulatory aspects of conventional and nanoscale chemical regulatory programs under the Federal Insecticide, Fungicide, and Rodenticide Act (FIFRA), the Toxic Substances Control Act (TSCA), and the Registration, Evaluation, Authorization and Restriction of Chemicals (REACH) regulation, and on issues pertinent to nanotechnology and other emerging transformative technologies. Ms. Bergeson is former chair of the American Bar Association Section of Environment, Energy, and Resources (2005–2006) and current vice chair of the Section's Committee on Pesticides, Chemical Regulation, and Right-to-Know, and serves in other ABA leadership capacities. Ms. Bergeson is listed in *The International Who's Who of Business Lawyers* (2006–2009) and *The Chambers USA: America's Leading Lawyers for Business* (2005–2009). Ms. Bergeson is a graduate of Michigan State University (B.A., magna cum laude), and the Columbus School of Law, Catholic University of America, where she was a member of the Law Review. She is admitted to the bar of the District of Columbia and several federal circuit courts.

CHAPTER I

Introduction

The rapidly expanding commercialization of nanotechnology is one of the most intriguing industrial phenomena of the early 21st century. Consumer products derived from the application of engineered nanotechnologies now number over a thousand[1] and run the gamut from sunscreens to paints to computer hard drives and beyond. As observed in Chapter 9 of this book, in less than ten years, nanomaterials are expected to evolve from today's stain-resistant treated fabrics and stronger tennis racquets to genetic therapies at the nano level and self-assembling molecules—at a projected level of some $1 trillion in goods and services by 2015.[2]

Just as the universe of applied nanotechnology is burgeoning, so are the questions raised about the potential impacts of exposure to nanoscale materials on human health and the environment. The properties of these materials are still imperfectly understood by science and health professionals, but inquiry is complicated because it goes beyond the substantial task of research into possible health and environmental effects. Nanotechnology also offers pathways for delivery—literally—of beneficial advances in both health care and environmental cleanup technologies. Because applied nanotechnology offers the potential for both positive and negative impacts on society and the environment, it eludes any simplistic or overly general assessment. The most challenging scenario is posed by beneficial applications that are accompanied by a downside of negative health or environmental effects. Future policy choices and value judgments—in other words, balancing acts—will affect how fully or freely, if at all, such technologies can be commercialized.

The commercialization of nanotechnology poses major challenges for environmental regulators and policymakers as well as the many government scientists, engineers, and lawyers who are now focusing on the implications and applications of nanotechnology. The environmental statutes that today are household names within the regulatory community (and

---

*This chapter was prepared by Lynn L. Bergeson, Bergeson & Campbell, P.C.

often beyond) were enacted through years-long efforts of blood, sweat, and compromise. Most of these statues have seldom been amended significantly, and little new environmental legislation of consequence (except in the area of food quality) has been enacted in recent years. As this introduction notes, and as discussed more fully in this volume, the existing environment laws and their implementing regulations generally are well equipped—in the abstract—to encompass nanomaterials in the context of their respective missions. Whether and how federal agencies deploy the broad statutory authority granted under these laws to adequately address concerns that have been raised regarding the implications of nanotechnology remains to be seen, as do questions going to health and environmental effects, exposure pathway, and persistence. Unique properties of nanoparticles, such as their large surface area relative to particle size, lend complexity to the task of regulation. The same is true of the increasingly ambitious plans by researchers and commercial venturers to develop nanotechnology-based approaches to health- and environment-enhancing tools, such as drug delivery devices or groundwater pollution sensors.

A threshold issue yet to be resolved is the definition of such basic terms as "nanotechnology," "nanomaterials," and "nanoparticles" themselves. While it is agreed that nanotechnology involves the design, structure, properties, manipulation, or control of materials no more than one-billionth of a meter in size,[3] standard-setting organizations (with participation by government agencies and other stakeholders) still are grappling with how the core terminology should be defined.[4] Questions of regulatory definition also remain to be addressed. For purposes of this book, "nanomaterials," "nanoparticles," and similar terms refer to those that do not exceed the size specified earlier and are engineered (intentionally produced) rather than naturally occurring or the by-product of an industrial process such as combustion. This definition is consistent with EPA's own approach.[5]

Among the federal environmental statutes covered in this book, the Toxic Substances Control Act (TSCA) is perhaps the one that policymakers and pundits alike point to first in analyzing the options for regulating engineered nanomaterials. TSCA offers a uniquely attractive regulatory option because, as Chapter 2 observes, it is by and large a front-loaded statute, directing the U.S. Environmental Protection Agency (EPA) to regulate chemicals before they come to market and while they are in use. In this respect, TSCA's basic focus differs from that of most other environmental statutes, which generally control the end products of industrial activity—thus the language of "discharge," "effluent," "emission," "waste," "pollutant," and so forth. TSCA creates a regulatory scheme for existing and new "chemical substances," a statutory term of art that is broadly defined to encompass "any organic or inorganic substances of a particular molecular identity," including chemical mixtures or elements.[6] Accordingly, nanomaterials that are "organic or inorganic" substances are amenable to regulation under TSCA. The unique physical properties or defining characteristics beyond molecular identity take on added significance when it comes to nanomaterials, however, and Chapter 2 discusses how the "particular molecular identity" definition may provide the flexibility to make it workable in this context.

A key provision from the standpoint of regulating nanomaterials is TSCA Section 5, which authorizes EPA to regulate "new chemical substances" (under Section 5(a)(1)) or "significant new uses" (under Section 5(a)(2)) of both new and "existing" substances—those already listed on TSCA's Chemical Substances Inventory—before they can be manufactured, imported, processed, or distributed for commercial purposes. EPA's Section 5(a)(1) premanufacture authority to address the health and environmental risk that new chemicals may pose applies to nanoscale chemical substances just as it does to other new chemicals. Additionally, under EPA's Section 5(a)(2) authority to regulate "significant new uses," TSCA can extend to nanoscale versions of such listed substances. TSCA defines "chemical substance" in terms of "molecular identity," and EPA points to molecular identity as the means for determining whether to proceed under Section 5(a)(1) or (a)(2); a nanoscale material with the same molecular identity as a substance on the TSCA Inventory is considered an "existing" chemical substance.[7]

As Chapter 2 explains, the application of these definitions and criteria is more straightforward in principle than in practice, particularly in view of the technical challenges that can arise in distinguishing between nanoscale and conventional-sized materials of the same molecular identity as well as the range of properties and risk profiles that characterize engineered nanomaterials. Despite the potential conundrums involved in sorting out "new" versus "existing" in the nano realm, the significant regulatory conclusion is that EPA has essentially the same oversight and risk assessment tools available in either case to address nanoscale materials under TSCA.

Chapter 3 discusses the regulatory tools available to EPA under the Federal Insecticide, Fungicide, and Rodenticide Act (FIFRA) to address health and environmental risks from nanopesticides—nano-sized particles of new or modified pesticidal active ingredients or other engineered nanostructures with useful pesticidal properties, such as the enhanced delivery of agrochemicals in the field. FIFRA bars the sale and use of unregistered pesticides. Significantly, EPA has affirmed that pesticide products containing nanomaterials are subject to FIFRA's core registration review process under Section 3.[8] Prospective registrants must submit or cite data to allow EPA to determine that the benefits will outweigh the risks of a pesticide and that unreasonable adverse effects either will not result or reliably can be avoided by conditions EPA attaches to the registration. EPA's enforcement tools in the face of a violation are varied and formidable.

For nanopesticides, threshold questions of interpretation remain, including whether the incorporation of a nanomaterial would change a pesticide product for which EPA already has issued a registration—and whether a nanopesticide would be considered unregistered if a registration has been issued for the conventional version. As Chapter 3 discusses, the inquiry goes to how the risk assessments for the two compare or whether the pesticide claims differ, rather than to a TSCA-like question of molecular identity, and thus is more squarely in the domain of EPA's discretion.

Despite the thousands of approved registrations extant, however, EPA has stated that no previously registered product would be considered a nanopesticide under current nanotechnology definitions.[9] EPA also has yet to determine whether registration requirements specifically designed to address nanopesticides are needed and whether a nano-appropriate data set for risk assessment purposes should be created. Surprisingly, despite the march of new consumer nanoproducts into the marketplace, through February 2009 EPA had not yet issued a notice indicating the receipt of any application for a pesticide product or active ingredient characterized as a "nanopesticide."[10]

The experimental use permit (EUP) provisions in FIFRA Section 5 enable EPA's regulatory reach to extend back as far as the preregistration research and development (R&D) activities by pesticide producers. In contrast to TSCA, which exempts R&D activities from premanufacture notice requirements, FIFRA requires pesticide developers to notify EPA and obtain a permit before conducting R&D.[11] Under Section 5 and its own implementing regulations, EPA is able to fashion a given EUP to address the circumstances of the research on the material involved.[12]

Unlike the product-directed focus of TSCA (on chemical substances) or FIFRA (on pesticide active ingredients), the Clean Air Act (CAA), discussed in Chapter 4, is directed largely toward controlling pollutant emissions from industrial processes and motor vehicles. Although EPA already regulates, through National Ambient Air Quality Standards (NAAQS) established under CAA Sections 108 and 109, emissions of very small particulates—those with a diameter of 25 microns or less

(PM$_{2.5}$)—these by-products of conventional combustion technologies are distinct in important ways from engineered nanoparticles.

As explained in Chapter 4, the minuscule size, negligible mass, and relatively larger surface area (resulting in higher reactivity) of nanoparticles makes them act quite differently from pollutants now regulated under the CAA, including those subject to the PM$_{2.5}$ standard. As a practical matter, this means that conventional methods are largely unsuited to identify, monitor, measure, or control engineered nanoparticulate emissions. For example, while EPA relies substantially on air pollution modeling to inform and support its regulatory effects, current models describe target pollutant behavior in terms of mass, which is not meaningful as applied to nanoparticles and thus precludes their reliable measurement or predictions as to their fate and transport in the atmosphere. Beyond this, while many types of air pollutant control standards authorized by the CAA are wholly or partially health based, the health risks posed by nanoparticles in general are not yet well defined, even as their study is an ongoing priority. Thus, while the CAA offers time-tested pathways for regulating a variety of air pollutants, whether characterized as "criteria" pollutants—such as PM$_{2.5}$—under Sections 108 and 109, or as hazardous air pollutants under Section 112, state-of-the-art information and tools are not yet adequate for regulating engineered nanoparticles.

While some environmental statutes may provide the means or the mandate to regulate nanomaterials directly, the Endangered Species Act (ESA) operates one step further removed: nanotechnology may come squarely into the ESA's purview through its potential impacts on the animal or plant species listed under Section 4 as "endangered" or "threatened" and on the "critical habitats" that such protected species depend upon.[13] As Chapter 5 explains, although ESA issues tend to arise most prominently where major land-disturbing activities are involved—such as construction, mining, and timber-harvesting projects—nothing prevents the ESA's broad reach and robust protections from extending to new technologies. Indeed, the application of the ESA to Navy sonar and wind energy turbines underscores its breadth.[14] It is fair to expect that impacts associated with the development, use, and disposal of nanomaterials will see increasing attention under the ESA as its uses become more widespread.[15]

Chapter 5 proceeds to consider the two most often employed protective measures under the ESA—the obligation to consult imposed on federal agencies by Section 7(a)(2) and the "take" prohibition under Section 9—and concludes that Section 7(a)(2) represents the more attractive pathway for addressing the potential impacts of nanotechnology on vulnerable species and habitats. Among other complications, the gaps in the current understanding of nanomaterials make it difficult to satisfy the "proximate cause" test that the Supreme Court articulated in the leading "take" decision.[16] The potential for harsh penalties under Section 9 may chill the development of nanomaterials if prosecutions are pursued aggressively against good-faith offenders.

By contrast, Section 7(a)(2) is less legalistic and more process oriented in requiring consultation with the appropriate "Service" to ensure that agency actions—those authorized, funded, or carried out by a federal agency—are unlikely to "jeopardize" listed species or "result in the destruction or adverse modification" of a critical habitat. Often private stakeholders are affected, as where the grant of a permit or license is involved; and the protection of listed species becomes an important part of a larger process, frequently at an early stage. At the same time, the Section 7(a)(2) requirement that each agency use "the best scientific and commercial data available" does not demand a no-risk determination at a level of certainty that would be unrealistic with the current level of knowledge about nanomaterials. The state-of-the-art focus does not lose sight of the strongly protective nature of the ESA but does not routinely result in a breakdown of the process while exhaustive data development obligations are satisfied.

The inevitable other side of the nanotechnology production coin is the generation of an ever-increasing variety of nanomaterial wastes that must be handled, stored, treated, and disposed of effectively and safely. Chapter 6 explores the key waste management challenges presented by such hazardous secondary waste nanomaterials and concludes that in most instances the Resource Conservation and Recovery Act (RCRA) and EPA's implementing regulations are a good fit for addressing these unique and challenging substances. But evolving nanotechnologies are more than another regulatory challenge; although part of the waste management problem, they also hold out promise as at least a small part of the solution. Among other projected uses, nanomaterials may well play a key role in the creation of sensors that can efficiently detect and identify small concentrations of toxic compounds harmful to the environment. Yet it is the risk posed by the releases—intended or not—of nanomaterials that necessarily takes center stage.

RCRA's comprehensive reach, together with EPA's implementing regulations, provide a workable framework for addressing the systematic management of secondary hazardous wastes that contain nanomaterials. So long as they meet the definitions for "solid" and "hazardous" wastes that are discarded, these wastes are amenable to regulation under RCRA.

EPA defines hazardous wastes as those that exhibit a "hazardous" characteristic or those it has specifically added to its regulatory hazardous waste list. The characteristic properties for which a waste will be deemed hazardous may well be affected by whether it is nano or conventional (i.e., reactivity, toxicity, ignitability, and corrosivity may all be affected by the size of the waste), and in most cases EPA's regulations will prove a good fit. Where a characteristic specific to the nanoscale of the material—for example, its unusually large surface area relative to particle size—may enhance its potential toxicity, EPA has the authority to add a new characteristic to capture this scenario.

EPA may determine to reexamine its listed hazardous wastes as well—for instance, to address a scenario in which a nanoscale chemical may lack the hazardous effects of the conventional version.[17] EPA can also address the potential for overregulation if a small amount of nanomaterial inappropriately triggers RCRA coverage. EPA also may need to revisit yet again its regulatory definition of "solid waste" under RCRA, for which it created an exclusion in 2008 for certain recycled materials not deemed to be discarded; as observed in Chapter 6, manufacturers may be expected to pursue the reclamation and reuse of valuable specialty nanomaterials, creating questions about whether they are or are not solid wastes within the purview of the 2008 revision. Chapter 6 identifies such potential instances of misfit, as well as the more prevalent scenarios in which RCRA can be expected to mesh more smoothly with the imperatives of regulating nanomaterial secondary wastes.

The Comprehensive Environmental Response, Compensation, and Liability Act (CERCLA) comes into play where hazardous substances are released uncontrolled into the environment. A wide and encompassing statutory definition of "hazardous substance" serves as the portal to the CERCLA's response, liability, funding, and reporting provisions; and EPA has authority to expand the list by designating additional substances. As Chapter 7 observes, however, it is uncertain today whether any existing nanomaterial meets the definition for listing—that is, whether, "when released into the environment," it "may present substantial danger to the public health or welfare or the environment."[18] As noted in connection with other statutes, characterizing nanomaterials for CERCLA purposes is complicated because the nano forms of some compounds may present concerns that conventional forms do not. On the other hand, nanomaterials may not persist in the environment as do some conventional substances, rendering them at least potentially less problematic in this respect. Today's incomplete data about risks posed by nanomaterials also affect how certain of CERCLA's requirements would operate in practice.

While CERCLA Section 103, for example, requires the reporting of hazardous substance releases that exceed a threshold "reportable quantity," the lack of data precludes EPA's making an informed decision about an appropriate threshold.

For other CERCLA core objectives, today's incomplete database should not prove an impediment. As Chapter 7 points out, EPA's authority to remediate contamination on its discovery is unaffected by whether the contamination was lawful or not when released. Additionally, when more data on health or environmental effects is available in the future, EPA could proceed to list a nanomaterial as hazardous, thus opening the door to CERCLA-authorized responsive actions, including the imposition of retroactive liability for cleanup costs, just as it has done—and was intended to do—since CERCLA was first enacted. Thus, assuming the requisite "hazardous substance" trigger can be supported, CERCLA can operate seamlessly in most instances to address uncontrolled releases and site contamination associated with nanomaterials.

The Clean Water Act (CWA), covered in Chapter 8, is a statutory umbrella extending to a variety of effluent discharge and water quality concerns. Nanoparticles may be expected increasingly to enter wastewater streams as commercialized nanotechnology grows and with it, sales of nano-containing consumer products. Chapter 8 describes several sources from which nanoparticles may end up in wastewater, including industrial processing and transportation; intentional use (such as sunscreens worn into the water and removed while showering); rinse water from laundered fabrics treated with nanomaterials; degradates from coatings applied to vessels and structures located near bodies of water; fertilizers and pesticides that contain nanomaterials designed to reduce runoff; and discard of consumer products.[19]

As with so many other environmental statutes where nanomaterials are involved, the challenge posed by insufficient data complicates regulatory efforts under the CWA as well. Further, the difficulties of detecting and reliably measuring aquatic nanoparticle levels also may confound the development of precisely tailored discharge permits and other tools in the CWA arsenal.[20] The definition of "pollutant" in Section 502 is broad enough to include nanomaterials among the many substances that are subject to the CWA when discharged into the "navigable waters," another term with an extensive reach. But, as Chapter 8 discusses, where nanoparticles are the "pollutants" in question, the mechanics of standard setting must skirt the unknowns; and regulators may need to be satisfied, at least in the near term, with a "best management practices" approach, coupled with information-gathering obligations on dischargers. A similar approach ("best professional judgment") may make sense for standards applicable to nanoparticle discharges that enter publicly owned treatment works (POTW) rather than the navigable waters.[21]

Chapter 12 explores the application of the National Environmental Policy Act (NEPA) in the nanotechnology context. Although it long predates today's flourishing commercial nanotechnologies, as Chapter 12 observes, this grandmother of environmental statutes has much to contribute to the informed analysis of decision making where federal agency approvals, funding, or other activities are involved. Indeed, NEPA did not necessarily contemplate developments in biotechnology either, but the D.C. Circuit Court of Appeals confirmed decades ago that it is no less applicable to newer technologies than to the highway building and other traditional projects that the term "Environmental Impact Statement" brings to mind.[22]

NEPA is triggered in the event of "major Federal actions significantly affecting the quality of the human environment."[23] The breadth of this nexus can be astonishing. NEPA review, including the exploration of alternatives to a contemplated "Federal action," is subject to the same practical constraint that affects regulatory activity under the other environmental statutes discussed in this book. Any review and findings relating to environmental impacts—and alternative pathways, including "no action"—necessarily is hobbled by the paucity of data needed to identify, describe, and quantify those impacts. Nevertheless, as Chapter 12 points out, even the acknowledgment of an incomplete database and the way decision making is affected as a result can inform an agency's review and provide an important reality check.

A significant limitation on NEPA and its potential applicability to nanotechnology are the exclusion of most EPA programs and actions, either through explicit statutory directives in the various environmental laws or as a matter of judicially created exemptions under the doctrine of "functional equivalence."[24] Other departments and agencies—most of them "project" agencies rather than "mission agencies," such as EPA— are extensively involved in activities that involve applied nanotechnology and/or the funding of nanotechnology-related research.[25] Many of these activities are potentially subject to NEPA review; whether the NEPA trigger is implicated and how review should proceed in the nanotechnology setting doubtless will be recurring issues for years to come.

The realities apparent in the chapters addressing regulatory approaches—explosive industry growth, a promising but imperfectly understood technology, and the lag between commercialization and data gathering on health and environmental effects—call for an approach to governance that goes beyond command, control, pick up the pieces, and punish. In the face of these circumstances, Chapter 9 proposes a systematic and multifaceted approach to governance that employs an array of management tools. In addition to traditional regulatory structures, this approach looks to performance and product standards and economic instruments; public dialogues, including interaction between industry, stakeholders, and an informed public; industry leadership in information collection and reporting; proactive approaches to responsibility and liability if products are released prematurely; and corporate self-regulation. Self-interest (enlightened or not), along with peer and public pressure and economic incentives would provide incentives to keep this multifaceted approach moving forward and producing results.

Because the growth of commercialized nanotechnology is outpacing health, safety, environmental, and other regulatory activity directed specifically at its products and their associated wastes, effluents, and emissions, stakeholders (including government agencies without their command-and-control hats) have stepped up to the plate. Chapter 10 describes initiatives led by industry standard-setting organizations, by government agencies, and by the private sector. Committees of both International Organization for Standardization (ISO) and ASTM International are working on international consensus standards on nomenclature, definitions, measurement, and other essentials. EPA, through its Nanoscale Materials Stewardship Program (NMSP), is affirmatively seeking to build a more robust database by reaching out to industry volunteers. International organizations also have initiated flourishing cooperative programs. Chapter 10 also describes a key private sector project in which the Environmental Defense Fund and DuPont have joined forces to develop a Nano Risk Framework that provides a standard for measuring best management practices within the industry.

Chapter 11 surveys the types of risks and potential liabilities facing companies in the business of nanotechnology. The very newness and aura of cutting-edge mystery that make nano-enhanced products attractive to consumers also may leave producers and others in the distribution and sales chain vulnerable to liability claims based on the various theories that apply to dangerous products, from design defects to gross negligence to failure to warn. The highly publicized 2006 "Magic Nano" recall in Germany involving a misleadingly named cleaning product—with no nano enhancements whatever—underscores the degree to which legitimate manufacturers need to be vigilant, informed, proactive, and transparent. Chapter 11 also emphasizes the need for commercialized nanotechnology business to be well versed in securities law reporting requirements for publicly traded companies, and in Generally Accepted Accounting Principles (GAAP) disclosure requirements for public and privately held companies, and—for public companies—attentive to shareholder issues relating to nanomaterials. Insurance coverage also may be problematic for commercialized nanotechnology firms, given the collective discomfort of the insurance industry in operating in the presence of so many unknowns and unquantifiable risks. Some insurers may insist on exclusions or impose caps on what they do agree to cover. Finally, the nanotechnology context calls for due diligence "plus," especially when a prospective purchaser explores potential liabilities it may acquire.

Collectively, the contributors to this volume have sought to identify regulatory, governance, and business issues of ongoing—and evolving—importance in an area that is as fascinating as it is challenging. Necessarily there is a moving target aspect to writing usefully about nanotechnology, whether from the perspective of science, business, law, or government. Still, the contributors have endeavored, and we believe have succeeded, in producing a treatise that will remain relevant for the foreseeable future even as commercialized technology—and those charged with regulating it—are moving forward.

Notes

1. *See* Chapter 6, note 1 (citing the database assembled by the Woodrow Wilson Institute's Project on Emerging Nanotechnology, which lists over 1,000 consumer products that claim to include nanomaterial components). *See also* Chapter 3, note 26 (citing an April 2008 report by the Project on Emerging Nanotechnologies (PEN), which estimated that over 600 nanotechnology-based consumer products are on the global market and three to four are being added each week).
2. *See* Chapter 9 at 181.
3. *See* U.S. Environmental Protection Agency (EPA), *Nanotechnology White Paper* (Feb. 2007, at 5), *available at* http://www.epa.gov/osa/pdfs/nanotech/epa-nanotechnology-whitepaper-0207.pdf. Hereinafter *EPA White Paper*.
4. *See, e.g.,* Chapter 2 at 16 and notes 6–8, and Chapter 6, note 7.
5. EPA White Paper at 7.
6. TSCA § 3(2)(A), 15 U.S.C. § 2602(2)(A).
7. *See* http://www.epa.gov/opptintr/nano/nmsp-inventorypaper2008.pdf at 6.
8. EPA White Paper at 66.
9. *See* Chapter 3, note 25.
10. *See* Chapter 3 at 83.

11. Additionally, EPA may solicit public comments or convene a public hearing when an EUP application raises potentially significant issues. *See* 40 C.F.R. § 172.11.

12. EPA may decide to develop a nanopesticide-specific provision within its EUP regulations to address the unique characteristics of these materials. EPA has done so previously for genetically modified microbial pesticides.

13. *See* 16 U.S.C. § 1531(b).

14. *See* Chapter 5 at 119.

15. The discussion in Chapter 5 also notes that nanotechnology may benefit biodiversity by offering new means to remediate environmental contamination or by enabling the development of smaller and more sophisticated medical or surveillance devices to protect threatened or endangered species.

16. Babbitt v. Sweet Home Chapter of Communities for a Great Oregon, 515 U.S. 687 (1995); see Chapter 5 at 118.

17. *See* Chapter 6, note 22 and the accompanying text.

18. CERCLA § 102(a), 42 U.S.C. § 9602(a).

19. *See* Chapter 8 at 162.

20. The National Pollutant Discharge Elimination System (NPDES) permit program established by CWA Section 402 implements the core CWA prohibition against discharging any pollutant into the navigable waters of the United States without a permit. *See* CWA §§ 301(a) and 402(a), 33 U.S.C. §§ 1311(a) and 1342(a).

21. *See* Chapter 8 at 172–173. As noted there, EPA's White Paper on nanotechnology acknowledges that the fate of nanoparticles in POTWs is "not well characterized." *Id.* at 173, note 17, citing EPA White Paper at 35.

22. *See* Chapter 12 at 236–237.

23. 42 U.S.C. § 4332(2)(C).

24. *See* Chapter 12 at 245–247. The nonexempt EPA activities include granting construction funding for wastewater treatment facilities under the CWA and the issuance of NPDES permits to new facilities. *See id.* at 239–241.

25. *See id.* at 241–245.

CHAPTER 2

TSCA and Nanomaterials

Executive Summary

Nanotechnology, loosely described as the creation or use of materials or processes at a scale of approximately 1 to 100 nanometers in at least one dimension, is a rapidly growing technology being utilized in virtually all major industrial sectors, including electronics, medicine, coatings, consumer products, aerospace, and specialty materials.[1] Nanotechnology holds promise for environmental protection as well, offering the possibility of increased energy efficiency, improved pollution controls, and more effective cleanup technologies. With these benefits, though, come concerns: the possibility that applications of nanotechnology may pose new or unusual risks to human health or the environment.[2]

This chapter addresses how the risks that may be associated with nanotechnology can be addressed under the Toxic Substances Control Act (TSCA). Unlike most other environmental statutes, which focus on controlling the end products of economic activity (e.g., emissions, discharges, and wastes), TSCA is largely a "front-loaded" statute that provides EPA with the authority and obligation to regulate chemicals before and during their use. In that sense, TSCA is essential to the concept of "cradle-to-grave" regulation of commercial activity. TSCA complements several other statutes available to EPA to regulate nanotechnology (e.g., the Clean Air Act, Clean Water Act, Resource Conservation and Recovery Act, and Federal Insecticide, Fungicide, and Rodenticide Act, or FIFRA).

This chapter expands upon the Section of Environment, Energy, and Resources' June 2006 paper entitled *Regulation of Nanoscale Materials under the Toxic Substances Control Act*. The Team Leader on that paper was Christopher L. Bell, Sidley Austin. Revisions are by Lynn L. Bergeson, Bergeson & Campbell, P.C.

Other federal agencies also have the authority to regulate nanotechnology, including but not limited to the Food and Drug Administration (FDA), the Consumer Product Safety Commission, and the Occupational Safety and Health Administration (OSHA).

This chapter comes to the following conclusions regarding the ability of EPA to regulate nanoscale materials under TSCA:

- Nanomaterials include chemical substances and mixtures that EPA can regulate pursuant to TSCA.
- TSCA, and the risk evaluation provisions of Section 5 in particular, was intended to address new health or environmental risks and the chemical products of new technologies. If a "new chemical substance" is manufactured at the nanoscale, it is subject to the same premanufacture notification (PMN) review requirements under TSCA Section 5(a)(1)(A) that are applicable to any new chemical.
- In addition to its Section 5(a)(1) PMN authority over "new chemical substances," EPA can regulate nanoscale versions of chemical substances already listed on the TSCA Chemical Substances Inventory (Inventory) as existing chemical substances under its Section 5(a)(2) authority to promulgate significant new use rules (SNUR). Promulgation of SNURs for individual nanomaterials or categories of nanomaterials would be feasible for EPA, as shown by its promulgation of approximately 40 existing chemical SNURs. Once such a SNUR is issued, EPA can then regulate individual nanomaterials in a manner identical to how it would regulate them under the Section 5(a)(1) PMN process as "new chemical substances."
- EPA also has other authorities under TSCA to regulate nanomaterials, including the authority to require health and environmental testing; collect production, health, and environmental information about nanomaterials; and promulgate rules regulating, and even prohibiting, the manufacture, processing, distribution, and use of nanomaterials.

Does EPA Have the Authority to Regulate Nanomaterials under TSCA?

A threshold question is whether EPA has the authority under TSCA to regulate nanomaterials. TSCA provides EPA with the authority to establish a regulatory framework governing "chemical substances." A "chemical substance" is "any organic or inorganic substance of a particular molecular identity, including—(i) any combination of such substances occurring in whole or in part as a result of a chemical reaction or occurring in nature and (ii) any element or uncombined radical." [3] Nanomaterials that fall within the broad sweep of "organic or inorganic" substances unquestionably are "chemical substances" that EPA has the authority to regulate under TSCA. [4]

Having established that nanomaterials can be "chemical substances" subject to regulation under TSCA, the next issue is determining the nature of EPA's TSCA authority. The most flexible authority provided under TSCA is that of Section 5. In considering action under Section 5, the first step is determining whether EPA can use its authority to regulate nanomaterials as "new" chemicals. To the extent that EPA's "new" chemical TSCA authority does not apply per se to nanoscale versions of existing chemicals, this does not preclude EPA's authority to regulate such nanomaterials as "existing" chemicals under Section 5(a)(2) or other provisions of TSCA.

Regulating Nanomaterials under TSCA Section 5

TSCA Section 5 gives EPA authority to assess the risks of individual chemical substances and to impose limitations on their manufacture, processing, distribution, and use in appropriate cases, including prohibiting their manufacture altogether. This TSCA section has twin provisions: Section 5(a)(1)(A) for "new chemical substances," and Section 5(a)(2) for significant new uses of both new and existing chemical substances. While the two provisions have different triggers, once triggered they operate almost identically. Much discussion and many papers from various stakeholders have focused on EPA's ability to use Section 5(a)(1)(A) to regulate as "new chemical substances" nanomaterials for which conventional-sized versions are already on the Inventory. Assuming that such distinctions reasonably can be drawn in individual cases, the arguments for this use of Section 5(a)(1)(A) were fraught with obstacles, and in any event EPA settled the debate on January 23, 2008, when it issued as part of the voluntary Nanoscale Materials Stewardship Program (NMSP) its so-called TSCA Inventory Paper. [5] In contrast, the Section 5(a)(2) SNUR process appears to offer EPA adequate authority to effectively regulate nanoscale versions of materials that are already on the TSCA Inventory.

Technical Challenges in Distinguishing between "Nanoscale" and Conventional-Sized Chemical Substances

As a preliminary matter, EPA must address the difficult task of defining key terms such as "nanotechnology," "nanomaterials," and "nanoparticles." As noted earlier, nano-size particles have generally been understood to involve those particles that are one-billionth of a meter in size or smaller. Size has not been the sole factor in defining "nanomaterials," however. For example, the U.S. National Nanotechnology Initiative (NNI) takes into account the properties of nanoscale particles in its definition of nanotechnology, while other definitions include the methods by which nanoscale materials are made. The International Organization for Standardization (ISO) has under way an initiative to develop, among other things, international consensus standards on terms, definitions, and nomenclature related to nanotechnology.[6] (In December 2006, ASTM International issued its own standard on such definitions.)[7] The United States is participating in the ISO effort, and several U.S. government entities—including NNI, EPA, OSHA, the National Institute of Standards and Technology, and the Department of Defense—are on the U.S. ISO delegation.[8]

The public discussion of EPA's authority to regulate nanomaterials typically presumes that "nanoscale" materials are clearly distinguishable from conventional-sized forms of materials with the same chemical structure. Neither particle size nor the form and structure of a chemical substance necessarily allows for easy distinctions between nanomaterials and conventional-sized materials, however.

Many chemical substances are comprised of or formed from nanoscale primary particles. These particles naturally aggregate and agglomerate to varying degrees, depending on the material and the process, into larger-scale particles. These aggregated or agglomerated nanoscale particles for the most part exist as micron-sized or larger particles as commercially produced (so-called conventional or bulk materials). This is also true of "engineered" (i.e., intentionally manufactured) nanoscale materials. Carbon nanotubes, for example, may be synthesized as nanoscale primary particles; but in the real world, natural physical forces that operate on any particle of that scale cause them to form aggregates and agglomerates in size ranges overlapping conventional particle sizes. As with conventional materials, the extent of aggregation and particle size are driven by process parameters, not molecular qualities. It is uncertain how one can articulate a nonarbitrary rationale distinguishing between "nanoscale" and "bulk" or "macroscale" substances based on either initial or final particle size.

Distinguishing between chemically similar materials on the basis of morphology (i.e., form or structure) presents similar challenges. EPA would have to define the morphology intended to be represented by the "existing" Inventory entry, determine which variations in form or structure should be deemed "new," and articulate a rationale for the criteria selected. It is difficult to see how this can be accomplished other than on a case-by-case basis. It also may be difficult to apply such principles consistently without casting doubt on the Inventory status of a great many existing chemical substances (e.g., carbon blacks) that reflect a multitude of engineered particle morphology variations designed to achieve particular particle properties (e.g., smaller aggregate size or greater conductivity).

This very brief summary suggests that the discussion of EPA's legal authority under TSCA to regulate nanomaterials, whether as "new" or "existing" chemical substances, should be carried out with an understanding of the technical difficulties in distinguishing between nanoscale and conventional-sized materials of the same molecular identity. In addition, while this chapter uses terms such as "nanomaterials" or "nanotechnology," it must be understood that these terms encompass a widely diverse range of materials, uses, and risk profiles that may be very difficult to regulate as a single class of chemical substances.

Whether Nanomaterials Qualify as "New Chemical Substances" Subject to Regulation under Section 5(a)(1)(A)

TSCA Section 8(b)(1) requires EPA to "compile, keep current, and publish a list of each chemical substance which is manufactured or processed in the United States," a list known as the TSCA Inventory.[9] A "new chemical substance" is any chemical substance that is not on the Inventory.[10]

With limited exceptions, "new chemical substances" cannot be manufactured unless the manufacturer first complies with the PMN provisions of TSCA Section 5(a)(1)(A).[11] A person who intends to manufacture or import a "new chemical substance" must submit to EPA certain information for EPA's review at least 90 days before manufacturing or importing the chemical. The outcomes of the PMN process can include placing the chemical substance on the Inventory and allowing it to be manufactured, processed, and used without limitation; placing it on the Inventory but subjecting the chemical substance to certain use restrictions; seeking more data about the substance before a decision is made; or a complete prohibition on manufacture (e.g., through a TSCA Section 5(e) order).

Nanomaterials that also are "new chemical substances" are subject to the PMN requirements of TSCA Section 5(a)(1) like any other new chemical.[12] For combinations of materials not presently reflected on the Inventory (e.g., EPA has given the example of a carbon-gold compound), the chemical substance is "new" and the requirement to submit a PMN clearly applies. The challenge in this context is determining when nanomaterials are "new." Many engineered nanomaterials share an identical or indistinguishable chemical structure with materials on the Inventory, such as silver or titanium, but may differ in primary particle morphology and typical particle size, depending on the material and when it is measured. These differences may result in very different physical characteristics and properties than those generally associated with the conventional form of the chemical, and this may cause the nanomaterials to have different risk profiles than their chemically identical brethren have. The question then arises whether EPA has the authority to require PMN review of such nanomaterials as "new chemical substances" or whether such materials are subject only to EPA's other TSCA authorities applicable to "existing" chemical substances.

TSCA defines a "chemical substance" in terms of its "particular molecular identity."[13] A "new" chemical is considered a chemical that does not have the same particular molecular identity as any chemical on the Inventory.[14] Applying contemporary TSCA nomenclature practices and conventions, the nanoscale versions of "existing" chemical substances are described identically, and their molecule identities are depicted identically to the conventional-sized version of the same chemical such that they can be said to have the same "particular molecular identity" as the existing chemical. Therefore, one would initially come to the conclusion that the nanoscale version of an "existing" chemical is not a "new" chemical and therefore is not subject to the TSCA Section 5(a)(1)(A) process.

EPA has now agreed with this conclusion. In the TSCA Inventory Paper, EPA explains that "[a]lthough a nanoscale substance that has the same molecular identity as a non-nanoscale substance listed on the Inventory differs in particle size and may differ in certain physical and/ or chemical properties resulting from the difference in particle size, EPA considers the two forms to be the same chemical substance because they have the same molecular identity."[15] EPA continues, "[t]he Inventory listing in this case is considered to represent both the nanoscale and non-nanoscale forms of the substance and, as such, does not distinguish between two forms having the same molecular identity that differ only in particle size and/or physical/chemical properties resulting from the difference in particle size."[16] A nanoscale substance whose particular molecular identity is not identical to any substance on the Inventory, EPA explains, constitutes a "new chemical substance."[17]

Arguments can be made that the statutory term "particular molecular identity" is sufficiently flexible as to take into account physical properties or other defining characteristics in addition to molecular identity, at least to a limited degree, while recognizing that molecular identity is the definitive characteristic in most instances.

The definition of "chemical substance" explicitly includes "any combination of such substances occurring in whole or in part as a result of a chemical reaction or occurring in nature."[18] Relying on that definition, EPA has included as individual entries on the Inventory many substances of unknown or variable composition, complex reaction products, and biological materials (UVCB substances). Some of these UVCB Inventory entries explicitly consider factors such as the manufacturing process and physical properties—factors that might be relevant to distinguishing nanoscale versions of macroscale existing chemical substances. For example, the following TSCA Inventory entries for UVCB materials include factors other than molecular structure:

> Naphtha (petroleum), light catalytic reformed, CAS No. 64741-63-5: A complex combination of hydrocarbons produced from the distillation of a catalytic reforming process. It consists primarily of hydrocarbons having carbon numbers predominantly in the range of C_5 through C_{11} and boiling in the range of approximately 35°C to 190°C (194°F to 446°F). It contains a relatively large proportion of aromatic and branched chain hydrocarbons. This stream may contain 10 vol. % or more benzene.

> Caramel (color), CAS No. 8028-89-5: The substance obtained by controlled heat treatment of food-grade carbohydrates ... Consists essentially of colloidal aggregates that are dispersible in water but only partly dispersible in alcohol-water solutions. Depending upon the particular caramelizing agent used, may have a positive or negative colloidal charge in solution.

It is important to recognize, however, that UVCB substances are "combinations" rather than discrete molecular entities. EPA developed the UVCB approach for complex reaction products for which there is no definite or known molecular formula or chemical structure information and considered a range of other information in the absence of a precise chemical description. EPA added them to the Inventory under the "combination" aspect of the definition of "chemical substance." That "combination" authority may not be applicable to most nanomaterials, however, since they typically are not combinations and usually have defined particular molecular identities. Thus, the UVCB precedent does not appear to support using physical properties to distinguish, for purposes of listing on the TSCA Inventory, between chemical substances with known, definite, and common molecular identities.

TSCA Section 5(e) provides EPA broad risk management authority (i.e., authority to restrict or prohibit the manufacture of a new chemical substance if there is inadequate data to permit a reasoned evaluation of the health or environmental effects of the new chemical substance and, in the absence of such information, activities involving the new chemical substance may present an unreasonable risk or there may be significant or substantial human exposure to the new chemical substance). In this situation, the general lack of data on the health or environmental effects of individual nanomaterials gives rise to the question of whether these risks can or should be addressed through EPA's new chemical PMN authority.[19]

According to an article that appeared in the Bureau of National Affairs' *Daily Environment Report*,[20] EPA exercised its TSCA Section 5(e) authority in October 2008 when it issued a TSCA Section 5(e) Consent Order regarding the manufacture of multi-walled carbon nanotubes.[21] The order requires the company to conduct an inhalation study on rats, prescribes the use of personal protective equipment for workers exposed to the nanotubes, and sets out other conditions as well. The order does not name the company, but the U.K.-based Thomas Swan & Co. Ltd. issued a press statement that a subsidiary in New Jersey had obtained a Consent Order to begin manufacturing a multi-walled carbon nanotube product. The order is most likely for the subsidiary, Swan Chemical Inc. of Lyndhurst. The Consent Order was issued in response to a PMN submitted by the company and the order states that nanotubes will be used as a property modifier in electronic applications and in polymer composites. According to the order, EPA approved the PMN even though the firm did not provide any data about the multi-walled carbon nanotubes in its submission. Under the Consent Order, the manufacturer must:

- conduct a 90-day inhalation toxicity study in rats;
- submit certain physical and chemical information about the multi-walled carbon nanotubes;
- deliver to EPA a 1-gram sample of the multi-walled carbon nanotubes along with a copy of the material safety data sheet that will accompany them;

- require workers to wear protective gloves, clothing, and a full-face respirator approved by the National Institute for Occupational Safety and Health;
- use the multi-walled carbon nanotubes only for one or more specific applications named in the Consent Order, but kept confidential;
- distribute the carbon nanotubes only to companies that agree to follow the same restrictions, with the exception of the testing requirements; and
- maintain for five years records of information including the volume made, customers that purchased them, and proof that a program to help workers use required equipment was established.

Previously, on May 7, 2008, EPA issued a *Federal Register* notice stating that Swan Chemical had submitted a PMN to make single-walled carbon nanotubes as property modifiers in electronics and polymer composites.[22] Similarly, on January 5, 2009, EPA announced receipt of several PMNs concerning multi-walled carbon nanotubes.[23]

EPA's PMN authority over "new chemical substances," however, is not its only source of legal authority to assess and manage such risks. As discussed in the next section, Congress gave EPA companion authority to its PMN authority that allows EPA to perform the same risk assessments and take the same risk management actions for existing chemical substances used for a significant new use as it can for new chemical substances. In particular, the risk management provisions of Section 5(e) apply to chemical substances "with respect to which notice is required by subsection (a)"; that notice can be a PMN or a significant new use notice (SNUN). Significantly, EPA uses the same form for both PMNs and SNUNs. Thus, the public policy interest in having EPA conduct risk assessments of individual nanomaterials, and impose appropriate risk management requirements, does not necessarily lead to the conclusion that nanomaterials must necessarily be "new" rather than "existing," since those goals can be met through either the PMN or SNUR authorities.

Whether Nanomaterial Uses Qualify as "Significant New Uses" of Existing Chemical Substances Subject to Regulation under Section 5(a)(2)

In light of the earlier discussion on Section 5(a)(1), it is important to note that EPA has risk assessment authority under its significant new use authority of Section 5(a)(2). This section of TSCA requires EPA first to promulgate a SNUR through rulemaking, but otherwise all of its PMN authority remains available. This SNUR authority offers EPA considerable flexibility to regulate nanomaterials.

The TSCA legislative history emphasized that EPA's authority under Section 5(a)(2) is a counterpart to its authority under Section 5(a)(1):

> If a new use of an existing substance has been specified by the Administrator in accordance with this subsection [Section 5(a)(2)], all of the premarket notification procedures and authority during the premarket notification period apply to such new use of an existing substance.[24]

For example, EPA may issue orders under Sections 5(e) and 5(f) with respect to chemicals notified under either Section 5(a)(1) or Section 5(a)(2), as both provisions refer to "a chemical substance with respect to which notice is required by subsection (a)."

Congress regarded both the PMN and the SNUR authority as suitable for addressing risks presented by new technology:

> The provisions of the section [Section 5, not simply Section 5(a)(1)] reflect the conferees['] recognition that the most desirable time to determine the health and environmental effects of a substance, and to take action to protect against any potential adverse effects, occurs before commercial production begins. Not only is human and environmental harm avoided or alleviated, but the cost of any regulatory action in terms of loss of jobs and capital investment is minimized. For these reasons the conferees have given the Administrator broad authority to act during the notification period.[25]

This determination of health and environmental effects must be made before a new chemical is manufactured, and it can be made before a new use of an existing chemical is undertaken. A key distinction between Section 5(a)(1) PMNs and Section 5(a)(2) SNURs is that under Section 5(a)(2), EPA must promulgate a rule subject to public notice and comment, whereas under Section 5(a)(1), EPA already has in place a generic rule requiring submission of a notice.[26] Once EPA has issued a rule under Section 5(a)(2), however, the two provisions operate in a very similar manner.

SNUR rulemakings proceed under the provisions of the Administrative Procedure Act.[27] This involves publication of a proposed rule, opportunity for public comment, and publication of a final rule together with a "concise general statement" of the SNUR's basis and purpose. EPA has already promulgated approximately 40 existing chemical SNURs using this procedure. This history of successful SNUR promulgation is strong evidence that EPA can practicably exercise its SNUR authority over nanoscale versions of existing chemicals.

In promulgating a SNUR, EPA must explain how the SNUR reflects EPA's consideration of the following statutory factors:

(A) the projected volume of manufacturing and processing of a chemical substance,

(B) the extent to which a use changes the type or form of exposure of human beings or the environment to a chemical substance,

(C) the extent to which a use increases the magnitude and duration of exposure of human beings or the environment to a chemical substance, and

(D) the reasonably anticipated manner and methods of manufacturing, processing, distribution in commerce, and disposal of a chemical substance.[28]

Nanomaterials may raise concerns under any of these factors, but (B), (C), and (D) seem particularly relevant to the unique characteristics of nanomaterials. Specifically, EPA's SNUR authority allows it to address new risks associated with manufacturing, processing, or using an existing chemical in a new way. Thus, the statutory factors that EPA must consider in issuing a SNUR are some of the very factors that would cause EPA to want to issue a SNUR for a nanomaterial or category of nanomaterials.

These statutory factors must simply be considered; specific findings are not required. These factors are considerably less burdensome for EPA in rulemaking than the requirements for issuing a rule under Section 6, which include both a finding that a chemical substance "presents, or will present an unreasonable risk of injury to health or the environment," and consideration of factors such as the chemical substance's effects, benefits, and substitutes and the economic impact of the rule. Whereas Section 6 rules are judicially reviewable under the "substantial evidence" test, SNURs are reviewable under the more deferential "arbitrary and capricious" test.[29]

EPA is not limited to issuing SNURs on individual nanomaterials, but may instead issue SNURs for categories of nanomaterials. The language of Section 5(a)(2) is not expressly limited to substance-by-substance rulemaking. EPA has already used Section 5(a)(2) to address chemical categories.[30] While such rulemaking has ultimately listed individual chemical substances within the categories, the rulemaking has been based on category characteristics. EPA's 1989 new chemical follow-up SNUR amendments addressed the category of PMN chemicals for which it had previously issued an order under Section 5(e)[31] and the category of non-Section 5(e) PMN chemicals for which EPA had concerns about actions by other manufacturers.[32] EPA issued rules setting up an expedited process for promulgating SNURs covering members of these broad categories. EPA's experience with categorical SNURs to date suggests that EPA can successfully promulgate categorical SNURs for nanomaterials.

In issuing the new chemical follow-up amendments, EPA cited Section 26(c) of TSCA as supporting a categorical approach.[33] TSCA Section 26(c), "Action with respect to categories," provides in part:

> (1) Any action authorized or required to be taken by the Administrator under any provision of this [Act] with respect to a chemical substance or mixture may be taken by the Administrator in accordance with that provision with respect to a category of chemical substances . . . .
> (2) For purposes of paragraph (1):
>> (A) The term 'category of chemical substances' means a group of chemical substances the members of which are similar in molecular structure, in physical, chemical, or biological properties, in use, or in mode of entrance into the human body or into the environment, or the members of which are in some other way suitable for classification as such for purposes of this [Act], except that such term does not mean a group of chemical substances which are grouped together solely on the basis of their being new chemical substances.[34]

Thus, the bottom-line criterion for qualifying as a category is being "in some . . . way suitable for classification as such" for purposes of TSCA, which is an extremely flexible test. EPA may be able to establish through rulemaking that particular classes of nanomaterials meet the definition of a "category of chemical substances" on the basis of their common characteristics, which are unique to nanomaterials. EPA could then conduct its risk assessments, and impose risk management controls, on individual nanomaterials in the same manner as it does through the PMN process.

One aspect of Section 5(a)(2) that may present a challenge to EPA in promulgating SNURs for some nanomaterials is the required determination that the particular use of the chemical substance for which a SNUR is promulgated be, in fact, a "new" use. EPA has consistently taken the position that if a substance is being used in a particular manner at the time that a SNUR is proposed, that specific use is not "new" and cannot be the subject of a SNUR.[35] Thus, to the extent that nanoscale versions of some chemical substances are already being distributed in commerce for certain uses, it may be difficult for EPA to make the requisite determination that those uses are "new."

One additional difference between Section 5(a)(1) PMNs and Section 5(a)(2) SNURs is that SNUR rulemakings under Section 5(a)(2) trigger Section 12(b) export notification requirements.[36] EPA has now amended its Section 12(b) regulations to limit export notifications for exports of SNUR chemicals to a one-time occurrence (per chemical per country, not per calendar year), as has been the case for Section 4 chemicals for several years.[37] This provision should minimize the impact of the export notification requirement for any nanomaterials covered by SNURs.

EPA issued SNURs for four nanoscale substances most recently on June 24, 2009.[38] According to EPA, four of these chemical substances, including multi-walled carbon nanotubes (generic) and single-walled carbon nanotubes, are subject to TSCA Section 5(e) consent orders issued by EPA. Under the SNURs, persons who intend to manufacture, import, or process any of these substances for an activity that is designated as a significant new use must notify EPA at least 90 days before commencing that activity. Once notified, EPA will evaluate the intended use and, if necessary, prohibit or limit that activity before it occurs. EPA states that, for the four PMN substances subject to consent orders, including multi-walled carbon nanotubes and single-walled carbon nanotubes, EPA determined that activities associated with the PMN substances "may present unreasonable risk to human health or the environment." The consent orders require protective measures intended to limit exposures or otherwise mitigate the potential unreasonable risk. The 5(e) SNURs designate as a "significant new use" the absence of the protective measures required in the corresponding consent orders.

Regulating Nanomaterials under Other Provisions of TSCA

TSCA Section 4 Test Rules

TSCA Section 4 authorizes EPA to require manufacturers and processors of existing chemicals to conduct tests "to develop data with respect to the health and environmental effects" of the chemical.[39] EPA may require such testing by rule if it determines that a chemical substance may present an unreasonable risk to human health or the environment. EPA also may promulgate a test rule without a risk-based finding if it determines that a chemical is produced in substantial quantities and there may be substantial human or environmental exposure to the chemical, that insufficient data are available to determine the environmental or health effects of the chemical, and that testing is necessary to provide such data. EPA also can obtain test data without going through the rulemaking process, by issuing consent decrees requiring testing where a consensus exists among EPA and interested parties and the public about the adequacy of a proposed testing program. Further, the statute contemplates that EPA will use its TSCA Section 4 authority to address EPA's own need for health and safety data as well as the health and safety data needs of other federal agencies such as the National Institute of Occupational Safety and Health, the Department of Labor, and the National Cancer Institute.[40]

EPA also has successfully used the threat of invoking its TSCA Section 4 authority to encourage manufacturers and processors to enter into voluntary agreements to test existing chemicals. The most notable instance of this is the High Production Volume (HPV) Challenge Program, which included over 2,200 chemicals with an annual production volume of over 1 million pounds.

Accordingly, neither the statute nor EPA's existing Section 4 regulations preclude EPA from exercising its authority under TSCA Section 4 to require manufacturers or processors of nanoscale versions of existing chemical substances to test those chemicals in an effort to better evaluate the potential environmental or health risks posed by them. Unless voluntary testing agreements are reached, however, EPA would need to demonstrate, through notice and comment rulemaking, that it can support either a risk- or exposure-based finding for a nanoscale substance that is subject to the test rule. EPA can base such a decision on risk, or on a determination that the nanomaterial is produced in substantial quantities and there may be substantial human or environmental exposure and that testing is necessary to fill data gaps. Further, consistent with EPA's HPV initiative, EPA may consider whether a voluntary approach to testing might be appropriate for certain classes of nanomaterials.[41]

Whether through voluntary efforts, negotiated testing agreements, or rulemaking, the authority to require the generation of health and safety data is available to EPA under TSCA Section 4. The importance of this tool with respect to nanomaterials is underscored by EPA's *Nanotechnology White Paper*, which identifies a considerable body of data that EPA and its sister agencies believe are important to understanding the health and safety implications of nanomaterials.

Importantly, EPA reported in early 2009 that it is preparing a draft TSCA Section 4 test rule for multi-walled carbon nanotubes. According to a notice in EPA's May 11, 2009, Regulatory Agenda, a TSCA Section 4(a) test rule "may be needed to determine the health effects" of multi-walled carbon nanotubes. EPA states that the results of the tests that could be required under the rule could assist in understanding the health effects of the substance to manage/minimize any potential risk and exposure. Results could also help with establishing a correlation between the chemical/physical properties and health effects needed to protect the health of workers handling the substance. EPA has not determined when it will publish a notice of proposed rulemaking (NPRM).

TSCA Section 6 Rules

TSCA Section 6(a) authorizes EPA to regulate the manufacture, processing, commercial distribution, use, and/or disposal of an existing chemical when there is a reasonable basis to conclude that the substance "presents or will present an unreasonable risk of injury to health or the environment."[42] EPA has the authority under TSCA Section 6 to promulgate regulations:

- prohibiting or limiting the manufacture, processing, or distribution in commerce of the chemical generally or for a particular use, as well as prohibiting or regulating the commercial use of a chemical;
- requiring that the chemical, or any article containing the chemical, be labeled or accompanied by warnings and instructions for use, distribution, or disposal;
- requiring creation and maintenance of records of manufacturing/ processing methods and reasonable monitoring or testing necessary to assure regulatory compliance;
- regulating disposal of the chemical, or any article containing the chemical; or
- requiring notification to distributors, other persons in possession of the chemical, and the general public of the unreasonable risk of injury.[43]

Unlike the Section 5 SNUR authority, Section 6 provides EPA with the capacity to prohibit or limit outright certain activities, but the exercise of that authority must be established through on-the-record rulemaking based upon a finding of unreasonable risk.[44] In addition, EPA is required to impose the least economically burdensome controls to manage that risk.

TSCA Section 7: EPA's Imminent Hazard Authority

TSCA Section 7 authorizes EPA to initiate a civil action to seize an imminently hazardous substance, mixture, or article containing them and to seek such other relief against any person who manufactures, processes, distributes, uses, or disposes of an imminently hazardous substance, mixture, or article containing them. EPA's authority under TSCA Section 7 is broad and authorizes EPA to seek a court order requiring recalls, replacements/repurchases, public notices of risk, or a combination of any of these requirements.

EPA's Information-Gathering Authorities

EPA has broad information-gathering powers regarding existing chemicals (i.e., in addition to the information it may gather through the review of "new" chemicals) under TSCA Sections 5, 6, and 8, some of which are self-implementing and do not require any new action by EPA to be applicable to nanomaterials. These include the following:

- TSCA Section 5—As part of the PMN and SNUR processes, EPA can issue TSCA Section 5(e) orders seeking additional information about chemicals for which PMNs or SNUNs have been submitted, but where EPA determines that it does not have sufficient information to evaluate the PMN or SNUN.
- TSCA Section 6(b)—Authorizes EPA to order a manufacturer or processor to provide certain information to EPA if EPA has a reasonable basis to conclude that the manufacture or processing of an existing chemical substance may present an unreasonable risk to human health or the environment. EPA may, for example, order the manufacturer or processor to submit a description of the chemical substance's quality control procedures. EPA can require the manufacturer or processor to modify those procedures to the extent EPA believes necessary to address any inadequacies. Further, if EPA determines that a chemical that has been distributed presents an unreasonable risk, EPA is authorized to order the manufacturer or processor to notify its customers and the public of the risk and to replace or repurchase the chemical, as appropriate, to abate the risk.
- TSCA Section 8(a)—EPA has promulgated a number of information-gathering rules under this provision, including rules to gather detailed information on specific chemicals and more generic rules such as the Inventory Update Rule, which collects basic

production information on chemicals on the Inventory every five years. EPA reportedly is preparing to issue a TSCA Section 8(a) rule on certain nanoscale materials in 2009.

- TSCA Section 8(c)—Manufacturers and processors of chemicals must create and maintain records of "allegations"—whether written or oral—that the chemical "caused a significant adverse reaction to health or the environment."[45] These records must be made available to EPA upon request. This is a very broad information-gathering tool because it encompasses allegations that can come from any source and that can be made without formal proof or regard for evidence. Thus EPA could, for example, request TSCA Section 8(c) records from certain sectors where nanomaterials are prevalent to determine if there are significant numbers of allegations regarding adverse reactions associated with nanomaterials or products containing nanomaterials.

- TSCA Section 8(d)—EPA can, by rule, designate chemicals for which manufacturers and processors must submit to EPA any health and safety studies conducted regarding the listed chemicals. Such rules are retrospective as well as prospective; qualifying studies that were conducted in the ten years prior to the listing and for the next ten years after the listing must be submitted.

- TSCA Section 8(e)—Manufacturers, processors, or distributors of chemicals must "immediately inform EPA if they obtain information that reasonably supports the conclusion that the chemical substance . . . presents a substantial risk of injury to health or the environment." This has been an important information-gathering tool for EPA and has also been the subject of recent enforcement actions. As nanomaterials are more broadly introduced into the economy, Section 8(e) will be a key mechanism for EPA to track the occurrence of adverse effects on human health or the environment.[46]

Nanoscale materials are not excluded from these various information-gathering authorities and may allow EPA to collect a broad range of production, health, and environmental risk information regarding nanomaterials. In particular, the "allegations of adverse effects" recordkeeping and the "substantial risk" reporting requirements together might form the basis of an "early warning" system for potential risks associated with the products of nanotechnology. EPA could then use this new information in assessing the risks and benefits of particular nanomaterials.

TSCA Section 21 Citizen Petitions

In addition to EPA's authorities, TSCA Section 21 allows citizens to petition EPA to initiate a proceeding for the issuance, amendment, or repeal of a rule under TSCA Section 4, 6, or 8 or an order under Section 5(e) or 6(b)(2) regarding chemical substances. A TSCA Section 21 petition must set forth facts that the petitioner believes establish the need for the action requested. Nanomaterials are not excluded from the scope of Section 21 petitions.

EPA is required to grant or deny the petition within 90 days of its filing. If EPA grants the petition, it must promptly commence an appropriate proceeding. If EPA denies the petition, it must publish its reasons for the denial in the *Federal Register*. Within 60 days of denial, or the expiration of the 90-day period, if no action is taken, the petitioner may commence a civil action in a U.S. district court to compel initiation of the requested rulemaking proceeding.

Conclusion

On January 28, 2008, EPA launched the NMSP "to complement and support its new and existing chemical efforts on nanoscale materials under [TSCA]."[47] EPA has emphasized that data from the NMSP "will provide important baseline information on health and environmental effects, exposures, risks, management practices, and data needs that will assist EPA and others in properly assessing and managing risks related to nanoscale materials."[48] EPA has further stated that "[d]ata submitted during the first 6 months of the [Basic] program will be a factor when [EPA] considers whether to use regulatory information gathering authority under TSCA,"[49] and that approximately two years after the NMSP's launch date, EPA will issue a detailed evaluation report on the NMSP that will "include consideration of [the] use of regulatory authorities under TSCA."[50]

On January 12, 2009, EPA released its interim report on the NMSP.[51] EPA states that, based on the current interim results, "the NMSP can be considered successful." EPA notes that a number of the environmental health and safety data gaps still exist, however, and "EPA is considering how to best use testing and information gathering authorities under the Toxic Substances Control Act to help address those gaps." According to EPA, it will continue to review new chemical nanoscale materials submitted under TSCA Sections 5(a) and 5(h)(4) and apply, as appropriate, testing requirements and exposure controls under Section 5(e) and SNURs under Section 5(a)(2). EPA continues to welcome new participants and information submissions for the NMSP, which will continue until January 2010. According to a notice in EPA's November 24, 2008, Regulatory Agenda, EPA intends to publish a final evaluation of the NMSP, including next steps, in April 2010.

With respect to its regulatory authorities under TSCA, the following conclusions can be made regarding EPA's ability to regulate nanotechnology: (1) nanomaterials include chemical substances and mixtures that EPA can regulate pursuant to TSCA; (2) if a "new chemical substance" is manufactured at the nanoscale, it is subject to the same PMN review requirements under TSCA Section 5(a)(1) that are applicable to any new chemical; and (3) as an alternative to its Section 5(a)(1) PMN authority over "new chemical substances," EPA may regulate nanomaterials as existing chemical substances under its Section 5(a)(2) authority to promulgate SNURs. In addition, EPA has other authorities under TSCA to regulate nanomaterials, including the authority to require health and environmental testing; collect production, health, and environmental information about nanomaterials; and promulgate rules regulating, and even prohibiting, the manufacture, processing, distribution, and use of nanomaterials.

Notes

1. A nanometer is one-billionth of a meter, or 10^{-9} m. *See* National Nanotechnology Initiative (NNI), "Frequently Asked Questions," http://www.nano.gov/html/facts/faqs.html.
2. An overview of the nature, benefits, and possible risks associated with nanotechnology can be found in U.S. Environmental Protection Agency (EPA), *Nanotechnology White Paper* (Feb. 2007), *available at* http://www.epa.gov/osa/pdfs/nanotech/epa-nanotechnology-whitepaper-0207.pdf.
3. TSCA § 3(2)(A), 15 U.S.C. § 2602(2)(A). There are a number of statutory exclusions from the definition of "chemical substance," including for pesticides that are regulated by EPA under FIFRA, foods and drugs regulated by the FDA, and tobacco.
4. *See, e.g.,* 72 Fed. Reg. 38083, 38084 (July 12, 2007) (stating that "[n]anoscale materials that meet the TSCA section 3(2)(A) definition of 'chemical substance' are subject to TSCA"). The fact that nanomaterials may present novel or unusual challenges does not vitiate EPA's TSCA jurisdiction. For example, EPA has under TSCA successfully regulated biotechnology, including microorganisms, that EPA has recognized are not traditional chemical substances. *See* 59 Fed. Reg. 45526, 45527 (Sept. 1, 1994) ("While the term 'chemical substance' has been interpreted to include

microorganisms, EPA acknowledges that microorganisms are not generally referred to as chemicals."). EPA reasoned that a microorganism is "[a] living organism [which] is [a] 'combination of such substances occurring in whole or in part as a result of a chemical reaction or occurring in nature . . . ." 49 Fed. Reg. 50880, 50886 (Dec. 31, 1984). With regard to DNA, EPA concluded that DNA "however created, is 'an organic substance of a particular molecular identity.'" *Id.*

5. *See* EPA, "TSCA Inventory Status of Nanoscale Substances—General Approach" (Jan. 23, 2008) (TSCA Inventory Paper), *available at* http://www.epa.gov/opptintr/nano/nmsp-inventorypaper2008.pdf.

6. *See* ISO, "TC 229—Nanotechnologies," *available at* http://www.iso.org/iso/standards_development/technical_committees/list_of_iso_technical_committees/iso_technical_committee.htm?commid=381983. In fact, on September 25, 2008, ISO's Technical Committee (TC) 229 announced the issuance of ISO/TS 27687:2008, a standard that provides definitions for various nanotechnology terms, including "nano-object," "nanoparticle," "nanofiber," and "nanoplate." *See* ISO, "New ISO/TS 27687 Will Help Defining Nanotechnologies" (Sept. 25, 2008), *available at* http://www.iso.org/iso/pressrelease.htm?refid=Ref1161.

7. *See* ASTM International, "Terminology for Nanotechnology Standard Now Available from ASTM International" (Dec. 2006), *available at* http://www.astmnewsroom.org/default.aspx?pageid=1192.

8. The National Technology Transfer Act of 1994 obligates U.S. government agencies to participate in relevant consensus standards writing activities and to use such standards in rulemakings where applicable (unless an agency explains why potentially applicable standards should not be used).

9. TSCA § 8(b)(1), 15 U.S.C. § 2607(b)(1).

10. TSCA § 3(9), 15 U.S.C. § 2602(9). EPA's regulatory definition of a "new chemical substance" tracks the statutory definition. *See* 40 C.F.R. §§ 710.3, 720.3(v), 720.25(a).

11. There are a variety of limitations on or exemptions from the PMN requirements, including those regarding chemicals used for research and development and chemicals manufactured in low volumes or for purposes of test marketing.

12. At least two engineered nanomaterials are known to be listed on the Inventory after having undergone PMN review. *See* 71 Fed. Reg. 46475, 46480 (Aug. 14, 2006) (P-05-0687, "siloxane coated alumina nanoparticles"); 71 Fed. Reg. 33449, 33454 (June 9, 2006) (P-05-0673, "siloxane coated silica nanoparticles").

13. TSCA § 3(2)(A), 15 U.S.C. § 2602(2)(A).

14. *See* TSCA Inventory Paper at 2–3.

15. *Id.* at 6.

16. *Id.*

17. *Id.* at 5. EPA cites "nanotubes and carbon fullerenes" as examples of new chemical substances. On October 31, 2008, EPA issued a *Federal Register* notice stating again its view that many carbon nanotubes will be considered new chemicals and thus subject to EPA premanufacture review. 73 Fed. Reg. 64946 (Oct. 31, 2008).
18. TSCA § 3(2)(A)(i), 15 U.S.C. § 2602(2)(A)(i).
19. For the reasons discussed at the beginning of this chapter, it may be difficult to assess the risks for nanomaterials as a class given the diversity of materials that arguably might fit in that category. The ISO initiative on nanotechnologies includes standards on the environmental, health, and safety (EHS) issues associated with nanotechnologies. The United States is leading the ISO TC 229 working group developing these EHS standards.
20. P. Rizzuto, *EPA Consent Order Allows Company to Produce Multi-Walled Carbon Nanotubes*, Env't Rep. (BNA) A-5 (Oct. 14, 2008).
21. A redacted copy of the Consent Order is reproduced in the appendix to this chapter.
22. 73 Fed. Reg. 25696 (May 7, 2008).
23. 74 Fed. Reg. 280 (Jan. 5, 2009).
24. S. Rep. No. 698, 94th Cong., 2nd Sess. 19 (1976), *reprinted in* Legislative History at 175.
25. H.R. Conf. Rep. No 1679, 94th Cong., 2nd Sess. (1976) 65, 66, *reprinted in* Legislative History at 678, 679 (emphasis added).
26. *See* 40 C.F.R. § 720.22.
27. 5 U.S.C. § 553.
28. TSCA § 5(a)(2)(A)–(D), 15 U.S.C. § 2604(a)(2)(A)–(D).
29. TSCA § 19(c)(1)(B), 15 U.S.C. § 2618(c)(1)(B).
30. *See, e.g.,* 40 C.F.R. § 721.9582, covering 88 perfluoroalkyl sulfonates; 72 Fed. Reg. 57222 (Oct. 9, 2007) (addition of 183 perfluoroalkyl sulfonates).
31. 40 C.F.R. § 721.160.
32. 40 C.F.R. § 721.170.
33. 52 Fed. Reg. 15594, 15597 (Apr. 29, 1987) (proposed rule); 54 Fed. Reg. 31298 (July 27, 1999) (final rule).
34. TSCA § 26(c), 15 U.S.C. § 2625(c).
35. *See, e.g.,* 68 Fed Reg. 35315 (June 13, 2003) (SNUR for *Burkholderia cepacia* complex, where EPA explains that existing uses of *Burkholderia* are not appropriate for inclusion in the SNUR for the microorganism); *see also* 55 Fed. Reg. 17376 (Apr. 24, 1990) (explaining that "[t]o establish a significant new use, EPA must determine that the use is not ongoing").
36. Export notification requirements would also be triggered for nanomaterials subject to rulemakings or proceedings under TSCA Section 4, 6, or 7.
37. 40 C.F.R. § 707.65(a)(2)(ii), 71 Fed. Reg. 66234, 66244 (Nov. 14, 2006).
38. 74 Fed. Reg. 29982 (June 24, 2009).

39. TSCA § 4(a), 15 U.S.C. § 2603(a).
40. *See* TSCA § 4(e), 15 U.S.C. § 2603(e), establishing an Interagency Testing Committee to recommend substances for testing under Section 4. An example of a test rule that was promulgated to address another agency's data needs is the 2004 *In Vitro* Dermal Absorption Rate test rule, which was promulgated under Section 4 to generate data of interest to OSHA. *See* 69 Fed. Reg. 22402 (Apr. 26, 2004).
41. One component of EPA's voluntary NMSP is the In-Depth Program, under which participants would "develop a plan and submit [testing and other] data over a longer period of time to be determined in the plan." 73 Fed. Reg. 4861, 4863 (Jan. 28, 2008).
42. TSCA § 6(a), 15 U.S.C. § 2605(a).
43. TSCA § 6(a)(1)–(7), 15 U.S.C. § 2605(a)(1)–(7).
44. EPA may take immediate action under TSCA Section 5(f) if it determines that a chemical that is the subject of a PMN or SNUN presents or will present an unreasonable risk before it is able to issue a TSCA Section 6 rule.
45. 40 C.F.R. § 717.3(a).
46. EPA's position has always been that Section 8(e) applies to nanoscale chemicals just as it does to bulk chemicals; *see, e.g.,* EPA, "Concept Paper for the Nanoscale Materials Stewardship Program Under TSCA," at 18 (undated) (including discussion of Section 8(e)), *available at* http:// www.epa.gov/oppt/nano/nmsp-conceptpaper.pdf, and several companies have made Section 8(e) submissions for nanoscale substances. *See, e.g.,* 8EHQ-1208-17079D (Dec. 4, 2008) (Sepiolite nanoclay), *available at* http://www.epa.gov/opptintr/tsca8e/pubs/8ehq/2008/dec08/ 8ehq_1208_17079d.pdf; 8EHQ-0708-17208B (Sept. 9, 2008) (carbon nano tube), *available at* http://www.epa.gov/opptintr/tsca8e/pubs/8ehq/2008/ sep08/8ehq_0908_17208b.pdf; FYI-0708-01611A (July 9, 2008) (multi-walled carbon nanotubes), *available at* http://www.epa.gov/opptintr/ tsca8e/pubs/8ehq/2008/jul08/fyi_0708_01611a.pdf; 8EHQ-0408-17079B (Mar. 31, 2008) (Sepiolite nanoclay), *available at* http://www.epa.gov/ opptintr/tsca8e/pubs/8ehq/2008/apr08/8ehq_0408_17079b.pdf; 8EHQ-0308-17109A (Mar. 24, 2008) (multi-walled carbon nanotubes), *available at* http://www.epa.gov/opptintr/tsca8e/pubs/8ehq/2008/mar08/ 8ehq_0308_17109a.pdf; 8EHQ-0308-17088A (Feb. 27, 2008) (submission by DuPont AirProducts NanoMaterials L.L.C.), *available at* http://www .epa.gov/opptintr/tsca8e/pubs/8ehq/2008/mar08/8ehq_0308_17088a .pdf; 8EHQ-0308-16999B (Feb. 27, 2008) (submission by DA Nano-Materials L.L.C.), *available at* http://www.epa.gov/opptintr/tsca8e/ pubs/8ehq/2008/mar08/8ehq_0308_16999b.pdf; 8EHQ-0707-16911A (July 19, 2007) (surface-modified nanoparticle), *available at* http:// www.epa.gov/oppt/tsca8e/pubs/8ehq/2007/jul07/8ehq_0707_169 11a_8807000000329.pdf; 8EHQ-0403-15319 (Apr. 10, 2003) (single-walled

carbon nanotubes); *see also* FYI-0708-01611A (July 9, 2008) (multi-walled carbon nanotubes), http://www.epa.gov/opptintr/tsca8e/pubs/8ehq/2008/jul08/fyi_0708_01611a.pdf.

47. 73 Fed. Reg. at 4861.
48. EPA, "Supporting Statement for an Information Collection Request (ICR)" (undated) at 2, *available at* http://www.epa.gov/oppt/nano/nmsp-icr-supportingstatement.pdf.
49. 73 Fed. Reg. at 4863.
50. EPA, "Nanoscale Materials Stewardship Program," *available at* http://www.epa.gov/oppt/nano/stewardship.htm.
51. EPA, Nanoscale Materials Stewardship Program Interim Report (Jan. 2009), *available at* http://www.epa.gov/oppt/nano/nmsp-interim-report-final.pdf.

APPENDIX

UNITED STATES ENVIRONMENTAL PROTECTION AGENCY

OFFICE OF POLLUTION PREVENTION AND TOXICS

REGULATION OF A NEW CHEMICAL SUBSTANCE

PENDING DEVELOPMENT OF INFORMATION

In the matter of:	)	Premanufacture Notice Number:
	)	
	)	
	)	
[ ]	)	P-08-0177
	)	
	)	
	)	
	)	
	)	
	)	
	)	
	)	
	)	
	)	
	)	
	)	
	)	
	)	
	)	
	)	
	)	
	)	

Consent Order and Determinations Supporting Consent Order

ii

TABLE OF CONTENTS

iii

PREAMBLE

I   INTRODUCTION

Under the authority of § 5(e) of the Toxic Substances Control Act ("TSCA") (15 U.S.C. 2604(e)), the Environmental Protection Agency ("EPA" or "the Agency") issues the attached Order, regarding premanufacture notice ("PMN") P-08-0177 for the chemical substance multiwalled carbon nano tubes, ("MWCNT" or the "PMN substance") submitted by [ ], ("the Company"), to take effect upon expiration of the PMN review period. The Company submitted the PMN to EPA pursuant to section 5(a)(1) of TSCA and 40 CFR Part 720.

Under § 15 of TSCA, it is unlawful for any person to fail or refuse to comply with any provision of § 5 or any order issued under § 5. Violators may be subject to various penalties and to both criminal and civil liability pursuant to § 16, and to specific enforcement and seizure pursuant to § 17. In addition, chemical substances subject to an Order issued under § 5 of TSCA, such as this one, are subject to the § 12(b) export notice requirement.

II.   SUMMARY OF TERMS OF THE ORDER

The Consent Order for this PMN substance requires the Company to:

(1) Deliver to EPA a 1 gram sample of the PMN substance along with a copy of MSDS;

(2) Submit to EPA the results of a 90-day inhalation toxicity study in rats with a post exposure observation period of up to 3 months, including bronchoalveolar lavage fluid ("BALF") analysis (OPPTS 870.3465 or OECD 413) at least 14 weeks before either (a) manufacturing or importing a total of [   ] kg of the PMN substance, or (b) [ ] years [ ] months

iv

after commencing non-exempt commercial manufacture of the PMN substance, whichever comes first. The production/time limit shall be calculated from a date 2 years after signing this Consent Order by the Company,

(3) Within 6 months of commencing non-exempt commercial manufacture of the PMN substance, submit certain material characterization data;

(4) Use gloves impervious to nanoscale particles and chemical protective clothing;

(5) Use a NIOSH–approved full-face respirator with an N -100 cartridge while exposed by inhalation in the work area;

(6) Use the PMN substance only as a [   ];

(7) distribute the PMN substance only to a person who agrees to follow the same restrictions (except the testing requirements); and

(8) maintain certain records.

III. CONTENTS OF PMN

Confidential Business Information Claims (Bracketed in the Preamble and Order): name of the technical contact, the name of the company, production volume, uses

Chemical Identity: multi-walled carbon nanotubes

Use:

Specific : [   ]

Generic: property modifier in electronic applications, contained use, property modifier in polymer composites, contained use.

Maximum 12-Month Production Volume: [   ] kg

v

Test Data Submitted with PMN: none

IV. EPA'S ASSESSMENT OF RISK

The following are EPA's predictions regarding the probable toxicity, human exposure and environmental release of the PMN substance, based on the information currently available to the Agency.

Human Health Effects Summary:

Absorption: Absorption of the PMN chemical is expected to be poor via all routes of exposure.

Toxicological Endpoints: There is a concern for health effects based on analogy to respirable, poorly soluble particulates and other carbon nanotubes and for lung irritation based on particle size.

Basis: chemical category, see www.epa.gov/oppt/newchems/chemcat.htm

Environmental Effects Summary: No significant effects expected.

Exposure and Environmental Release Summary:

Scenario	No. of Sites	No. of Workers	Inhal (mg/d)	Dermal (mg/d)	Release to water (kg/y)
Use 1	[ ]	[ ] [ ]	0.02	1600 3100	13
Use 2	[ ]	[ ] [ ]	0.02	1600 3100	13

During Use 1 and Use 2, [ ] workers are expected to be exposed by both inhalation and dermal vi

routes, and [ ] workers are expected to be exposed via the dermal route only.

Risk to Workers: health risk to workers exposed to the PMN chemical via the
inhalation route and via the dermal route.

Risk to General Public: potential risk to the general population from water, landfill and/or
incineration releases.

V.   EPA'S CONCLUSIONS OF LAW

The following findings constitute the basis of the Consent Order:

(A) EPA is unable to determine the potential for human health effects from exposure to the
PMN substance. EPA therefore concludes, pursuant to § 5(e)(1)(A)(i) of TSCA, that the
information available to the Agency is insufficient to permit a reasoned evaluation of the human
health effects of the PMN substance.

(B) In light of the potential risk to human health posed by the uncontrolled manufacture, import,
processing, distribution in commerce, use, and disposal of the PMN substance, EPA has
concluded, pursuant to § 5(e)(1)(A)(ii)(I) of TSCA, that uncontrolled manufacture, import,
processing, distribution in commerce, use, and disposal of the PMN substance may present an
unreasonable risk of injury to human health.

VI.   INFORMATION REQUIRED TO EVALUATE HEALTH EFFECTS

Triggered Testing. The Order prohibits the Company from exceeding a specified

vii

production time period or production volume unless the Company submits the information

described in the Testing section of this Order in accordance with the conditions specified in the

Testing section. The Order requires submission of the following triggered testing:

Information	Effects	Guidelines
90-day inhalation toxicity	lung	OPPTS 870.3465 or OECD 413

study on rats with a post-exposure

observation period of up to 3 months,

including bronchoalveolar lavage fluid

("BALF") analysis.

The Order's restrictions on manufacture, import, processing, distribution in commerce, use, and

disposal of the PMN substance will remain in effect until the Order is modified or revoked by

EPA based on submission of that or other relevant information.

EPA encourages the Company to develop additional health effects testing in coordination with

other multi-walled carbon nanotube (MWCNT) manufacturers. This can be done under the in-

depth portion of EPA's Nanoscale Materials Stewardship Program or through independent

testing. If, for example, a consortium of companies commit to testing a representative set of

MWCNT for subchronic mammalian toxicity, EPA may consider waiving the triggered testing

requirement. EPA would be willing to facilitate the process in coordination with other ongoing

health effects testing for MWCNT nationally and internationally. EPA would consider accepting

the results of such testing in lieu of triggered testing in this order.

CONSENT ORDER

I. SCOPE OF APPLICABILITY AND EXEMPTIONS

(a) Scope. The requirements of this Order apply to all commercial manufacturing, processing, distribution in commerce, use and disposal of the chemical substance, multi-walled carbon nanotubes (MWCNT), P-08-0177 ("the PMN substance"), in the United States by [   ] ("the Company"), except to the extent that those activities are exempted by paragraph (b).

(b) Exemptions. Manufacturing, processing, distribution in commerce, use and disposal of the PMN substance is exempt from the requirements of this Order (except the requirements in the Recordkeeping and Successor Liability Upon Transfer Of Consent Order sections) only to the extent that (1) these activities are conducted in full compliance with all applicable requirements of the following exemptions, and (2) such compliance is documented by appropriate recordkeeping as required in the Recordkeeping section of this Order.

   (1) Completely Reacted (Cured). The requirements of this Order do not apply to quantities of the PMN substance that have been completely reacted (cured).

   (2) Export. Until the Company begins commercial manufacture of the PMN substance for use in the United States, the requirements of this Order do not apply to manufacture, processing or distribution in commerce of the PMN substance solely for export in accordance

2

with TSCA §12(a) and (b), 40 CFR 720.3(s) and 40 CFR Part 707. However, once the Company

begins to manufacture the PMN substance for use in the United States, no further activity by the

Company involving the PMN substance is exempt as "solely for export" even if some amount of

the PMN substance is later exported. At that point, the requirements of this Order apply to all

activities associated with the PMN substance while in the territory of the United States. Prior to

leaving U.S. territory, even those quantities or batches of the PMN substance that are destined

for export are subject to terms of the Order, and count towards any production volume test

triggers in the Testing section of this Order.

(3) Research & Development ("R&D"). The requirements of this Order do not apply to

manufacturing, processing, distribution in commerce, use and disposal of the PMN substance in

small quantities solely for research and development in accordance with TSCA §5(h)(3), 40 CFR

720.3(cc), and 40 CFR 720.36.

(4) Byproducts. The requirements of this Order do not apply to the PMN substance

when it is produced, without separate commercial intent, only as a "byproduct" as defined at 40

CFR 720.3(d) and in compliance with 40 CFR 720.30(g).

(5) No Separate Commercial Purpose. The requirements of this Order do not apply to

the PMN substance when it is manufactured, pursuant to any of the exemptions in 40 CFR

720.30(h), with no commercial purpose separate from the substance, mixture, or article of which

it is a part.

(c) Automatic Sunset. If the Company has obtained for the PMN substance a Test Market

Exemption ("TME") under TSCA §5(h)(1) and 40 CFR 720.38 or a Low Volume Exemption

3

(LVE) or Low Release and Exposure Exemption ("LoREx") under TSCA §5(h)(4) and 40 CFR 723.50(c)(1) and (2) respectively, any such exemption is automatically rendered null and void as of the effective date of this Consent Order.

II. TERMS OF MANUFACTURE, IMPORT, PROCESSING, DISTRIBUTION IN COMMERCE, USE, AND DISPOSAL PENDING SUBMISSION AND EVALUATION OF INFORMATION

PROHIBITION

The Company is prohibited from manufacturing, importing, processing, distributing in commerce, using, or disposing of the PMN substance in the United States, for any nonexempt commercial purpose, pending the development of information necessary for a reasoned evaluation of the human health and environmental effects of the substance, and the completion of EPA's review of, and regulatory action based on, that information, except in accordance with the conditions described in this Order.

TESTING

(a) Section 8(e) Reporting. Any information on the PMN substance which reasonably supports the conclusion that the PMN substance presents a substantial risk of injury to health or the environment required to be reported under EPA's section 8(e) policy statement at 43 Federal Register 11110 (March 16, 1978) as amended at 52 Federal Register 20083 (May 29, 1987), shall reference the appropriate PMN identification number for this substance and shall contain a statement that the substance is subject to this Consent Order. Additional information regarding section 8(e) reporting requirements can be found in the reporting guide referenced at 56 Federal

4

Register 28458 (June 20, 1991).

(b) Notice of Study Scheduling. The Company shall notify, in writing, the EPA Laboratory

Data Integrity Branch (2225A), Office of Enforcement and Compliance Assurance, U.S.

Environmental Protection Agency, 1200 Pennsylvania Avenue, N.W., Washington, D.C. 20460,

of the following information within 10 days of scheduling any study required to be performed

pursuant to this Order, or within 15 days after the effective date of this Order, whichever is later:

(1) The date when the study is scheduled to commence;

(2) The name and address of the laboratory which will conduct the study;

(3) The name and telephone number of a person at the Company or the laboratory whom

EPA may contact regarding the study; and

(4) The appropriate PMN identification number for the substance and a statement that

the substance is subject to this Consent Order.

(c) Good Laboratory Practice Standards and Test Protocols. Each study required to be

performed pursuant to this Order must be conducted according to TSCA Good Laboratory

Practice Standards at 40 CFR Part 792 and using methodologies generally accepted in the

relevant scientific community at the time the study is initiated. Before starting to conduct any

such study, the Company must obtain approval of test protocols from EPA by submitting written

protocols. EPA will respond to the Company within 4 weeks of receiving the written protocols.

Published test guidelines specified in paragraph (d) provide general guidance for development of

test protocols, but are not themselves acceptable protocols. Approval of the test protocol does

not mean pre-acceptance of test results.

5

(d) <u>Triggered Testing Requirements.</u>

    (1) <u>90-day inhalation toxicity study.</u> The Company is prohibited from manufacturing or importing the PMN substance beyond the following aggregate manufacture and import volumes ("the production limits"), unless the Company conducts the following studies on the PMN substance and submits all final reports and underlying data in accordance with the conditions specified in this Testing section. The production/time limit shall be calculated from the date 2 years after signing this Consent Order by the Company.

<u>Production/Time Limit</u>	<u>Study</u>	<u>Guideline</u>
[ ] years [ ] months,	90-day inhalation toxicity	OPPTS 870.3465
or [ ] kg	study on rats with a post-exposure	or OECD 413
whichever comes first	observation period of up to 3 months,	
	including bronchoalveolar lavage	
	fluid (BALF) analysis	

If an appropriate adaptation of the 90-day inhalation study for the evaluation of MWCNT is not developed within two years of the date the Company signs this Consent Order or if the Company commits to an appropriate program to test representative MWCNTs, e.g., under the in-depth portion of the Nanoscale Materials Stewardship program, the Company may petition EPA, pursuant to Section IV of this Consent Order, to modify the above testing requirement. If a consortium of companies commit to test a representative set of MWCNT for subchronic mammalian toxicity, EPA will consider waiving the above requirement.

6

(2) Material Characterization. Within 6 months of commencing non-exempt commercial

manufacture of the PMN substance, the Company must submit the following material

characterization data (including data summaries and procedures) obtained from *(1)* microscopy

analysis (scanning electron microscopy, SEM, or transmission electron microscopy, TEM), and

(2) X-Ray analysis (X-ray diffraction, XRD, X-ray fluorescence, XRF, or X-ray spectroscopy,

EDX):

A. type of multi-walled carbon nanotube

- concentric cylinders or scrolled tubes

- number of walls/tubes

B. configuration of nanotube ends (e.g., open, capped)

C. description of any branching

D. width/diameter of inner most wall/tube (average and range)

E. carbon unit cell ring size and connectivity (e.g., typically 6 membered rings but can
    include other ring sizes)

F. alignment of nanotube along long axis (e.g., straight, bent, buckled)

G. hexagonal array orientation when rolled up (e.g., armchair, chiral, zig-zag)

- chiral or twist angle (the angle between the axis of the hexagonal pattern and the
  long axis of the nanotube)

H. particle size of catalyst used in the manufacture of the nanotube

I. molecular weight (average and range)

7

J. Particle properties: shape, size (average and distribution), weight (average and

distribution), count, surface area (average and distribution), surface to volume ratio,

aggregation/agglomeration.

(e) Test Reports. The Company shall: (1) conduct each study in good faith, with due care, and

in a scientifically valid manner; (2) promptly furnish to EPA the results of any interim phase of

each study; and (3) submit, in triplicate (with an additional sanitized copy, if confidential

business information is involved), the final report of each study and all underlying data ("the

report and data") to EPA no later than 14 weeks prior to exceeding the applicable production

limit. The final report shall contain the contents specified in 40 CFR 792.185. Underlying data

shall be submitted to EPA in accordance with the applicable "Reporting", "Data and Reporting",

and "Test Report" subparagraphs in the applicable test guidelines. However, for purposes of this

Consent Order, the word "should" in those subparagraphs shall be interpreted to mean "shall" to

make clear that the submission of such information is mandatory. EPA will not require the

submission of raw data such as slides and laboratory notebooks unless if EPA finds, on the basis

of professional judgment, that an adequate evaluation of the study cannot take place in the

absence of these items.

(f) Testing Waivers. The Company is not required to conduct a study specified in paragraph (d)

of this Testing section if notified in writing by EPA that it is unnecessary to conduct that study.

(g) Equivocal Data. If EPA finds that the data generated by a study are scientifically equivocal,

the Company may continue to manufacture and import the PMN substance beyond the applicable

8

production limit.   To seek relief from any other restrictions of this Order, the Company may

make a second attempt to obtain unequivocal data by reconducting the study under the conditions

specified in paragraphs (b), (c), and (e)(1) and (2).   The testing requirements may be modified, as

necessary to permit a reasoned evaluation of the risks presented by the PMN substance, only by

mutual consent of EPA and the Company.

(h) EPA Determination of Invalid Data.

    (1) Except as described in subparagraph (h)(2), if, within 6 weeks of EPA's receipt of a

test report and data, the Company receives written notice that EPA finds that the data generated

by a study are scientifically invalid, the Company is prohibited from further manufacture and

import of the PMN substance beyond the applicable production limit.

    (2) The Company may continue to manufacture and import the PMN substance beyond

the applicable production limit only if so notified, in writing, by EPA in response to the

Company's compliance with either of the following subparagraphs (h)(2)(i) or (h)(2)(ii).

        (i) The Company may reconduct the study in compliance with paragraphs (b),

(c), and (e)(1) and (2). If there is sufficient time to reconduct the study and submit the report and

data to EPA at least 14 weeks before exceeding the production limit as required by subparagraph

(e)(3), the Company shall comply with subparagraph (e)(3). If there is insufficient time for the

Company to comply with subparagraph (f)(3), the Company may exceed the production limit and

shall submit the report and data in triplicate to EPA within a reasonable period of time, all as

specified by EPA in the notice described in subparagraph (h)(1). EPA will respond to the

Company, in writing, within 6 weeks of receiving the Company's report and data.

        (ii) The Company may, within 4 weeks of receiving from EPA the notice

9

described in subparagraph (h)(1), submit to EPA a written report refuting EPA's finding. EPA will respond to the Company, in writing, within 4 weeks of receiving the Company's report.

(i) Company Determination of Invalid Data.

(1)Except as described in subparagraph (i)(2), if the Company becomes aware that circumstances clearly beyond the control of the Company or laboratory will prevent, or have prevented, development of scientifically valid data under the conditions specified in paragraphs (c) and (e), the Company remains prohibited from further manufacture and import of the PMN substance beyond the applicable production limit.

(2)   The Company may submit to EPA, within 2 weeks of first becoming aware of such circumstances, a written statement explaining why circumstances clearly beyond the control of the Company or laboratory will cause or have caused development of scientifically invalid data. EPA will notify the Company of its response, in writing, within 4 weeks of receiving the Company's report. EPA's written response may either:

(i)   allow the Company to continue to manufacture and import the PMN substance beyond the applicable production limit, or

(ii)   require the Company to continue to conduct, or to reconduct, the study in compliance with paragraphs (b), (c), and (e)(1) and (2). If there is sufficient time to conduct or reconduct the study and submit the report and data to EPA at least 14 weeks before exceeding the production limit as required by subparagraph (e)(3), the Company shall comply with subparagraph (e)(3). If there is insufficient time for the Company to comply with subparagraph (e)(3), the Company may exceed the production limit and shall submit the report and data in triplicate to EPA within a reasonable period of time, all as specified by EPA in the notice

10

described in subparagraph (i)(2). EPA will respond to the Company, in writing, within 6 weeks

of receiving the Company's report and data, as to whether the Company may continue to

manufacture and import beyond the applicable production limit.

(j) Unreasonable Risk.

(1) EPA may notify the Company in writing that EPA finds that the data generated by a

study are scientifically valid and unequivocal and indicate that, despite the terms of this Order,

the PMN substance will or may present an unreasonable risk of injury to human health or the

environment. EPA's notice may specify that the Company undertake certain actions concerning

further testing, manufacture, import, processing, distribution, use and/or disposal of the PMN

substance to mitigate exposures to or to better characterize the risks presented by the PMN

substance. Within 2 weeks from receipt of such a notice, the Company must cease all

manufacture, import, processing, distribution, use and disposal of the PMN substance, unless

either:

(2) within 2 weeks from receipt of the notice described in subparagraph (j)(1), the

Company complies with such requirements as EPA's notice specifies; or

(3) within 4 weeks from receipt of the notice described in subparagraph (j)(1), the

Company submits to EPA a written report refuting EPA's finding and/or the appropriateness of

any additional requirements imposed by EPA. The Company may continue to manufacture,

import, process, distribute, use and dispose of the PMN substance in accordance with the terms

of this Order pending EPA's response to the Company's written report. EPA will respond to the

Company, in writing, within 4 weeks of receiving the Company's report. Within 2 weeks of

receipt of EPA's written response, the Company shall comply with any requirements imposed by

11

EPA's response or cease all manufacture, import, processing, distribution, use and disposal of the PMN substance.

(k) <u>Other Requirements.</u> Regardless of the satisfaction of any other conditions in this Testing section, the Company must continue to obey all the terms of this Consent Order until otherwise notified in writing by EPA. The Company may, based upon submitted test data or other relevant information, petition EPA to modify or revoke provisions of this Consent Order pursuant to Part VI of this Consent Order.

PROTECTION IN THE WORKPLACE

(a) <u>Establishment of Program.</u> During manufacturing, processing, and use of the PMN substance at any site controlled by the Company (including any associated packaging and storage and during any cleaning or maintenance of equipment associated with the PMN substance), the Company must establish a program whereby:

(1) <u>General Dermal Protection.</u> Each person who is reasonably likely to be dermally exposed in the work area to the PMN substance through direct handling of the substance or through contact with equipment on which the substance may exist, or because the substance becomes airborne in a form listed in subparagraph (a)(5) of this section, is provided with, and is required to wear, personal protective equipment that provides a barrier to prevent dermal exposure to the substance in the specific work area where it is selected for use. Each such item of personal protective equipment must be selected and used in accordance with OSHA dermal protection requirements at 29 CFR 1910.132, 1910.133, and 1910.138.

12

(2) <u>Specific Dermal P rotective Equipment</u>.   The dermal personal protective equipment required

by subparagraph (a)(1) of this section must include, but is not limited to, the following items:

   (i)   Gloves impervious to the PMN substance

   (ii) full body clothing impervious to the PMN substance

(3) <u>Demonstration of Imperviousness.</u> The Company is able to demonstrate that each

item of chemical protective clothing selected, including gloves, provides an impervious barrier to

prevent dermal exposure during normal and expected duration and conditions of exposure within

the work area by any one or a combination of the following:

   (i) <u>Permeation Testing</u>. Testing the material used to make the chemical protective

clothing and the construction of the clothing to establish that the protective clothing will be

impervious for the expected duration and conditions of exposure. The testing must subject the

chemical protective clothing to the expected conditions of exposure, including the likely

combinations of chemical substances to which the clothing may be exposed in the work area.

Permeation testing shall be conducted according to the American Society for Testing and

Materials (ASTM) F739 "Standard Test Method for Resistance of Protective Clothing materials

to Permeation by Liquids or Gases." Results shall be recorded as a cumulative permeation rate

as a function of time, and shall be documented in accordance with ASTM F739 using the format

specified in ASTM F1194-89 "Guide for Documenting the Results of Chemical Permeation

Testing on Protective Clothing Materials." Gloves may not be used for a time period longer than

they are actually tested and must be replaced at the end of each work shift during which they are

exposed to the PMN substance.

   (ii) <u>Manufacturer's Specifications</u>. Evaluating the specifications from the

13

manufacturer or supplier of the chemical protective clothing, or of the material used in construction of the clothing, to establish that the chemical protective clothing will be impervious to the PMN substance alone and in likely combination with other chemical substances in the work area.

(4) Respiratory Protection. Each person who is reasonably likely to be exposed by inhalation in the work area to the PMN substance in the form listed in subparagraph (a)(5) of this section, is provided with, and is required to wear, at a minimum, a NIOSH-certified respirator with an APF of 50, from the respirators listed in subparagraph (a)(6) of this section, and the respirator is used in accordance with OSHA and NIOSH respiratory protection requirements at 29 CFR 1910.134 and 42 CFR Part 84. All respirators must be issued, used, and maintained according to an appropriate respiratory protection program under the Occupational Safety and Health Administration (OSHA) requirements in 29 CFR 1910.134.

(5) Physical States. The following physical states of airborne chemical substances are listed for subparagraphs (a)(1) and (4) of this section:

      (i) Particulate (including solids or liquid droplets).

(6) Authorized Respirators. The following NIOSH-certified respirators meet the minimum requirements for subparagraph (a)(4) of this section: Particulate/Aerosol/Mist Exposures, NIOSH-certified air-purifying, tight-fitting full-face respirator equipped with N100 filters.

MANUFACTURING

(a)(1) Prohibition. The Company shall not cause, encourage, or suggest the manufacture or import of the PMN substance by any other person.

14

(2) <u>Sunset Following SNUR.</u> Subparagraph (a)(1) shall expire 75 days after promulgation of a final significant new use rule ("SNUR") governing the PMN substance under section 5(a)(2) of TSCA unless the Company is notified on or before that day of an action in a Federal Court seeking judicial review of the SNUR. If the Company is so notified, subparagraph (a)(1) shall not expire until EPA notifies the Company in writing that all Federal Court actions involving the SNUR have been resolved and the validity of the SNUR affirmed.

(3) <u>Notice of SNUR.</u> When EPA promulgates a final SNUR for the PMN substance and subparagraph (a)(1) expires in accordance with subparagraph (a)(2), the Company shall notify each person whom it causes, encourages or suggests to manufacture or import the PMN substance of the existence of the SNUR.

(b)   The Company shall not manufacture the PMN substance other than as [   ].

(c)   The Company shall provide to EPA a 1 gram sample of the PMN substance as specified by EPA in a future written request along with a copy of MSDS for the substance.

PROCESSIN G AND USE

The Company shall not process or use the PMN substance other than as [   ].

DISTRIBUTION

(a) <u>Distribution Requirements.</u> Except after the PMN has been completely reacted , the Company shall distribute the PMN substance outside the Company, other than for disposal, only to a person who has agreed in writing prior to the date of distribution, to:

15

(1) Not further distribute the PMN substance to any other person, other than for disposal, until after the PMN substance has been completely reacted.

(2) Comply with the same requirements and restrictions, if any, required of the Company in the Protection in the Workplace.

(3) Not process and use the PMN substance other than as [   ].

(b) Temporary Transport and Storage. Notwithstanding paragraph (a), the Company may distribute the PMN substance outside the Company for temporary transport and storage in sealed containers (labeled in accordance with paragraph (b)(2) of the Hazard Communication Program section of this Order) provided the following two conditions are met:

(1) Subsequent to any such exempt temporary transport or storage of sealed containers, the PMN substance may be distributed only to the Company or a person who has given the Company the written agreement required by paragraph (a).

(2) Any human exposure or environmental release resulting from opening the sealed containers and removing or washing out the PMN substance may occur only while the PMN substance is in the possession and control of the Company or a person who has given the Company the written agreement required by paragraph (a).

(c) Recipient Non-Compliance. If, at any time after commencing distribution in commerce of the PMN substance, the Company obtains knowledge that a recipient of the substance has failed to comply with any of the conditions specified in paragraph (a) of this Distribution section or, after paragraph (a)(1) expires in accordance with subparagraph (d)(1), has engaged in a significant new use of the PMN substance (as defined in 40 CFR Part 721, Subpart E) without submitting a

16

significant new use notice to EPA, the Company shall cease supplying the substance to that recipient, unless the Company is able to document each of the following:

(1) That the Company has, within 5 working days, notified the recipient in writing that the recipient has failed to comply with any of the conditions specified in paragraph (a) of this Distribution section, or has engaged in a significant new use of the PMN substance without submitting a significant new use notice to EPA.

(2) That, within 15 working days of notifying the recipient of the noncompliance, the Company received from the recipient, in writing, a statement of assurance that the recipient is aware of the terms of paragraph (a) of this Distribution section and will comply with those terms, or is aware of the terms of the significant new use rule for the PMN substance and will not engage in a significant new use without submitting a significant new use notice to EPA.

(3) If, after receiving a statement of assurance from a recipient under subparagraph (c)(2) of this Distribution section, the Company obtains knowledge that the recipient has failed to comply with any of the conditions specified in paragraph (a) of this Distribution section, or has engaged in a significant new use of the PMN substance without submitting a significant new use notice to EPA, the Company shall cease supplying the PMN substance to that recipient, shall notify EPA of the failure to comply, and shall resume supplying the PMN substance to that recipient only upon written notification from the Agency.

(d) Sunset Following SNUR. (1) Paragraph (a)(1) of this Distribution section shall expire 75 days after promulgation of a final SNUR for the PMN substance under section 5(a)(2) of TSCA, unless the Company is notified on or before that day of an action in a Federal Court seeking judicial review of the SNUR. If the Company is so notified, paragraph (a)(1) of this Distribution

17

section shall not expire until EPA notifies the Company in writing that all Federal Court actions involving the SNUR have been resolved and the validity of the SNUR affirmed.

(2) When EPA promulgates a final SNUR for the PMN substance and paragraph (a)(1) of this Distribution section expires in accordance with subparagraph (d)(1), the Company shall notify each person to whom it distributes the PMN substance of the existence of the SNUR. Such notification must be in writing and must specifically include all limitations contained in the SNUR which are defined as significant new uses, and which would invoke significant new use notification to EPA for the PMN substance. Such notice must also reference the publication of the SNUR for this PMN substance in either the Federal Register or the Code of Federal Regulations. After promulgation of a SNUR and expiration of subparagraph (a)(1), such notice may substitute for the written agreement required in the introductory clause of paragraph (a); so that, if the Company provides such notice to the persons to whom it distributes the PMN substance, then the Company is not required to obtain from such persons the written agreement specified in paragraph (a).

III. RECORDKEEPING

(a) Records. The Company shall maintain the following records until 5 years after the date they are created and shall make them available for inspection and copying by EPA in accordance with section 11 of TSCA:

(1) Exemptions. Records documenting that the PMN substance did in fact qualify for any one or more of the exemptions described in Section I, Paragraph (b) of this Order. Such records must satisfy all the statutory and regulatory recordkeeping requirements applicable to the exemption being claimed by the Company. Any amounts or batches of the PMN substance

18

eligible for the Export exemption in Section I, Paragraph (b)(3) of this Order, are exempt from all the requirements in this Recordkeeping section, if the Company maintains, for 5 years from the date of their creation, copies of the export label and export notice to EPA, required by TSCA sections 12(a)(1)(B) and 12(b), respectively. Any amounts or batches of the PMN substance eligible for the Research and Development exemption in Section I, Paragraph (b)(4) of this Order, are exempt from all the requirements in this Recordkeeping section, if the Company maintains, for 5 years from the date of their creation, the records required by 40 CFR 720.78(b). For any amounts or batches of the PMN substance claimed to be eligible for any other exemption described in Section I, Paragraph (b) of this Order, the Company shall keep records demonstrating qualification for that exemption as well as the records specified in paragraphs (2) and (3) below, but is exempt from the other recordkeeping requirements in this Recordkeeping section;

(2) Records documenting the manufacture and importation volume of the PMN substance and the corresponding dates of manufacture and import;

(3) Records documenting the names and addresses (including shipment destination address, if different) of all persons outside the site of manufacture or import to whom the Company directly sells or transfers the PMN substance, the date of each sale or transfer, and the quantity of the substance sold or transferred on such date;

(4) Records documenting the addresses of all sites of manufacture, import, processing, and use;

(5) Records documenting establishment and implementation of a program for the use of any applicable personal protective equipment required pursuant to the Protection in the Workplace section of this Order;

(6) Records documenting the determinations required by the Protection in the Workplace

19

section of this Order that chemical protective clothing is impervious to the PMN substance;

(7) Records documenting compliance with any applicable manufacturing, processing, use, and distribution restrictions in the Manufacturing, Processing, Use, and Distribution sections of this Order, including distributees' written agreement to comply with the Distribution section of this Order;

(8) Copies of any Transfer Documents and notices required by the Successor Liability section of this Order, if applicable; and

(9) The Company shall keep a copy of this Order at each of its sites where the PMN substance is manufactured of imported.

(a) Applicability. The provisions of this Recordkeeping Section are applicable only to activities of the Company and its Contract Manufacturer, if applicable, and not to activities of the Company's customers.

(b) OMB Control Number. Under the Paperwork Reduction Act and its regulations at 5 CFR Part 1320, particularly 5 CFR 1320.5(b), the Company is not required to respond to this "collection of information" unless this Order displays a currently valid control number from the Office of Management and Budget ("OMB"), and EPA so informs the Company. The "collection of information" required in this TSCA §5(e) Consent Orders has been approved under currently valid **OMB Control Number 2070-0012.**

IV. REQUESTS FOR PRE-INSPECTION INFORMATION

(a) EPA's Request for Information. Pursuant to section 11 of TSCA and 40 CFR 720.122, EPA

20

may occasionally conduct on-site compliance inspections of Company facilities and conveyances associated with the PMN substance. To facilitate such inspections, EPA personnel may contact the Company in advance to request information pertinent to the scheduling and conduct of such inspections. Such requests may be written or oral. The types of information that EPA may request may include, but are not limited to, the following:

(i) Expected dates and times when the PMN substance will be in production within the subsequent 12 months;

(ii) Current workshift schedules for workers who are involved in activities associated with the PMN substance and may reasonably be exposed to the PMN substance;

(iii) Current job titles or categories for workers who are involved in activities associated with the PMN substance and may reasonably be exposed to the PMN substance;

(iv) Existing exposure monitoring data for workers who are involved in activities associated with the PMN substance and may reasonably be exposed to the PMN substance;

(v) Records required by the Recordkeeping section of this Order; and/or

(vi) Any other information reasonably related to determining compliance with this Order or conducting an inspection for that purpose.

(b) Company's Response. The Company shall respond to such requests within a reasonable period of time, but in no event later than 30 days after receiving EPA's request. When requested in writing by EPA, the Company's response shall be in writing. To the extent the information is known to or reasonably ascertainable to the Company at the time of the request, the Company's response shall demonstrate a good faith effort to provide reasonably accurate and detailed answers to all of EPA's requests.

21

(c) <u>Confidential Business Information</u>. Any Confidential Business Information ("CBI") that the Company submits to EPA pursuant to paragraph (b) shall be protected in accordance with §14 of TSCA and 40 CFR Part 2.

V. SUCCESSOR LIABILITY UPON TRANSFER OF CONSENT ORDER

(a) <u>Scope.</u> This section sets forth the procedures by which the Company's rights and obligations under this Order may be transferred when the Company transfers its interests in the PMN substance, including the right to manufacture the PMN substance, to another person outside the Company (the "Successor in Interest").

(b) <u>Relation of Transfer Date to Notice of Commencement ("NOC").</u>

(1) <u>Before NOC.</u> If the transfer from the Company to the Successor in Interest is effective before EPA receives a notice of commencement of manufacture or import ("NOC") for the PMN substance from the Company pursuant to 40 CFR 720.102, the Successor in Interest must submit a new PMN to EPA and comply fully with Section 5(a)(1) of TSCA and 40 CFR part 720 before commencing manufacture or import of the PMN substance.

(2) <u>After NOC.</u> If the transfer from the Company to the Successor in Interest is effective after EPA receives a NOC, the Successor in Interest shall comply with the terms of this Order and shall not be required to submit a new PMN to EPA.

(c) <u>Definitions.</u> The following definitions apply to this Successor Liability section of the Order:

(1) "Successor in Interest" means a person outside the Company who has acquired the

22

Company's full interest in the rights to manufacture the PMN substance, including all ownership rights and legal liabilities, through a transfer document signed by the Company, as transferor, and the Successor in Interest, as transferee. The term excludes persons who acquire less than the full interest of the Company in the PMN substance, such as a licensee who has acquired a limited license to the patent or manufacturing rights associated with the PMN substance. A Successor in Interest must be incorporated, licensed, or doing business in the United States in accordance with 40 CFR 720.22(a)(3).

(2) "Transfer Document" means the legal instrument(s) used to convey the interests in the PMN substance, including the right to manufacture the PMN substance, from the Company to the Successor in Interest.

(d) Notices.

(1) Notice to Successor in Interest. On or before the effective date of the transfer, the Company shall provide to the Successor in Interest, by registered mail, a copy of the Consent Order and the "Notice of Transfer" document which is incorporated by reference as Attachment C to this Order.

(2) Notice to EPA. Within 10 business days of the effective date of the transfer, the Company shall, by registered mail, submit the fully executed Notice of Transfer document to: U.S. Environmental Protection Agency, New Chemicals Branch (7405), 1200 Pennsylvania Avenue, N.W., Washington, D.C. 20460.

(3) Transfer Document. Copies of the Transfer Document must be maintained by the Successor in Interest at its principal place of business, and at all sites where the PMN substance is manufactured or imported. Copies of the Transfer Document must also be made available for

23

inspection pursuant to Section 11 of TSCA, must state the effective date of transfer, and must contain provisions which expressly transfer liability for the PMN substance under the terms of this Order from the Company to the Successor in Interest.

(e) Liability.

(1) The Company shall be liable for compliance with the requirements of this Order until the effective date of the transfer described above.

(2) The Successor in Interest shall be liable for compliance with the requirements of this Order effective as of the date of transfer.

(3) Nothing in this section shall be construed to prohibit the Agency from taking enforcement action against the Company after the effective date of the transfer for actions taken, or omissions made, during the time in which the Company manufactured, processed, used, distributed in commerce, or disposed of the PMN substance pursuant to the terms of this Consent Order.

(f) Obligations to Submit Test Data under Consent Order. If paragraph (d) of the Testing section of this Consent Order requires the Company to submit test data to EPA at a specified production volume ("test trigger"), the aggregate volume of the PMN substance manufactured and imported by the Company up to the date of transfer shall count towards the test trigger applicable to the Successor in Interest.

24

VI. **MODIFICATION AND REVOCATION OF CONSENT ORDER**

The Company may petition EPA at any time, based upon new information on the health effects of, or human exposure to, the PMN substance, to modify or revoke substantive provisions of this Order. The exposures and risks identified by EPA during its review of the PMN substance and the information EPA determined to be necessary to evaluate those exposures and risks are described in the preamble to this Order. However, in determining whether to amend or revoke this Order, EPA will consider all relevant information available at the time the Agency makes that determination, including, where appropriate, any reassessment of the test data or other information that supports the findings in this Order, an examination of new test data or other information or analysis, and any other relevant information.

EPA will issue a modification or revocation if EPA determines that the activities proposed therein will not present an unreasonable risk of injury to health or the environment and will not result in significant or substantial human exposure or substantial environmental release in the absence of data sufficient to permit a reasoned evaluation of the health or environmental effects of the PMN substance.

In addition, the Company may petition EPA at any time to make other modifications to the language of this Order. EPA will issue such a modification if EPA determines that the modification is useful, appropriate, and consistent with the structure and intent of this Order as issued.

25

VII. EFFECT OF CONSENT ORDER

By consenting to the entry of this Order, the Company waives its rights to file objections to this

Order pursuant to section 5(e)(1)(C) of TSCA, to receive service of this Order no later than 45

days before the end of the review period pursuant to section 5(e)(1)(B) of TSCA, and to challenge

the validity of this Order in any subsequent action. Consenting to the entry of this Order, and

agreeing to be bound by its terms, do not constitute an admission by the Company as to, the facts

or conclusions underlying the Agency's determinations in this proceeding. This waiver does not

affect any other rights that the Company may have under TSCA.

_____   _____

Date   Jim Willis, Director
Chemical Control Division
Office of Pollution Prevention and Toxics

_____   _____

Date   Name:
Title:
Company: [ ]

ATTACHMENT A

DEFINITIONS

[Note: The attached Order may not contain some of the terms defined below.]

"Chemical name" means the scientific designation of a chemical substance in accordance with the nomenclature system developed by the International Union of Pure and Applied Chemistry or the Chemical Abstracts Service's rules of nomenclature, or a name which will clearly identify a chemical substance for the purpose of conducting a hazard evaluation.

"Chemical protective clothing" means items of clothing that provide a protective barrier to prevent dermal contact with chemical substances of concern. Examples can include, but are not limited to: full body protective clothing, boots, coveralls, gloves, jackets, and pants.

"Company" means the person or persons subject to this Order.

"Commercial use" means the use of a chemical substance or any mixture containing the chemical substance in a commercial enterprise providing saleable goods or a service to consumers (e.g., a commercial dry cleaning establishment or painting contractor).

"Common name" means any designation or identification such as code name, code number, trade name, brand name, or generic chemical name used to identify a chemical substance other than by its chemical name.

"Consumer" means a private individual who uses a chemical substance or any product containing the chemical substance in or around a permanent or temporary household or residence, during recreation, or for any personal use or enjoyment.

"Consumer product" means a chemical substance that is directly, or as part of a mixture, sold or made available to consumers for their use in or around a permanent or temporary household or residence, in or around a school, or in recreation.

"Container" means any bag, barrel, bottle, box, can, cylinder, drum, reaction vessel, storage tank, or the like that contains a hazardous chemical. For purposes of this section, pipes or piping systems, and engines, fuel tanks, or other operating systems in a vehicle, are not considered to be containers.

"Contract Manufacturer" means a person, outside the Company, who is authorized to manufacture and import the PMN substance under the conditions specified in Part II. of this Consent Order and in the Consent Order for Contract Manufacturer.

"Identity" means any chemical or common name used to identify a chemical substance or a mixture containing that substance.

"Immediate use." A chemical substance is for the "immediate use" of a person if it is under

2

the control of, and used only by, the person who transferred it from a labeled container and will only be used by that person within the work shift in which it is transferred from the labelled container.

"Impervious." Chemical protective clothing is "impervious" to a chemical substance if the substance causes no chemical or mechanical degradation, permeation, or penetration of the chemical protective clothing under the conditions of, and the duration of, exposure.

"Manufacturing stream" means all reasonably anticipated transfer, flow, or disposal of a chemical substance, regardless of physical state or concentration, through all intended operations of manufacture, including the cleaning of equipment.

"MSDS" means material safety data sheet, the written listing of data for the chemical substance.

"NIOSH" means the National Institute for Occupational Safety and Health of the U.S. Department of Health and Human Services.

"Non-enclosed process" means any equipment system (such as an open-top reactor, storage tank, or mixing vessel) in which a chemical substance is manufactured, processed, or otherwise used where significant direct contact of the bulk chemical substance and the workplace air may occur.

"Non-industrial use" means use other than at a facility where chemical substances or mixtures are manufactured, imported, or processed.

"PMN substance" means the chemical substance described in the Premanufacture notice submitted by the Company relevant to this Order.

"Personal protective equipment" means any chemical protective clothing or device placed on the body to prevent contact with, and exposure to, an identified chemical substance or substances in the work area. Examples include, but are not limited to, chemical protective clothing, aprons, hoods, chemical goggles, face splash shields, or equivalent eye protection, and various types of respirators. Barrier creams are not included in this definition.

"Process stream" means all reasonably anticipated transfer, flow, or disposal of a chemical substance, regardless of physical state or concentration, through all intended operations of processing, including the cleaning of equipment.

"Scientifically invalid" means any significant departure from the EPA-approved protocol or the Good Laboratory Practice Standards at 40 CFR Part 792 without prior or subsequent Agency approval that prevents a reasoned evaluation of the health or environmental effects of the PMN substance.

"Scientifically equivocal data" means data which, although developed in apparent

3

conformity with the Good Laboratory Practice Standards and EPA-approved protocols, are inconclusive, internally inconsistent, or otherwise insufficient to permit a reasoned evaluation of the potential risk of injury to human health or the environment of the PMN substance.

"Sealed container" means a closed container that is physically and chemically suitable for long-term containment of the PMN substance, and from which there will be no human exposure to, nor environmental release of, the PMN substance during transport and storage.

"Use stream" means all reasonably anticipated transfer, flow, or disposal of a chemical substance, regardless of physical state or concentration, through all intended operations of industrial, commercial, or consumer use.

"Waters of the United States" has the meaning set forth in 40 CFR 122.2.

"Work area" means a room or defined space in a workplace where the PMN substance is manufactured, processed, or used and where employees are present.

"Workplace" means an establishment at one geographic location containing one or more work areas.

ATTACHMENT B
NOTICE OF TRANSFER OF
TOXIC SUBSTANCES CONTROL ACT
SECTION 5(e) CONSENT ORDER

_____   _____
Company (Transferor)   PMN Number

1. Transfer of Manufacture Rights. Effective on _____, the Company did sell or otherwise transfer to _____, ("Successor in Interest") the rights and liabilities associated with manufacture of the above-referenced chemical substance, which was the subject of a premanufacture notice (PMN) and is governed by a Consent Order issued by the U.S. Environmental Protection Agency (EPA) under the authority of §5(e) of the Toxic Substances Control Act (TSCA, 15 U.S.C. §2604(e)).

2. Assumption of Liability. The Successor in Interest hereby certifies that, as of the effective date of transfer, all actions or omissions governed by the applicable Consent Order limiting manufacture, processing, use, distribution in commerce and disposal of the PMN substance, shall be the responsibility of the Successor in Interest. Successor in Interest also certifies that it is incorporated, licensed, or doing business in the United States in accordance with 40 CFR 720.22(a)(3).

3. Confidential Business Information. The Successor in Interest hereby:

____ reasserts,

____ relinquishes, or

____ modifies

all Confidential Business Information (CBI) claims made by the Company, pursuant to Section 14 of TSCA and 40 CFR part 2, for the PMN substance(s). Where "reasserts" or "relinquishes" is indicated, that designation shall be deemed to apply to all such claims. Where "modifies" is indicated, such modification shall be explained in detail in an attachment to this Notice of Transfer. Information which has been previously disclosed to the public (e.g., a chemical identity that was not claimed as CBI by the original submitter) would not subsequently be eligible for confidential treatment under this Notice of Transfer.

_____   _____
Company (Transferor)   PMN Number

_____   _____
Signature of Authorized Official   Date

_____

2

Printed Name of Authorized Official

_____
Title of Authorized Official

_____
Successor in Interest

_____   _____
Signature of Authorized Official   Date

_____
Printed Name of Authorized Official

_____
Title of Authorized Official

_____
Address

_____
City, State, Zip Code

_____
Successor's Technical Contact

_____
Address

_____
City, State, Zip Code

_____
Phone

CHAPTER 3

FIFRA/FQPA and Nanotechnology

Executive Summary

As applied to pesticides, the new and developing area of nanotechnology has the potential to bring real benefits as well as regulatory challenges. Consumer products on the market today are using engineered nanoparticles of active ingredients such as silver to achieve antimicrobial effects, and many more such products are likely.[1] Even as these consumer products are introduced, agricultural chemical producers are developing new pesticide products using nanotechnology to enhance the effectiveness or delivery of those pesticides. Among the uses of nanotechnology in agriculture currently being explored are agrochemical delivery (delivery of pesticides and other chemicals only when needed or for better absorption), nanosensors, and new or modified active pesticidal ingredients.[2]

Under the Federal Insecticide, Fungicide, and Rodenticide Act (FIFRA), as amended by the Food Quality Protection Act (FQPA), the U.S. Environmental Protection Agency (EPA) has the authority and responsibility to determine whether the benefits of pesticidal products developed using nanotechnology (referred to herein as "nanopesticides") outweigh any risks and to determine the conditions under which a nanopesticide may be registered so as to limit potential risks. EPA has stated that "[p]esticide products containing nanomaterials will be subject to FIFRA's review and registration requirements."[3] Yet it has also acknowledged questions about how FIFRA can be applied to nanopesticides, such as whether use

This chapter expands upon the Section of Environment, Energy, and Resources' May 2006 paper entitled *The Adequacy of FIFRA to Regulate Nanotechnology-Based Pesticides*. The Team Leader on that paper was Mark N. Duvall, Beveridge & Diamond, P.C. Revisions are by Lynn L. Bergeson and Timothy D. Backstrom, Bergeson & Campbell, P.C., and Charles L. Franklin, Akin Gump Strauss Hauer & Feld, LLP.

of a nanoscale material results in a change to a pesticide product already registered under FIFRA.

This chapter addresses those and other challenging issues relating to the application of FIFRA to nanopesticides. It discusses the extent to which FIFRA and EPA's implementing regulations and programs are adequate to address the regulatory challenges of such products.

In summary, EPA has considerable authority under FIFRA to prohibit, condition, or allow the manufacture and use of nanopesticides. Its regulatory tools include regulation of preregistration research and development (R&D) through experimental use permits (EUP); requirements for preregistration testing; the registration requirement, which requires development of data and can impose limits on the use and handling of a nanopesticide; requirements for registrants to submit post-registration adverse effects information; possible requirements for post-registration testing; and reregistration requirements. Additionally, EPA has strong enforcement options under FIFRA to proceed against unregistered nanopesticides or those found to cause unreasonable adverse effects on human health or the environment. EPA may therefore prohibit the use of nanopesticides presenting unreasonable adverse effects, and may restrict other nanopesticides so as to ensure that risks do not become unreasonable.

General Comments on FIFRA Regulation of Nanopesticides

What Is a Nanopesticide?

One of the challenges for EPA in developing a regulatory framework for "nanopesticides" is that there is no universally accepted definition of what constitutes a "nanopesticide."[4] Although there is no rigorous basis for any one definition of nanotechnology, a rough consensus has nevertheless emerged. Both EPA and the National Nanotechnology Initiative, a U.S. government project to coordinate nanotechnology research and development launched by Congress in 2001, define nanotechnology to involve a length scale of approximately 1 to 100 nanometers in any dimension.[5]

Small size alone is not sufficient, however, as very small things have always existed in nature. For example, volcanic ash can involve particles in the specified size range. To constitute nanotechnology as that term is generally used by EPA, the small structures must have been deliberately engineered through use of specific chemical or physical processes. This can include "bottom-up" processes that create structures from atoms and molecules, as well as "top-down" processes such as milling or machining larger particles into smaller particles.[6]

Moreover, some very small things involve conventional chemical processes that have long been in commercial use, rather than resulting from the more advanced engineering and fabrication techniques that are typically associated with nanotechnology. One familiar example of very small particles that have long been in commercial use is ions in solution. This example is also quite relevant to pesticide regulation because EPA determined that a washing machine that generates silver ions for antimicrobial purposes, as well as other devices that generate free ions for a pesticidal purpose, are pesticides that must be registered.[7] While the release of such ions may present significant environmental issues such as potential effects on wastewater treatment, it is doubtful whether there is any good reason to construe the equipment that generates such ions as nanotechnology. In contrast, very small solid particles of metals like silver and zinc that can be created by modern milling technology also have useful antimicrobial properties and may have utility for a variety of pesticidal purposes.

Nanopesticides may involve either very small particles of pesticidal active ingredients or other small engineered structures with useful pesticidal properties. In addition, nanotechnology may be used to produce the inert constituents in pesticide products. The latter category could include engineered nanocontainers or nanocapsules, which are already being studied as a technology for drug delivery but may also facilitate targeted delivery of pesticides to pest organisms.

FIFRA Provides Considerable Authority to Regulate Nanopesticides

FIFRA offers EPA ample statutory authority to regulate nanopesticides. This authority covers the entire scope of regulatory interest, from preregistration research and development to registration to post-registration marketing and use.

As discussed in greater detail under FIFRA Section 5, EPA regulates preregistration activities such as R&D. For example, EPA currently regulates R&D on conventional pesticides through EUPs. Pesticide developers must notify EPA and obtain a permit before conducting R&D on pesticides, except where the Agency has expressly chosen to exempt certain classes of R&D. EUPs themselves can be tailored to address the particular circumstances of the R&D activities or the material involved. Thus, EPA can ensure that the risks of testing unregistered nanopesticides are managed appropriately.

The degree of control that EPA has under FIFRA is in marked contrast to the Agency's regulation of R&D under the Toxic Substances Control

Act (TSCA). For example, under the premanufacture notice (PMN) R&D exemption, developers of new chemical substances have no obligation to notify EPA of any aspect of their R&D activities. EPA has limited means of controlling research risks beyond enforcing certain minimal requirements. Instead, the TSCA regulation simply requires that hazards are communicated; that the amount produced for R&D does not exceed that reasonably necessary for the research purpose; that a technically qualified individual supervises the research; and that records are maintained.[8]

As noted above, EPA has chosen to promulgate several limitations on the requirement to obtain an EUP before conducting R&D. Stringent controls have not been deemed necessary in the past for such research on conventional pesticides; however, they may or may not be necessary for R&D on nanopesticides. Theoretically, workers would be protected by applicable Occupational Safety and Health Administration (OSHA) requirements. Nevertheless, EPA could cut back on or eliminate its self-imposed restrictions on the scope of the EUP requirement with respect to nanopesticides if appropriate.

EPA's most powerful tool for controlling the potential risks posed by nanopesticides is the registration requirement. Registration review provides EPA with the opportunity to prohibit, condition, or allow the manufacture and use of nanopesticides and prescribe the conditions of that manufacture or use. The registration requirement in FIFRA Section 3 is backed up by strong enforcement powers that EPA can exercise over unregistered pesticides under FIFRA Sections 12, 13, 14, and 19.

The registration requirement expressly provides EPA authority to require the generation of data necessary for risk assessment on the candidate nanopesticide; to conduct a risk assessment balancing the risks and benefits of the nanopesticide; to prohibit the use of a nanopesticide that is determined to present unreasonable adverse effects to human health or the environment; and to condition the use of a nanopesticide to ensure that it does not present the threat of unreasonable adverse effects. The authority afforded under FIFRA is far more flexible than that provided for existing chemicals under TSCA Sections 4, 6, and 7. Instead, EPA's FIFRA authority is more akin to EPA's authority under TSCA Section 5(a)(1) regulating new chemicals, but it is even more comprehensive than this PMN authority.

EPA's authority to regulate nanopesticides under FIFRA continues post-registration as well. After a period of years, reregistration is required under FIFRA Sections 3(g) and 4. EPA can require post-registration testing of nanopesticides under FIFRA Sections 3(c)(2)(B) and 4. Nanopesticide registrants remain under an obligation to notify the Agency of adverse effects discovered after registration under FIFRA Section 6(a)(2). If EPA should determine that the balance of risks and benefits of a nanopesticide has shifted since its original risk assessment, the Agency has a variety of tools to halt further use of the nanopesticide under FIFRA Sections 12, 13, 14, and 19.

Nanopesticides Provide EPA with Regulatory Challenges

Although the Agency has considerable authority to regulate nanopesticides under FIFRA, exercising that authority appropriately will require rethinking its decisions on issues that are settled with respect to conventional pesticides. Among the challenges are the following:

- EPA may want to reconsider its exemptions from EUP requirements for nanopesticides.
- EPA may need to identify an appropriate data set for EPA's risk assessment of nanopesticides.
- EPA may want to develop registration requirements specifically for nanopesticides.

OPP Workgroup on Nanotechnology

To assist EPA in working through these challenging issues, the Office of Pesticide Programs (OPP) established an internal OPP Nanotechnology Workgroup (Workgroup) in late 2006.[9] Cochaired by senior managers in OPP's Antimicrobials Division and Health Effects Division, the Workgroup includes legal, science, and policy experts from across OPP and the Office of General Counsel.[10] The Workgroup has dual purposes: first, to help OPP develop a regulatory and technical framework (including data needs) for reviewing nanopesticides submitted for registration under FIFRA,[11] and second, to advise OPP decisionmakers on technical and policy issues raised on a case-by-case basis with specific applications.[12] In keeping with these objectives, the Workgroup's stated duties include

- working with and learning from other agencies within the government and internationally in figuring out the best way to evaluate potential risks to nanomaterials;
- placing OPP in the best position to evaluate a nanopesticide submission when it is received;
- providing information to the public on how the Agency is assuring the safety of future nanopesticides;

- providing clear guidance to pesticide registrants of any additional data needs for nanopesticides as soon as possible; and
- providing a scientifically sound and transparent process.[13]

As of September 2009, OPP had not issued or proposed any specific details of a national regulatory framework for FIFRA applications, nor had OPP acknowledged receipt of any formal, publicly noticed registration application for a new nanotechnology-derived pesticide. As such, it remains to be seen what the long-term impact of the Workgroup will be on OPP's general or product-specific nanotech policy.

EPA Authority to Regulate Nanopesticides before Registration

EPA has authority to regulate any substance or mixture of substances intended to be a pesticide before registration. Existing authorities under FIFRA in the preregistration regulatory arena do not distinguish regulated products by size, but by intended function (i.e., as a pesticide). Accordingly, the Agency is well poised to regulate nanopesticides before their registration either immediately or upon modification of existing regulations or policies.

EPA's EUP Authority

EPA's authority to regulate preregistration activities for pesticides has generally focused on R&D activities, particularly with respect to those persons wishing to accumulate the necessary information to register a pesticide under FIFRA Section 3. Under FIFRA Section 5(a), EPA has established a number of requirements for the preregistration activities under an EUP. These requirements are set forth generally in the regulations at 40 C.F.R. Part 172.

Many requirements of Part 172 may apply directly or with some minor modification to nanopesticides. For example, EPA has prescribed data submission requirements for EUPs at 40 C.F.R. Section 172.4(b). Since those requirements set forth the information needed by the Agency in general terms, EPA likely would not need to conduct additional rulemaking to address EUP data requirements for nanopesticides. Regardless, EPA may still wish to review those requirements in light of the unique properties of nanopesticides and make modifications as necessary. Specifically, as a matter of practical application, EPA may want to notify applicants of the specific nanopesticide information that the Agency believes is appropriate to meet the requirements of 40 C.F.R. Sections 172.4(b)(1)(iii), (vi), and (vii) regarding the details of the testing, scope of testing to be conducted, purpose of the testing, any prior testing or knowledge of existing properties or toxicity of the nanopesticides, and the planned storage and disposal plans for the nanopesticides. Section 172.4(b)(1)(viii) provides EPA with authority even beyond the scope of the information described, in that this provision allows EPA to seek any "other additional pertinent information as the Administrator may require." Accordingly, EPA has the authority in existing regulations to require additional testing or information necessary to appropriately review any EUP application associated with nanopesticides.

In addition, EPA can solicit public comment and even hold a public hearing on any EUP permit applications that may be of regional or national significance.[14] On several occasions EPA has solicited public comment on EUP applications related to small-scale field testing of genetically engineered microbial pesticides,[15] and the Agency may wish to do so for nanopesticides as well.

Based on the information submitted under 40 C.F.R. Section 172.4(b) and the Agency's analysis of such information, EPA may impose appropriate limitations on a nanopesticide's EUP to address any potential risks.[16] As to whether an EUP would be needed for a nanopesticide for which a macro version has been registered, see the discussion of pesticide registration below.

As an alternative to direct application of existing provisions, should EPA determine that nanopesticides warrant specific regulatory provisions, the Agency may wish to consider a special nanopesticide provision on EUPs that addresses the unique characteristics of those substances. EPA has done this in the past with genetically modified microbial pesticides.[17] EPA would need to support the decision for special provisions with evidence demonstrating this need. Given the new and unique properties of nanopesticides, this step would likely not be needed.

Exemptions from EUP Requirements and Corresponding Controls

Currently, under 40 C.F.R. Section 172.3, certain types of R&D activities are exempt from the EUP requirements. Examples include tests conducted in laboratories or greenhouses and replicated field trials or other tests intended solely to assess a pesticide's potential efficacy, toxicity, or other properties.[18]

Given the unique properties of nanopesticides, EPA may wish to reconsider that general presumption as applied to these new types of pesticides, especially with respect to tests assessing toxicity. EPA has expressly reserved the right to revoke the general presumptions on a case-by-case basis. Specifically, pursuant to 40 C.F.R. Section 172.3(e), EPA may require that any type of testing for a particular pesticide or class of pesticides, including tests generally exempt from EUP requirements, be conducted under an EUP through notification to the pesticide developer. Given the unique characteristics of nanopesticides, EPA may wish to consider invoking the provisions of 40 C.F.R. Section 172.3(e) should Agency analyses justify such action. Depending on the Agency's evaluation of the risks, such action could be for particular nanopesticides, particular subclasses of nanopesticides, or for the entire class of nanopesticides.

Other controls under FIFRA also exist for unregistered pesticides. For example, under FIFRA Section 3(a), EPA may through regulation limit the distribution, sale, and use of any unregistered pesticides undergoing R&D that are not the subject of an EUP or emergency exemption. To do so, however, EPA must demonstrate that such regulation is necessary to prevent unreasonable adverse effects on the environment.

Other Preregistration Exemptions Potentially Applicable to Nanopesticides

In addition to the general EUP exemptions, FIFRA Section 12(b)(5) provides an exemption from civil penalties where an unregistered pesticide (such as an R&D nanopesticide) is being shipped for testing. Typically, the reasons involved with the testing include determining the potential value of the product as a pesticide or the product's toxicity or other properties. Although this exemption may be of concern to EPA for nanopesticides, this provision relates solely to shipment of R&D pesticides. Accordingly, any concerns that EPA may have with respect to appropriate labeling or use can be addressed through other FIFRA provisions as discussed in this chapter.

Temporary Tolerance Level

Testing nanopesticides may result in nanopesticide residues on or in foods. In such situations, EPA may issue a temporary tolerance level for the expected nanopesticide residue before issuing an EUP. The Agency would need to determine whether a temporary tolerance level would be required for nanopesticides under FIFRA Section 5(b), just as EPA would for any other R&D pesticide. Regarding its application to nanopesticides, the terms of Section 5(b) do not appear otherwise to restrict EPA's regulatory authority in this regard simply because of the unique characteristics of nanopesticides. Accordingly, FIFRA appears to grant EPA wide latitude in this area.

In the case where a temporary tolerance already exists for the conventional version of a nanopesticide, EPA may wish to consider whether the Agency would need to revise the applicable tolerance—or issue a separate tolerance altogether—to address the nanopesticide version and the particular circumstances associated with that pesticide.

Studies

Under FIFRA Section 5(d), EPA may determine whether to require certain studies to be performed during the EUP period. Thus, EPA can sometimes require testing as a condition of granting an EUP. This provision, however, applies only to "a pesticide containing any chemical or combination of chemicals which has not been included in any previously registered pesticide." Where a conventional registered pesticide contains the same "chemical or combination of chemicals" used in a nanopesticide, this provision apparently would not apply.

State Issuance of EUPs

Under FIFRA Section 5(f) and 40 C.F.R. Part 172, Subpart B, EPA has authorized states to issue EUPs under state authority. A number of states have applied for and received EPA authorization. Given the unique properties of nanopesticides and the authorization given to states to issue EUPs, EPA may wish to consider whether it should amend that authorization and its regulations in light of the unique characteristics of nanopesticides.

Regardless of whether EPA chooses to amend those regulations, the Agency still retains broad authority over state-issued EUPs under 40 C.F.R. Section 172.26. Specifically, those provisions require states issuing, amending, or revoking state-level EUPs to provide EPA with notification of such actions. EPA retains the ability to amend or revoke such EUPs provided sufficient justification. Accordingly, while EPA may wish to revisit whether the provisions of 40 C.F.R. Section 172.26 require revision in light of the unique properties of nanopesticides, existing regulatory authority already provides a significant degree of post-issuance oversight. Any subsequent changes deemed appropriate or necessary would likely be more effective before being issued by the authorized state.

EPA Authority to Require Registration of Nanopesticides

The centerpiece of EPA's FIFRA authority to regulate nanopesticides is the registration requirement of FIFRA Section 3. Subject to limited exceptions, no one may distribute or sell any unregistered pesticide, a prohibition backed up by strong enforcement tools. As part of the registration process, EPA can require applicants to develop extensive information relevant to an assessment of the pesticide's risks and benefits. Registration itself is not a simple up-or-down decision, but rather is always a limited approval that conditions the use of a pesticide in a manner designed to prevent unreasonable adverse effects. Thus, through the registration requirement, EPA may prohibit the use of nanopesticides presenting unreasonable adverse effects on human health or the environment; and EPA may restrict other nanopesticides in a tailored manner to ensure that the risks do not become unreasonable.

If a nanopesticide is unregistered, it may not be distributed or sold in the United States (except under exceptions such as that for R&D discussed above and certain export exemptions).[19] Moreover, distribution and sale of a registered nanopesticide is also prohibited if the pesticide is distributed, sold, or used in a manner that departs from the conditions of EPA's approval, such as claims substantially different than those approved in a registration,[20] a composition different from that reviewed in the registration[21] or that is adulterated,[22] or a use inconsistent with the product's labeling.[23] Violation of these prohibitions can bring civil or criminal penalties under FIFRA Section 14 as well as orders for stop sale, removal, or seizure under FIFRA Section 13. EPA can suspend or cancel the registration or change its classification under FIFRA Section 6 and can order a recall under FIFRA Section 19(b). It can inspect for compliance under FIFRA Section 9. These enforcement tools give EPA authority to ensure that its ability to control nanopesticides through registration is effective.

Before exercising its enforcement authority against distributors and sellers of unregistered nanopesticides, EPA may wish to consider educating them about the application of FIFRA to nanopesticides. As can be seen with some nanotechnology-based consumer products, nontraditional pesticide producers are entering the market. Due to the unique characteristics of nanopesticides, some producers and sellers may not recognize that FIFRA applies to their products and may be unaware of their obligations under FIFRA.

Whether Existing Registered Products Are Nanopesticides

More than 1,000 active ingredients, and thousands of pesticide products, are currently registered under EPA's pesticide registration program and reflect a wide variety of proposed uses, manufacturing processes, and modes of action.[24] According to EPA, none of these previously approved registrations would qualify as nanopesticides under EPA's current "nanotechnology" definitions.[25] Moreover, as of February 2009, EPA had yet to publish any notice acknowledging receipt of an application for any pesticide product or active ingredient characterized as a "nanopesticide."

The lack of formal regulatory activity regarding nanopesticides is notable given that an April 2008 report by the Project on Emerging Nanotechnologies (PEN) estimated that over 600 nanotech-based consumer products are on the global market, and 3 to 4 products are being added *each week.*[26] While the rigorous registration procedures applied to *all* FIFRA-regulated substances are likely one reason the U.S. pesticide industry would lag behind other chemical and consumer product sectors in commercializing nanomaterials, some stakeholders have argued that nanopesticides may already be on the U.S. market—just absent any nanotechnology claim or the requisite regulatory approvals.

For example, on May 1, 2008, a coalition of nongovernmental organizations joined the International Center for Technology Assessment (ICTA) in filing a petition with EPA's Office of Enforcement and Compliance Assurance (OECA) identifying 260 products in the U.S. marketplace that ICTA claimed contain "nanosilver" and that, ICTA alleges, "either expressly make pesticidal claims or imply pesticidal effectiveness—none of which are currently registered with EPA."[27] On November 19, 2008, EPA issued a *Federal Register* notice seeking comment on the petition.[28] EPA extended the comment period until March 20, 2009, allowing the submission of many comments.

Whether Nanopesticides Are Covered by Existing Registrations of Conventional Pesticides

A threshold question is whether a nanopesticide is deemed unregistered solely because of the size of the active ingredient. This question arises where a conventional version of a nanopesticide is already registered. It also arises where a registrant has reengineered a conventional-sized nanopesticide registered active to a nanoscale unbeknownst to EPA. Both scenarios under FIFRA resemble that under TSCA as to whether a nanomaterial is an existing or new chemical substance, but the resolution under FIFRA is clearer than that under TSCA.

Under FIFRA Section 3(c)(5)(D), registration decisions depend in part upon an EPA determination that a pesticide "will not generally cause unreasonable adverse effects on the environment." Thus, EPA has both the authority and responsibility to determine whether the benefits of a nanopesticide outweigh its risks and to determine the conditions under which a nanopesticide may be registered so as to limit those risks appropriately. Key factors in that determination are the claims and composition of the nanopesticide. Since the precise balancing of risks and benefits of a nanopesticide is likely to be different than that for a corresponding registered conventional pesticide, EPA likely would take the position that use of nanoscale ingredients in place of conventional ingredients in a registered pesticide would necessitate the need for a new or amended registration.

In contrast, regulation under TSCA Section 5(a)(1) depends on whether a prospective PMN chemical has the same "particular molecular identity" as an existing chemical,[29] a determination that is independent of risk assessment considerations. Under TSCA the question turns on chemistry, which is not under EPA's control; but under FIFRA the question turns on risk assessment, which is under EPA's control.

Under FIFRA, a pesticide is considered unregistered if its claims differ substantially from claims made for the registered pesticide or if its composition differs from the composition of the registered pesticide.[30] On the other hand, a pesticide with the same formulation and claims as a registered pesticide may be added to the registration by supplemental statement (i.e., without a separate risk assessment).[31]

The claims made for a nanopesticide may well differ from those made for a corresponding registered conventional pesticide, since nanotechnology allows for many new applications. Taking the antimicrobial active ingredient silver as an example, macro versions of silver-based pesticides are registered for use in swimming pools and other applications. Silver-based nanopesticides are being used as antimicrobials in fabrics, appliances, and other consumer applications.[32] Although both sets of uses involve antimicrobial activity, the details on the claims may well differ. Such differences may support an EPA determination that registrations for macro versions may not apply to nano versions.

Composition includes the identity of both active and inert ingredients and their ratios. Thus, the issue of whether or not a nanopesticide has the same composition as a corresponding registered conventional pesticide is not simply a function of whether the nano ingredient is an active or an inert. Given the unique characteristics of nanomaterials, a nanopesticide is unlikely to have the same composition as the corresponding registered macro version.

Even where the claims and composition of a nanopesticide are ostensibly identical to that of its macro version, EPA could take the position that the substitution of a nanoscale ingredient for its macro counterpart constitutes a change in composition per se. Moreover, the product chemistry, toxicology, and other information submitted for the macro version under 40 C.F.R. Part 158, Subparts C and D, almost certainly would not apply to the nano version.

The unique characteristics of a nanopesticide will most likely result in different risks and benefits than those of its macro version. Thus, EPA's previous resolution of the balance of risks and benefits, and appropriate control measures, for the corresponding conventional pesticide is likely to differ from that for the nanopesticide even where the composition and claims are ostensibly identical.

Thus, a new or amended registration application will be needed for a nanopesticide, at least in most cases. Where the registrant of a conventional pesticide applies for registration of a nano version of that pesticide, an application for an amended registration of the corresponding macro pesticide under FIFRA Section 3(c)(7) and 40 C.F.R. Section 152.44 might be appropriate. An amended registration application could be required to provide additional information specific to the nanopesticide's risks and benefits.

Data Requirements for Registration of Nanopesticides

To perform the statutorily mandated risk assessment for a nanopesticide, EPA needs information on the potential risks and benefits of the nanopesticide. Under FIFRA Section 3, EPA may obtain the necessary data from prospective registrants. This authority contrasts with EPA's inability to require testing of PMN chemicals except through a consent order under TSCA Section 5(e). Risk assessments under TSCA Section 5(a)(1) necessarily rely on structure-activity relationships and other assumptions in many instances, which may create difficulties for EPA where the unique characteristics of nanomaterials make analogies to conventional chemical substances unreliable. Under FIFRA, however, EPA can ensure that the Agency has all the data on the specific nanopesticide necessary to perform its risk assessment.

For a number of reasons, EPA might elect to require additional or different data for nanopesticides. Pesticidal materials deliberately engineered to be nanoscale may exhibit materially different physical, chemical, and biological properties from those of otherwise similar conventional pesticides. Because the ratio of surface atoms or molecules to total atoms or molecules increases with decreasing particle size, active ingredients that have been milled to a smaller particle size may have increased reactivity and greater biological activity than their conventional-sized counterparts. Smaller particles of a pesticidal active ingredient may also be absorbed, metabolized, and excreted differently than conventional pesticides are. In the case of nanomaterials engineered on the molecular level, these materials may present unique toxicologic hazards. For example, carbon nanotubes have been shown to cause inflammation and fibrogenic pulmonary responses and thus have greater pulmonary toxicity than do carbon nanoparticles.[33] Moreover, nanopesticides may differ in their environmental persistence and mobility.

EPA has indicated that its OPP Nanotechnology Workgroup is considering "whether or not existing data are sufficient to support licensing/registration or if the unique characteristics associated with nanopesticides warrant additional yet undefined testing."[34] Unique physical data requirements for nanopesticides could include physical characteristics such as particle size and size distribution, shape, surface-to-volume ratio, and electrical properties.[35] Unique toxicologic requirements for nanopesticides might include studies to measure reactivity or biological activity, pharmacokinetic studies, and bioassays using test animals to evaluate potential adverse effects such as local inflammation, tumor promotion, and neurotoxicity. EPA will also need to consider whether nanopesticides should be tested separately under the endocrine testing program established pursuant to FQPA Section 405(p).[36]

Under FIFRA Section 3(c)(2)(A), EPA may publish guidelines for the kinds of information that it needs to support registration, and it may revise those guidelines from time to time. EPA's current data guidelines appear in 40 C.F.R. Part 158. EPA could develop guideline provisions directed specifically at nanopesticides. It has done so for genetically modified biochemical pesticides and microbial pesticides.[37] To date, EPA has not promulgated data requirements specifically for plant-incorporated protectants,[38] although it is considering doing so.[39] EPA may wish to consider whether adopting data guidelines specifically for nanopesticides would be helpful for the Agency in conducting its risk assessments.[40]

For example, EPA's current data guidelines for physical and chemical characteristics (color, melting point, vapor pressure, etc.) do not address the key characteristics that denote the unique character of nanomaterials.[41] Also, since nanomaterials may be used in nanopesticides at extremely low levels, current thresholds and exemptions may not be appropriate.[42] EPA may also wish to revisit testing guidelines for application to nanopesticides.

The current uncertainty facing applicants concerning special data requirements that EPA may elect to impose for registration of nanopesticides could be exacerbated by the Pesticide Registration Improvement

Renewal Act (PRIA 2),[43] which requires EPA to conduct more stringent reviews of the "completeness" of registration applications and imposes financial penalties for submission of incomplete applications. Since most early applications for registration of nanopesticides are expected to be antimicrobial products, further uncertainty is created by the lack of finality of its proposed registration requirements for antimicrobial products.[44] Given the current lack of any clear guidance from EPA on any unique data requirements EPA may impose for nanopesticides, it would be helpful for EPA to state clearly that no application for registration of a nanopesticide will be deemed incomplete under PRIA 2 for failure to include such data.

Tolerances for Nanopesticides

EPA has authority to establish tolerances for pesticide residues in or on food or feed commodities under the Federal Food, Drug, and Cosmetic Act (FFDCA). FFDCA Section 408(b)(2)(A)(i), as amended by Section 405 of the FQPA, allows EPA to "establish or leave in effect a tolerance for a pesticide chemical residue in or on a food only if the Administrator determines that the tolerance is safe."[45] FFDCA Section 408(b)(2)(A)(ii), as amended, defines the term "safe" to require that EPA assess the "harm [that] will result from aggregate exposure to the pesticide residue."[46] In establishing tolerances, EPA is also required to consider a number of factors enumerated in FFDCA Section 408(b)(2)(D).[47]

EPA generally exercises broad discretion in defining the residue for which a particular tolerance will be established and in specifying the analytic methodology to be utilized in determining compliance with the tolerance. Thus, it would be hypothetically possible for EPA to establish a separate tolerance for nanoscale residues of a particular pesticide in or on treated commodities. Nevertheless, EPA would first need to consider whether any residues in or on food or feed from application of a nanopesticide would still be present in a nanoscale form. While applicators or agricultural workers may be directly exposed to nanoscale particles of an active ingredient, any residues of the active ingredient, or of degradation products or metabolites, that ultimately remain in commodities may no longer retain these characteristics. Moreover, EPA will need to consider whether particle size would be a material factor in determining any potential risks following ingestion of a treated commodity with nanoscale residues.

As in the ongoing discussions of regulation of nanotechnology under TSCA, the question of whether nanoscale particles of a pesticidal active ingredient should be deemed to be a different chemical substance than conventional-size particles of the same active ingredient may arise. EPA's 2001 guidance document on performing aggregate exposure and risk assessments under the FQPA states: "'Aggregate exposure' refers to the combined exposures to a single chemical across multiple routes (oral, dermal, inhalation) and across multiple pathways (food, drinking water, residential)." [48] In any case, even if EPA were to decide to treat a nanopesticide as a discrete substance for purposes of determining aggregate exposure, EPA would likely retain discretion where appropriate to combine such estimates with exposure to conventional-size particles of the same active ingredient in determining aggregate risk. EPA is explicitly authorized to consider "other substances that have a common mechanism of toxicity" and "related substances" by FFDCA Section 408(b)(2)(D)(v) and (vi).[49]

Registration Decisions for Nanopesticides

Where a candidate nanopesticide presents some data gaps (which appears likely for most nanopesticides, at least for the near term), EPA has discretion to review the nanopesticide registration application under criteria that allow for the conditional registration of the pesticide, pending the development of additional required data, under FIFRA Section 3(c)(7).[50]

In addition, when making registration decisions, EPA may impose appropriate restrictions on the registration of a nanopesticide to prevent it from causing unreasonable adverse effects. Among the restrictions available to EPA for nanopesticide registrations in appropriate cases are the following:

- Registration for general use or restricted use under FIFRA Section 3(d) and 40 C.F.R. Part 152, Subpart I.
- Labeling restrictions under FIFRA Section 3(c)(5)(B) and 40 C.F.R. Part 156. These may include use of personal protective equipment, disposal restrictions, use restrictions, etc.
- Worker protection standards under FIFRA Section 25(a) and 40 C.F.R. Part 170.
- Packaging standards under FIFRA Section 25(c)(3) and 40 C.F.R. Part 157.

As appropriate, EPA may want to revise its implementing regulations for these provisions to address the unique circumstances of nanopesticides.

Other Uses of Nanotechnology in Pesticide Application

Nanocontainers and Capsules for Pesticide Delivery

As discussed earlier, nanoscale structures that are not themselves pesticidal in character might be used as containers or capsules to deliver nanoscale particles of a pesticide active ingredient to target pests. This type of structure is often described as one part of the "second generation" of nanotechnology.[51] Such nanocontainers are likely to be dendrimers, which are nano-sized polymers built at the molecular level from branched units.[52] These structures are already being studied as candidates for drug delivery systems and may also have potential as vehicles for delivery of nanoscale pesticide particles. It is uncertain whether EPA would view such nanocontainers or nanocapsules as inert ingredients or as a component of a composite active ingredient, but any unique risks and benefits attributable to use of this technology should be considered in either case.

Nanosensors for Monitoring Pests or Residues

Another "second generation" product of nanotechnology that may have utility in pesticide application is nanosensors. Nanoscale sensors are being developed that can detect the presence of chemical substances in the environment at very low concentrations.[53] These sensors may have a role in detecting the presence or abundance of pest species or in monitoring environmental levels of pesticidal substances. If used separately, such sensors would probably not be considered to be pesticides as that term is defined by FIFRA,[54] but they might still be evaluated as part of the registration process if they are an integral component of a registered product.

EPA's Post-Registration Authority to Regulate Nanopesticides

Nanotechnology is both new and rapidly developing. EPA may anticipate that significant information relevant to nanopesticides will continue to become available for years. As EPA approves registrations for nanopesticides, it may do so with the assurance that it has substantial authority under FIFRA to amend its regulation of those nanopesticides even after granting registration.

EPA can expect to receive relevant information directly from nanopesticide registrants. FIFRA Section 6(a)(2) imposes on each registrant of a nanopesticide the obligation to notify EPA promptly of "additional factual information regarding unreasonable adverse effects on the environment of the pesticide." EPA regulations under 40 C.F.R. Part 159 specify particular kinds of information required to be submitted. The information may relate to a class of registered pesticides rather than to a particular pesticide.[55] In addition, there is a catchall provision for information that the registrant knows or should know that EPA might regard as raising concerns about the continued registration of the pesticide or about the terms and conditions of that registration.[56] This threshold for reporting is arguably lesser than, or at least comparable to, the "substantial risk" criterion for reporting of information under TSCA Section 8(e).

EPA may also exercise other post-registration authority. For example, EPA chose to develop a tailored requirement for reporting post-registration information for plant-incorporated protectants.[57] EPA also has issued a reminder to registrants of genetically engineered microbial pesticides of the need to report adverse effects information under FIFRA Section 6(a)(2).[58] EPA may wish to undertake similar action for nanopesticides as well.

EPA can also require nanopesticide registrants to develop new data post-registration. FIFRA Section 3(c)(2)(B) authorizes EPA to require registrants to conduct new studies, and FIFRA Section 4(d)(3) allows EPA to require submission of missing or inadequate data in connection with reregistration. Section 3(c)(2)(B) can be triggered whenever EPA determines that such new data are "required to maintain in effect an existing registration of a pesticide." This is a lesser threshold than the thresholds under TSCA Section 4(a) for EPA to issue a test rule.

Under FIFRA Section 3(g)(1)(A), EPA is required to review a pesticide's registration every 15 years. Thus, EPA must eventually reconsider its registration decisions in light of post-registration developments. The 15-year review interval does not preclude any earlier review of the registration.[59] Reregistration is required under FIFRA Section 4(a) for pesticides containing active ingredients also contained in any pesticide initially registered before November 1, 1984. As EPA conducts its reregistration reviews, the Agency can consider the particular hazards presented by nano versions of those active ingredients. While reconsideration of a new registration of a nanopesticide may not occur for many years, EPA may grant initial registrations for nanopesticides knowing that reregistration will eventually be required. Reregistration decisions have a lower threshold for EPA action than does TSCA Section 6(a), with its requirement for EPA to determine that a chemical substance or mixture "presents or will present an unreasonable risk of injury to health or the environment."

In appropriate cases, EPA may also act to protect the public from nanopesticides without waiting for reregistration. Based on sufficient evidence, under FIFRA Section 6, EPA may by order cancel or suspend a registration or change its classification. Under FIFRA Section 13, EPA may issue stop sale, use, or removal orders for pesticides whose registrations have been canceled or suspended. EPA may also order a recall under FIFRA Section 19(b) for such pesticides. Experience demonstrates that EPA's recall authority has proven easier to use than its "imminent hazard" authority under TSCA Section 7.

Conclusion

The preceding discussion supports the view that EPA can regulate nanopesticides adequately through its existing statutory authority. EPA may wish, however, to revisit its current regulations and guidance to address the unique characteristics of nanopesticides.

Congress did provide additional statutory authority to regulate antimicrobials under the FQPA, but that authority mostly addressed procedure rather than substantive criteria for registration.[60] The FQPA does not establish a precedent for EPA needing legislative action to address particular classes of pesticides presenting different characteristics than the pesticides traditionally addressed by FIFRA.

The better precedent is genetically engineered microorganisms used as pesticides. In 1986, EPA determined that it could regulate the pesticidal products of biotechnology through FIFRA, despite the Agency's recognition that at least some of those products were likely to exhibit new traits. EPA addressed such factors as EUP exemptions, data requirements for registration, and post-registration reporting of adverse effects information for bioengineered microbial pesticides under FIFRA without the need for new legislative authority.[61] In 2001, EPA promulgated regulations to address a particular class of bioengineered pesticides—plant-incorporated protectants—again without additional legislative authority.[62] These examples suggest that EPA can regulate nanopesticides effectively under FIFRA.

Notes

1. *See, e.g.,* Woodrow Wilson International Center for Scholars, Project on Emerging Technologies, Nanotechnology Consumer Products Inventory, http://www.nanotechproject.org/inventories/consumer/.

2. *See, e.g.,* Woodrow Wilson International Center for Scholars, Project on Emerging Technologies, Inventory of Agrifood Nanotechnology, http://www.nanotechproject.org/inventories/agrifood/; Center for Science, Technology, and Public Policy, University of Minnesota, The Nanotechnology-Biology Interface: Exploring Models for Oversight (Sept. 15,

2005), Workshop Report, *available at* http://www.hhh.umn.edu/img/assets/9685/nanotech_jan06.pdf.

3. U.S. Environmental Protection Agency (EPA), *Nanotechnology White Paper* (Feb. 2007) at 66, *available at* http://www.epa.gov/osa/pdfs/nanotech/epa-nanotechnology-whitepaper-0207.pdf.

4. *See, e.g.*, J. Clarence Davies, *EPA and Nanotechnology for the 21st Century*, Woodrow Wilson International Center for Scholars, May 2007 ("EPA needs to craft a category of nanopesticides and decide how to regulate them."), *available at* http://www.nanotechproject.org/file_download/files/Nano&EPA_PEN9.pdf.

5. *Nanotechnology White Paper* at 5.

6. *Nanotechnology White Paper* at 7.

7. 72 Fed. Reg. 54039 (Sept. 21, 2007).

8. 40 C.F.R. §§ 720.3(cc) and (ee), 720.36.

9. *See* OPP Presentation to the OPP's Presentation to the Pesticide Program Dialogue Committee on Nov. 9, 2006, http://www.epa.gov/pesticides/ppdc/2006/november06/session7-nanotec.pdf.

10. *Id*. at Slide 26 (listing members of the OPP Nanotech Workgroup).

11. *Id*. at Slide 25.

12. *See id.*

13. *Id*. at Slide 28.

14. 40 C.F.R. § 172.11.

15. *See, e.g.*, 69 Fed. Reg. 23193 (Apr. 28, 2004); 66 Fed. Reg. 30458 (June 6, 2001).

16. *See* 40 C.F.R. § 172.5(c).

17. *See, e.g.*, 40 C.F.R. Part 172, Subpart C.

18. *See, e.g.*, 40 C.F.R. § 172.3(b) and (c).

19. FIFRA §§ 12(a)(1)(A), 17(a), 7 U.S.C. §§ 136j(a)(1)(A), 136o(a).

20. FIFRA § 12(a)(1)(B), 7 U.S.C. § 136j(a)(1)(B).

21. FIFRA § 12(a)(1)(C), 7 U.S.C. § 136j(a)(1)(C).

22. FIFRA § 12(a)(1)(E), 7 U.S.C. § 136j(a)(1)(E).

23. FIFRA § 12(a)(2)(G), 7 U.S.C. § 136j(a)(2)(G).

24. *See* EPA, *Pesticides: Registration Review—Program Highlights* (updated Dec. 18, 2008) ("By law, the Agency must complete the first 15-year cycle of registration review by October 1, 2022. To meet this requirement, EPA will begin opening about 70 dockets annually beginning in fiscal year 2009 and continuing through 2017, so that almost all currently-registered pesticides will have dockets opened by 2017. As of fiscal year 2008, EPA expects 722 pesticide cases comprising 1,135 active ingredients to undergo registration review."), http://www.epa.gov/oppsrrd1/registration_review/highlights.htm; EPA, *Pesticide Reregistration Facts* (updated Nov. 24, 2008) ("The reregistration program encompasses approximately 1,150 pesticide active ingredients organized into 613 'cases' or related groups."), http://www.epa.gov/pesticides/reregistration/reregistration

_facts.htm; EPA, *Economic Assessment of Proposed Procedural Regulations for the Registration Review of Pesticides* (May 20, 2005) ("The Agency currently regulates about 18–20,000 pesticide products containing 1,160 active ingredients."), Docket No. EPA-HQ-OPP-2004-0404-0002.

25. *See, e.g.*, Statement of Jack Housenger, Associate Director, OPP Health Effects Division and Co-chair of OPP's Nanotechnology Workgroup, Transcript of Meeting of Pesticide Program Dialogue Committee (Nov. 8 & 9, 2006) at 313, lines 11–19 ("[W]e're not currently aware of any [registered nanopesticides]. Some companies have claimed that nanopesticides—that they have nanopesticides and we have been informed by others that they think their competitors' products are nanos. However, when we checked on these, we found that they did not fit the definition of nanotechnology."), *available at* http://www.epa.gov/pesticides/ppdc/2006/november06/nov06-transcript.pdf.

26. See PEN, *New Nanotech Products Hitting the Market at the Rate of 3–4 Per Week: Nanotechnology Consumer Products Are in Your Mouth and On Your Face*, http://www.nanotechproject.org/news/archive/6697/.

27. *See ICTA v. Johnson, Petition for Rulemaking Requesting EPA Regulate Nano-Silver Products as Pesticides* (May 1, 2008), http://www.icta.org/nanoaction/doc/CTA_nano-silver%20petition__final_5_1_08.pdf.

28. 73 Fed. Reg. 69644 (Nov. 19, 2008).

29. *See* TSCA § 3(2)(A)(i), 15 U.S.C. § 2602(2)(A)(i).

30. FIFRA § 12(a)(1)(B) and (C), 7 U.S.C. § 136j(a)(1)(B) and (C).

31. FIFRA § 3(e), 7 U.S.C. § 136a(e).

32. *See* Nanotechnology Consumer Products Inventory, *supra* note 1.

33. *Nanotechnology White Paper* at 54.

34. *Id.* at 20.

35. *Id.* at 31.

36. Codified as Section 408(p) of the Federal Food, Drug, and Cosmetic Act (FFDCA), 21 U.S.C. § 346a(p).

37. 40 C.F.R. §§ 158.690, 158.740.

38. *See* 40 C.F.R. Part 174, Subpart H (data requirements for plant-incorporated protectants—reserved).

39. EPA has indicated that it intends to propose data requirements for the registration of plant-incorporated protectants in Dec. 2009. 73 Fed. Reg. 91424 (Nov. 24, 2008) (the semiannual regulatory agenda is published online at http://www.reginfo.gov).

40. EPA has issued in final its data requirements for biochemical and microbial pesticides, 72 Fed. Reg. 60988 (Oct. 26, 2007), and for conventional pesticides, 72 Fed. Reg. 60934 (Oct. 26, 2007).

41. 40 C.F.R. §§ 158.310 and 161.190.

42. *See, e.g.*, 40 C.F.R. §§ 158.320(d) and 161.155(d) (0.1% threshold for impurities); 40 C.F.R. §§ 158.320(e) and 161.155(e) (no information required for impurities associated with inerts, even inerts that may be nanoparticles);

40 C.F.R. §§ 158.350(b)(2) and 161.175(b)(2) (table of standard certified limits); Pesticide Registration (PR) Notice 96-8, "Toxicologically Significant Levels of Pesticide Active Ingredients" (Oct. 31, 1996), § IV (guidance on levels considered toxicologically significant), *available at* http://www.epa.gov/opppmsd1/PR_Notices/pr96-8.html.

43. Pub. L. No. 110–94 (enacted Oct. 9, 2007).
44. *See* 64 Fed. Reg. 50672 (Sept. 17, 1999). Although this proposed rule was not adopted, EPA often advises applicants wishing to register antimicrobial products to consult it for guidance on EPA requirements. EPA promulgated antimicrobial data requirements at 40 C.F.R. Part 161, however.
45. 21 U.S.C. § 346a(b)(2)(A)(i), as amended by FQPA Section 405.
46. 21 U.S.C. § 346a(b)(2)(A)(ii).
47. 21 U.S.C. § 346a(b)(2)(D).
48. EPA Office of Pesticide Programs, *General Principles for Performing Aggregate Exposure and Risk Assessments* (Nov. 28, 2001), at 8, *available at* http://www.epa.gov/opp00001/trac/science/aggregate.pdf.
49. 21 U.S.C. § 346a(b)(2)(D)(v) and (vi).
50. *See* 40 C.F.R. § 152.111.
51. *Nanotechnology White Paper* at 12–13.
52. *Id*. at 9.
53. *Id*. at 23–24.
54. FIFRA § 2(u), 7 U.S.C. § 136(u).
55. *See* PR Notice 98-3, "Guidance on Final FIFRA Section 6(A)(2) Regulations for Pesticide Product Registrants" (Apr. 3, 1998), § X, *available at* http://www.epa.gov/opppmsd1/PR_Notices/pr98-3.pdf.
56. *See* 40 C.F.R. § 159.195(a).
57. *See* 40 C.F.R. § 174.71.
58. 51 Fed. Reg. 23313, 23320 (June 26, 1986).
59. *See* FIFRA § 3(g)(1)(B), 7 U.S.C. § 136a(g)(1)(B).
60. Food Quality Protection Act of 1996, Pub. L. No. 104–170, Title II, Subpart B, amended by the Antimicrobial Regulation Technical Corrections Act of 1998, Pub. L. No. 105–324. *See* 64 Fed. Reg. 50672 (Sept. 17, 1999) (proposed rule to implement this aspect of the FQPA).
61. *See* 51 Fed. Reg. at 23313.
62. 66 Fed. Reg. 37772 (July 19, 2001) (40 C.F.R. Part 174). The passage of the FQPA in 1996 had an incidental impact on this rulemaking.

CHAPTER 4

The Clean Air Act and Nanotechnology

Executive Summary

The Clean Air Act (CAA), first enacted in 1970, is a mature statute under which the U.S. Environmental Protection Agency (EPA) regulates emissions into the ambient air from a wide variety of sources of pollutants that may adversely affect human health or the environment. The regulatory strategies required or available under the CAA are not the same for all types of sources or air pollutants, but typically the processes include identifying the types of pollutants involved; characterizing the associated exposure risks and potential health and environmental impacts once released to the atmosphere; adopting and implementing health- or technology-based emissions control strategies; and monitoring the success of regulated entities in reducing emissions by meeting applicable pollutant limits or complying with other control requirements.

Engineered nanoparticles pose a number of regulatory challenges from the CAA standpoint.[1] Methods of practically identifying nanoparticles that may be released as air pollutant emissions are not currently developed, nor are methods of controlling or monitoring these releases developed sufficiently to rely on them with any confidence. Most critically, the health risks posed by nanoparticles in general are not yet well defined, despite the work done to characterize the risk posed by certain types of nanoparticles—particularly those produced by conventional combustion technologies used, for example, by mobile sources and power plants.

This chapter expands upon the Section of Environment, Energy, and Resources' June 2006 paper entitled *ABA EER CAA Nanotechnology Briefing Paper*. The Team Leader and primary author of that paper was Mary Ellen Ternes, McAfee & Taft. Revisions are by Mary Ellen Ternes.

While nanoparticles may consist of constituents that are currently regulated pursuant to the CAA, their unique nature poses regulatory hurdles. Due to their minuscule size, negligible mass, and higher reactivity resulting from relatively larger surface areas, nanoparticles behave very differently than pollutants now regulated under the CAA. Given these unique characteristics, nanoparticulate emissions in most instances are not amenable to the application of conventional methods to identify, monitor and measure, and control them.

The CAA may offer both statutory framework and the authority to regulate (or further interpret existing regulations) emissions of engineered nanoparticles when more is known about them and there is adequate scientific basis to develop appropriate tools to identify, monitor, and measure these emissions. The following discussion addresses the CAA provisions that may be relevant to EPA's regulation of engineered nanoparticle emissions.

Subchapter I, Part A—Air Quality and Emission Limitations Sections 101, 103, 108, 109, 111, 112, and 123

Section 101—Findings and Purpose

In enacting the CAA, Congress found, in relevant part, that the growth in the amount and complexity of air pollution brought about by industrial development had resulted in mounting dangers to the public health and welfare, including hazards to air. Congress additionally found that federal leadership would be essential for the development of cooperative federal, state, regional, and local programs to prevent and control air pollution.

Congress thus declared the purpose of the CAA was to protect and enhance the quality of the nation's air resources so as to promote the public health and welfare and the productive capacity of its population as well as to initiate and accelerate a national research and development program to achieve the prevention and control of air pollution. This statutory authority applies with equal force to regulation of nanoparticle emissions where such emissions present a threat to the public health and welfare.

Section 103—Research, Investigation, Training, and Other Activities

With Section 103, Congress directed EPA to establish a national research and development program for the prevention and control of air pollution. The program also has broad authority to coordinate with other federal departments and agencies. EPA's research, development, and testing authority encompasses methods for sampling, measurement, monitoring, analysis, and modeling of air pollutants, including "[c]onsideration of individual as well as complex mixtures of, air pollutants and their chemical transformations in the atmosphere."

Nanoparticulate emissions certainly would seem to fall well within "complex mixtures" and "their chemical transformations in the atmosphere." Certainly, too, EPA's current regulatory and policy development structure created in reliance on Section 103 is well suited to take an active role in investigating the health and welfare impacts as well as potential pathways for addressing air emissions associated with the emerging nanotech industry.

Air Pollutant Emissions Measurement

The Emission Measurement Center (EMC) in the EPA Office of Air Quality Planning and Standards (OAQPS) develops procedural methods used to characterize and measure air pollutant emissions. Part of the Emissions Monitoring and Analysis Division in OAQPS, the EMC is divided into two groups—the Source Measurement Analysis Group and the Source Measurement Technology Group. Bringing together research scientists in EPA's Office for Research and Development (ORD) and those in OAQPS responsible for developing national performance and emissions standards, EMC has developed methods for measuring air pollutants generated by the entire spectrum of industrial stationary sources. EMC also serves as a conduit between regulators and the regulated community in providing technical expertise and guidance necessary to implement EPA's rules, especially in specifying emission testing methods for pollution control evaluations, compliance determinations, and performance testing. EMC is the EPA's focal point for planning and conducting field test programs to provide quality data in support of regulatory development, validated emissions test methods, and expert technical assistance for EPA, state, and local air enforcement officials and industrial representatives involved in emissions testing.

EMC publishes methods for emissions testing and monitoring in five categories differentiated by (1) the legal status of the methods with regard to their application under federally enforceable regulations and (2) the validation information available on the method and EPA's corresponding confidence in application of the method for its intended use. EMC has published methods in the *Federal Register* that have been codified in 40 C.F.R. Parts 51 (State Implementation Plan (SIP)), 60 (New Source Performance Standards (NSPS)), 61 (National Emission Standards for Hazardous Air

Pollutants (NESHAP)), and 63 (Maximum Achievable Control Technology (MACT)). In addition, EMC also develops source category approved alternative methods (EPA approved alternatives to promulgated methods), conditional methods (methods reviewed and potentially applicable to specific source categories), preliminary methods (not well defined but potentially useful in specific scenarios as gap-filling methods), and "idea box" methods (intended to promote information exchange only).[2] Methods developed by EMC to date cover a wide variety of industry sectors and air pollutants.

Given the breadth of the methods developed to date and the depth of its technical expertise, EMC is well positioned—using and building upon state-of-the-art laboratory procedures—to investigate and develop methods that could apply to a wider variety of possible air pollutants. In view of the fundamental differences between nanoscale particulate and engineered nanoscale structures, however, it is not yet clear how much of this previous experience will be relevant in developing appropriate methods for engineered nanoscale structures.

Any effort to develop appropriate methods faces significant challenges. For example, there are detailed discussions in the docket materials supporting EPA's $PM_{2.5}$ rule[3] regarding the difficulty of capturing and quantifying simple nanoscale particulate (a less complex task than if engineered nanoscale structures were involved). Though EPA recognizes several categories of ultrafine particles less than 1 µm in diameter (these include "ultrafine particles" less than 0.1 µm in diameter that grow by coagulation or condensation and accumulate; "Aitkin-Mode Particles" between 0.01 and 0.1 µm; and "Nucleation-Mode Particles" less than 0.01 µm), EPA's own draft Staff Paper addressing $PM_{2.5}$ monitoring[4] acknowledges the challenges in controlling and monitoring these particles. As the draft Staff Paper observes, the $PM_{2.5}$ rule essentially requires the use of ambient monitoring technology capable of capturing merely 50 percent of particles with an aerodynamic diameter of 2.5 µm, 50 percent collection efficiency being deemed the effective cutoff point.[5] The Staff Paper notes various types of non-mass-reliant, ultrafine monitoring devices that count number rather than capture and weigh mass.[6] The devices include the nano-scanning mobility particle sizer (NSMPS), which counts particles in the 0.003- to 0.15-µm range, in contrast to a standard scanning mobility particle sizer (SMPS), which counts particles in the 0.01- to 1-µm range. All of these techniques are described as "widely used in aerosol research."[7]

EPA's Staff Paper also recognizes, however, that while it may be possible to count ultrafine particles, they change so quickly that the time distribution over the counting process may render the final count meaningless.[8] These changes affect the distribution of size, volume, and surface area of nanoparticles. For example, while the Staff Paper discusses "typical distribution" of ambient particles,[9] in reality all of these distributions may vary across locations, conditions, and time due to differences in sources, atmospheric conditions, topography, and age of the particulate.

Air Pollutant Emissions Modeling

EPA devotes a wide variety of resources to air pollution modeling. Key among them are its Support Center for Regulatory Air Models (SCRAM) site, which provides information (e.g., computer codes, meteorological input data, and documentation and guidance on usage) about mathematical models used to predict the dispersion of air pollution. EPA's Regional Modeling Center provides information and data associated with regional applications, including a description of modeling projects, tabular and graphical summaries of the emissions scenarios, simulated model results, and access to emissions and meteorological inputs and predictions. EPA's Modeling Clearinghouse provides reviews of modeling techniques in specific applications.

EPA utilizes Models-3, a flexible software design system, to simplify the development and use of environmental assessment and decision support tools for a range of applications from regulatory and policy analysis to understanding the interactions of atmospheric chemistry and physics. The initial version of Models-3 employs a Community Multiscale Air Quality (CMAQ) system with capabilities for urban- to regional-scale air quality simulations of tropospheric ozone, acid deposition, visibility, and fine particulate. EPA's Air Quality Modeling Group provides support in atmospheric and mathematical technique.

EPA also has models specifically designed for air toxics, including the Industrial Source Complex (ISC3) model, or, for more simple screening, the TSCREEN model. Stationary sources can also utilize EPA's "Guidance on the Application of Refined Dispersion Models for Hazardous/Toxic Air Releases,"[10] which provides guidance on the use of dense gas models.

The major barrier preventing use of EPA's current modeling resources to characterize the fate and transport of nanoparticle pollutant emissions in the atmosphere is that the current set of models use parameters (i.e., follow rules) that describe the behavior of target pollutants that are either measurable particulate in steady state or are chemicals, in each case regulated by mass. Because nanoparticles are neither steady state nor properly regulated as mass, these models simply cannot be used for purposes of modeling nanoparticles. Thus, until measurement and modeling methods are developed for nanoparticles that take into account the unique nature of these pollutants, nanoparticulate emissions cannot be reliably measured, and their fate and transport in the atmosphere cannot be predicted. Because there are so many different types of nanoparticles that can vary so widely, the development of proper measurement and modeling parameters will pose unique technical challenges and accompanying demands on limited EPA resources, despite its considerable expertise and experience in air pollution modeling.

Section 108—Air Quality Criteria and Control Techniques

Section 108(a) requires EPA to publish a list including each "criteria" air pollutant[11] for the purpose of establishing primary and secondary NAAQS within 30 days after December 31, 1970, to be revised "from time to time, thereafter." Under Section 108(a)(1), pollutants are to be included on the list if they are emitted from "numerous or diverse mobile or stationary or sources" and if, in EPA's judgment, those emissions "cause or contribute to air pollution which may reasonably be anticipated to endanger public health or welfare." Theoretically EPA could revise the Section 108(a) list and the NAAQS to include nanoparticles, assuming that the Section 108(a)(1) test for listing is satisfied. This pathway, however, seems unwieldy given the time-consuming process for designating criteria pollutants and the incredible variety of engineered nanostructures. A simpler path forward may be to revise the tools used to monitor the current NAAQS for $PM_{2.5}$ so that nanoparticles are included in the $PM_{2.5}$ compliance requirements.

Section 108(b)(1) requires EPA to publish "information on air pollution control techniques" simultaneously with the publication of the criteria pollutants list or a revision to that list. Therefore, if EPA should decide to designate nanoparticles as a criteria pollutant, it would also be required to publish the relevant information on air pollution control techniques. Apart from developing and identifying specific air pollution control techniques, EPA also enforces air pollution control efficiencies and, in some instances, even specific technologies in implementing many sections of the CAA, as discussed in the next section.

Conventional Air Pollution Control Technology

The CAA may effectively require the use of specific pollution control technologies and work practices at stationary sources in implementing several different sections of the CAA, including Standards of

Performance for New Stationary Sources (NSPS pursuant to Section 111), Prevention of Significant Deterioration/New Source Review (PSD/NSR pursuant to Sections 108 and 109, and 160 through 193), and NESHAPs (pursuant to Section 112, which include MACT). Each of these statutory programs requires certain control technologies and work practices and/or, frequently, control efficiencies based on the application of a specific control technology.

In terms of their relevance for controlling nanoparticle emissions, conventional air pollution control methods implemented through these programs are probably tested most vigorously at regulated hazardous and solid waste combustion facilities. These industrial-scale processes combust extremely varied waste streams creating nanoparticles (non-engineered) of every type. Air pollution control methods used at waste combustion sources are designed to control chlorides and other halogen acid gases; criteria pollutants, such as nitrogen oxides and sulfur dioxides; volatile organic compounds (VOC), which are photoreactive and can form ozone; and particulate emissions. Any attempt to control nanoparticulate emissions, however, must focus on ultrafine particles that are much less than 2.5 µm (2,500 nanometers) in diameter. Using conventional pollutants as a reference, ultrafine particulates would be about the size of fumes, mists, dusts, sprays, smokes, fly ash, coal dust, metal fumes and dust, carbon black, pulverized coal, and alkali fumes.

Technologies employed to remove these fine particulates include cyclones, scrubbers, electrostatic precipitators, fabric filters, and HEPA filters. Specific techniques utilized by these types of control equipment include ultrasonic venturi scrubbers (which work by highly accelerating the stack gas and then creating an impact zone, causing the particulate to stick together or "agglomerate," followed by a settling chamber that allows gravity to pull down the particulate, now a larger size); liquid countercurrent scrubbers; cloth particulate filters; packed beds; high-efficiency air filters; thermal precipitation; and electrical precipitators.[12]

All of the gas-scrubbing techniques utilize one of four types of mechanisms for capturing particulate matter: interception; gravitational force; impingement; or contraction and expansion. Interception causes an effective increase in the size of the fine particle, allowing it to be affected by gravity and thus make it easier to remove through settling, or slowing of the gas stream sufficiently to allow particles to fall from it. Impingement occurs when an obstacle is placed in the gas stream; the particles are too heavy to flow around the obstacle and consequently strike the obstacle itself. Finally, contraction causes condensation of the moisture in the stream, while high turbulence in a contracted area results in improved contact between solid and liquid particles that, through agglomeration, become heavy enough to separate from the gas stream.[13]

The removal efficiency achieved by all of these methods is dictated largely by particle size—either the initial size itself or the larger particle created through ability of the gas-scrubbing technique to agglomerate the smaller particles into larger ones that can efficiently be removed through one of the conventional removal techniques.[14] Particles of less than 100 nanometers, however, defy these removal efforts because their chemical and physical characteristics prevent their behaving as do larger particles, rendering such conventional techniques ineffective for use with nanoparticles.

As an example, solid waste incinerator emissions treated with multistage controls—including a venturi and spray scrubber—achieved particulate removal efficiencies approaching 100 percent for all particulate matter over 5 μm in diameter, but only 54.6 percent for the particulates less than 760 nanometers in size. Nearly half of these very small particles, therefore, still were emitted into the ambient air. Literature describing a study of venturi scrubbers using a fine-water mist spray to achieve nucleation and agglomeration did achieve reportable removal efficiencies of particles between 1 and 100 nanometers.[15] With the aid of the fine-water mist spray to first cause the ultrafine particulate to stick together into larger particles, the scrubbers achieved 40 percent removal efficiency for 50-nanometer particulate and 80 percent removal for 100-nanometer particulate.[16] These results show some potential, but significant improvements are still needed.

Enhancements Benefiting Nanoparticulate Removal

Devices relying primarily on impact and agglomeration have not yet been developed for nanoparticulate removal in industry, though devices such as cyclones enhanced through operation at low pressures or addition of electrical fields may show some promise.[17] Filtration systems, such as conventional high-efficiency particulate air (HEPA) filters and ultralow particulate air-rated filters, have achieved relatively high removal efficiencies of fine particulate—such as 99.97 percent removal at 7,300 nanometers and 99.9999 percent removal at 100 nanometers—through the use of very substantial pressure drops.[18] The performance of these filters can be enhanced without such great drops in pressure by using electrostatically augmented air filters and dielectric screens.[19] These applications are expensive and used only where absolutely necessary, such as in ultraclean rooms for microelectronics component assembly or hospital surgeries. It is not yet clear whether filtration will be adequate or practical for industrial applications.

A nonintuitive method of nanoparticulate control stems from the lack of gravitational effect, allowing a temperature gradient to govern nanoparticulate direction. In areas with higher temperatures, the nitrogen and oxygen molecules in the air are more excited and thus move around more. This movement effectively pushes the nanoparticle to an area of lesser molecular excitation—that is, a cooler area. In the nano arena, the benefit of this type of particulate collection, called "thermophoretic collection," is that the effect is independent of particle size, as long as the size is nanoscale. Another benefit of thermophoretic collection is that many nanoscale synthesis systems use high temperatures to enhance chemical reactions necessary to achieve the molecular state from which the desired nanoparticle can be assembled through nucleation (preferred joining together, as in agglomeration or crystallization). The nucleation process occurs in a quench zone with temperature gradients from hot to cool. Thus, thermophoretic collection systems seem to offer a "natural" method for nanoparticulate control.[20]

Another promising method for nanoparticulate removal, especially for systems with low-pressure drops (relatively constant pressure systems with low gas stream velocity) is through the use of electrical fields. In this method, the particles become charged and are subjected to an electric field that causes them to become attracted to collector walls. Studies have indicated that with standard methods some particles fail to achieve a charge, resulting in less efficient capture and efficiencies in the area of 90 percent for 60-nanometer particulate to less than 10 percent for 10-nanometer particulate. Enhancement of the process with additional directed ionization sources ("soft X-ray irradiation and unipolar coronas"), however, has greatly improved the capture efficiencies, raising them to greater than 99.99 percent for 5- to 100-nanometer particles.[21]

Section 109—NAAQS

Under Section 109(a), EPA is required to establish numerical primary (protecting public health) and secondary (protecting public welfare) NAAQS for each of the criteria pollutants listed under Section 108. The primary standard must be stringent enough to protect the public health with an "adequate margin of safety." EPA has established NAAQS for six such criteria pollutants, including particulate matter. The current standards for particulate matter were developed without reference to engineered nanostructures, and it would be necessary to revisit the existing standard if EPA should determine to incorporate the regulation of nanoparticles within its scope.

Alternatively, if EPA determined to regulate emissions of engineered nanostructures as a new criteria pollutant, a fundamentally different approach would be in order. The criteria pollutants for which EPA already has set NAAQS under Section 109 are regulated in terms of mass per volume of air. As previously observed, however, nanoparticles are unique in their characteristics. While they very well may be $PM_{2.5}$ for purposes of the fine-particle NAAQS currently in effect, at the same time they may behave like VOC ozone precursors or may contain lead. The mass limitation approach currently in use may not adequately protect the public from the health impacts of ambient concentrations of these nanoparticles. This does not preclude EPA from regulating nanoparticles as new criteria pollutants; Section 109 does not require the NAAQS set for criteria pollutants to be based upon mass limitations or concentrations determined by mass in any case. Therefore, Section 109 does not expressly prevent EPA from adopting primary or secondary standards for nanostructures based upon "number" of particles, rather than mass—though again, as discussed previously, the practical aspects of adopting a criteria pollutant approach appear unwieldy at best.

Section 111—Standards of Performance for New Stationary Sources

Section 111 requires EPA to establish technology-based standards for air pollutant emissions from new stationary sources (New Source Performance Standards, or NSPS), by category. In effect, these standards are built upon and typically require new sources to "engineer in" specific types of pollution control technologies. If EPA decided to regulate nanoparticles as criteria pollutants—presumably as $PM_{.001-1.0}$, to specifically address particles an order of magnitude smaller than $PM_{2.5}$—new sources of these nanoparticles also would be subject to regulation under Section 111, assuming the necessary findings were made. Under Section 111(b)(1)(A), the standard-setting process begins at the source level with EPA publishing, and periodically revising, a list of stationary sources for regulation. The regulatory trigger for inclusion of a source category on the NSPS list is whether, in EPA's judgment, the source category "causes, or contributes significantly to, air pollution which may reasonably be anticipated to endanger public health or welfare." Source categories that emit criteria pollutants, for example, are amenable to such a finding. Thus, if nanoparticles are regulated as criteria pollutants, EPA could be expected to establish NSPS for these sources.

Section 112—NESHAPs

Section 112 establishes an extensive regulatory scheme for addressing "hazardous air pollutants" (HAP) from existing and new stationary sources. Because the program progressed slowly in its first 20 years, Congress in 1990 inserted a list of nearly 200 pollutants in Section 112(b)(1) for which it required EPA to establish national emissions standards (NESHAP). The pollutants included by congressional action are by definition "hazardous" for purposes of Section 112, and no further findings of hazard must be made by EPA as a prerequisite to regulating them. Nanoparticles are not specifically listed in Section 112(b)(1). Constituents contained in nanoparticles may be listed; the list does not address the physical form of any of the included pollutants, but only the constituents themselves.

Pollutants not previously listed by Congress, however, still may be added by EPA. Section 112(b)(2) provides the EPA Administrator with the authority to revise the list as follows:

> (b)(2) Revision of the list.—The Administrator shall periodically review the list established by this subsection and publish the results thereof and, where appropriate, revise such list by rule, **adding pollutants which present, or may present, through inhalation or other routes of exposure, a threat of adverse human health effects** (including, but not limited to, substances which are known to be, or may reasonably be anticipated to be, carcinogenic, mutagenic, teratogenic, neurotoxic, which cause reproductive dysfunction, or which are acutely or chronically toxic) or adverse environmental effects whether through ambient concentrations, bioaccumulation, deposition, or otherwise, but not including releases subject to regulation under subsection (r) as a result of emissions to the air. **No air pollutant which is listed under section 108(a) may be added to the list under this section, except that the prohibition of this sentence shall not apply to any pollutant which independently meets the listing criteria of this paragraph and is a precursor to a pollutant which is listed under section 108(a) or to any pollutant which is in a class of pollutants listed under such section.** No substance, practice, process or activity regulated under title VI of this Act shall be subject to regulation under this section solely due to its adverse effects on the environment.[22]

Although both are aimed primarily at protecting human health, the statutory test for what constitutes a HAP under Section 112 differs from tests for listing and standard setting for criteria pollutants under Sections 108 and 109. As stated in the quoted language the CAA does not contemplate overlap between criteria pollutants and HAPs; no criteria pollutant may be listed under Section 112 unless it independently meets the Section 112(b)(2) test for listing and is a precursor to a Section 108 pollutant.

Section 112(b)(4) allows EPA to use "any authority available" to acquire information on the health or environmental effects of a substance—which would include engineered nanoparticles—if there is insufficient information available to decide whether they should be regulated as HAPs. If EPA should decide to list manufactured nanoparticles under the HAP provision, Section (b)(5) provides the further authority to establish, by rule, test measures and other analytic procedures for monitoring and measuring emissions, ambient concentrations, deposition, and bioaccumulation. In the event that EPA decided to regulate nanoparticles as HAPs, it would identify the source category or categories that emit them and then develop technology-based MACT standards for the particular manufacturing industry involved. If these proved insufficient to address the associated health risk, Section 112(f) allows EPA to adopt additional, health-based standards for the source categories.

Section 112(r)—Accidental Release Prevention of Extremely Hazardous Substances

Section 112 addresses accidental releases as well as more predictable process emissions from sources of HAPs. Section 112(r) specifically provides for additional protections to prevent, and minimize the impacts of, accidental releases into the ambient air from stationary sources of regulated chemical substances or of "other extremely hazardous substances." Here again the first step was the preparation of an initial list of 100 substances that "in the case of an accidental release, are known to cause or may reasonably be anticipated to cause death, injury, or serious adverse effects to human health or the environment,"[23] and thus, if released, could result in potentially catastrophic consequences for surrounding communities. Congress specified certain substances to be among those included on the initial list and gave EPA both the power and responsibility to review the list and add and delete substances. Thus the authority exists to include manufactured nanoparticles should their accidental release pose the level of harm to human health that this provision contemplates.

Section 112(r)(1) contains a "general duty clause," which provides in part:

The owners and operators of stationary sources producing, processing, handling or storing [a chemical in 40 C.F.R. Part 68 or any other extremely hazardous substance] have a general duty [in the same manner and to the same extent as the general duty clause in the Occupational Safety and Health Act (OSHA)], to identify hazards which may result from . . . releases using appropriate hazard assessment techniques, to design and maintain a safe facility taking such steps as are necessary to prevent releases, and to minimize the consequences of accidental releases which do occur.

Beginning with the list of extremely hazardous substances published under the Emergency Planning and Community Right-to-Know Act (EPCRA), EPA has developed a list of 77 toxic substances and 63 flammable substances promulgated in 40 C.F.R. Part 68, based on consideration of the following factors:

(i) the severity of any acute adverse health effects associated with an accidental release;
(ii) the likelihood of an accidental release of the substance; and
(iii) the potential magnitude of human exposure to accidental releases of the substance.[24]

For these substances, EPA has established threshold quantities (TQs) that, if met, trigger the application of the Section 112(r) risk management program requirements provided by 40 C.F.R. Part 68. The established TQs for these substances range from a minimum of 500 pounds to a maximum of 20,000 pounds.[25]

In reviewing Section 112(r) in the context of nanotechnology, it is clear that this provision, like the rest of the CAA, does not distinguish between conventional and nano-sized particles. With Section 112(r), however, EPA would appear to have flexibility to distinguish between conventional and nano-sized particles in designating additional chemicals for its list and establishing appropriate mass thresholds that might be triggered by current nanoscale manufacturers in the event of an accidental release. EPA appears to have more flexibility in adding to the list of Section 112(r) constituents than in revising the original list of HAPs mandated by Section 112(b)(1).[26]

To add to the Section 112(r) list, EPA may initiate an addition on its own or may act on the basis of a petition from any person, considering the factors set out above.[27] In making a listing decision, EPA requires documentation of literature searches as well as effects data indicating the potential for death, injury, or serious adverse human and environmental impacts from acute exposure following an accidental release. EPA also requires exposure data or previous accident history data, which may include physical and chemical properties of the petitioned substance.[28]

Given the specificity involved in a Section 112(r) listing determination, EPA should have sufficient discretion to properly review and, if warranted, add to the list a nanoscale version of any known or newly manufactured chemical. The general duty clause in the statute, moreover, is not specifically limited to chemicals listed in 40 C.F.R. Part 68, but expressly includes "any other extremely hazardous substance," a term that is not limited to the definition in CAA Section 112(r)(1).[29] The applicability of the general duty clause does not depend on whether mass thresholds are met. Thus, existing nanoscale manufacturers in possession of sufficient quantities of a nanoscale material that if accidentally released, could have catastrophic results to human health and the environment may be subject to the Section 112(r) general duty clause.

Section 123—Stack Heights

Section 123 prohibits the use of stack height as a means of circumventing emission limitations, thereby ensuring that sources cannot engineer a stack to exceed stack height above that dictated by "good engineering practices," relying on dispersion rather than emissions limitations to reduce the impact of emitted pollutants on human health and the environment. This is not to say that some dispersion is not included when assessing emission impacts and potential control strategies; rather, the prohibition is intended to ensure that artificially high stacks are not used as a control strategy.

For some transient forms of nanoparticulate emissions—particularly those forms that quickly change sunlight and other atmospheric conditions—such dispersion may be an appropriate method of control. For this reason, the intentional use of stack height as a control technology for nanoparticles might be considered, causing EPA to revisit its stack height regulations in connection with this approach.

Subchapter I, Part C—Prevention of Significant Deterioration of Air Quality, Sections 160 through 193

The CAA's Prevention of Significant Deterioration (PSD) provisions require EPA to limit emissions of criteria pollutants into the ambient air to maintain compliance with the NAAQS in geographic areas that have achieved compliance status or better. Nanoparticles could fall into many different regulatory categories (NAAQS, as in VOCs—ozone precursors; ultrafine particles not counted as $PM_{2.5}$; and/or HAPs). Thus, regulation of each type of nanoparticle will fall into place depending upon EPA's categorization—and, whether EPA determines that ultrafine particles should count as part of $PM_{2.5}$ for NAAQS purposes.

Monitoring poses an obstacle to the potential inclusion of ultrafine particles within the NAAQS for $PM_{2.5}$. Currently, $PM_{2.5}$ monitors demonstrate low capture efficiency below 1 μm, and none below 0.5 μm, and even then there is no particle size distribution. Thus, the smaller nanoparticles and precursors of larger particulate are not addressed by the current $PM_{2.5}$ monitoring method and fall outside the scope of the current $PM_{2.5}$ standard.

Through extension of its current $PM_{2.5}$ standard, assuming future developments in monitoring technology, EPA could propose revisions to the $PM_{2.5}$ monitoring regulations to include monitors that capture submicron particulate. Inclusion of submicron particulate in the $PM_{2.5}$ standard—which is simply a mass limitation per volume of air—alone, however, will not adequately protect public health if forms of the submicron particulate are extremely harmful at exposures more properly characterized as numbers of particles, rather than mass of particles. Here again, the unique properties of submicron particulates will challenge straightforward regulatory answers.

Subchapter II, Part A—Motor Vehicle Emission and Fuel Standards, Sections 202 and 211

A significant percentage of nanoparticles in the ambient air of developed countries currently is combustion particulate generated by mobile sources. As discussed, particulate emissions greater than 1,000 nanometers now are regulated by the $PM_{2.5}$ NAAQS. As observed earlier, however, the smaller nanoparticles and precursors of larger particulate are not captured by the current monitoring technology and thus not adequately addressed by the $PM_{2.5}$ standard.

Consequently, one type of nanoparticle from mobile sources currently is unregulated simply due to its size. The types of nanoparticles normally emitted from mobile sources, without considering nanoparticle fuel additives, are generally carbonaceous combustion by-product and nitrogen oxides. This smaller particulate could be regulated through an additional PM standard, should EPA choose to do so. EPA also could utilize developments in technology to enforce existing auto emission standards while including nanoparticulate emissions pursuant to its standards-setting authority for motor vehicles under Section 202.

Additional issues arise from the industry developing fuel additives to enhance motor vehicle performance. Now on the market are many different types of fuel additives developed through what is purported to be "nanotechnology." Some of these may be harmless—such as the H2OIL Corporation's "F2-21" fuel additives, which appear to be merely water with a small amount of surfactant creating an emulsion that results in water droplets with diameters less than 100 nanometers.[30] Other types of "nano-fuel additives," such as cerium oxide, may pose more risk. According to Azonano.com, the Oxonica nano-fuel additive "Envirox" is essentially cerium oxide in particles of 10-nanometer diameters, which create a larger surface area for catalysis.[31] Cerium oxide is a lung irritant, however, and at nanometer particle sizes may be even more irritating because the greater surface area causes more reactivity.[32] Thus, nanoparticulate fuel additives will need to be carefully evaluated to avoid the possibility of a recurrence of a tetraethyl lead scenario, in which a ubiquitous gasoline additive was found to be toxic to humans (and problematic for catalytic converters in automobiles as well) and necessitated regulatory action, industry resistance, and an ultimate across-the-board phaseout. Fortunately, the provisions Congress already has included in the CAA to address tetraethyl lead should be equally applicable, as needed, to any new nanotechnology fuel or fuel additive.

Section 211 authorizes EPA to require manufacturers to provide information regarding all fuels and fuel additives and to address concerns arising from this information.[33] Sections 211(a), (b), and (c) authorize EPA to require fuel additive manufacturers to provide health effects data for both fuels and fuel additives, while (c) allows EPA to regulate fuels and fuel additives generally if, in its judgment, any emission product of the fuel or fuel additives will cause or contribute to air pollution, or if the fuel or fuel additive will damage the vehicle's emissions control equipment or impair its performance.

Two other fuel-related provisions may be relevant to nanoparticles. Section 211(f) prohibits regulated fuel and fuel additive manufacturers from distributing new fuels or fuel additives unless the fuel or fuel additive is "substantially similar" to any fuel or fuel additive used in vehicle certification. EPA may waive the prohibition if the manufacturer can prove that the new fuel or fuel additive and its emission products will not cause a violation of the vehicle's emission standards.

Section 211(l) requires that gasoline contain detergent additives to prevent accumulation of material deposits in the engine. Ironically, it may be these detergent additives that raise health risk issues as nanoparticle mobile source emissions.

Subchapter III—General Provisions, Sections 302, 303, and 304

The general provisions of the CAA give EPA broad authority to protect public health and welfare from air pollutant emissions. For example, the definitions in Section 302 authorize the Administrator to regulate any "air pollution agent or combination of such agents," including their precursors.[34] The statutory definition of "welfare" similarly is very broad and expands the concept of causation to include transformation, conversion, or combination with other air pollutants,[35] which is a characteristic of the behavior of nanoparticles in the atmosphere.

Section 303 empowers EPA to take emergency regulatory action when presented with "evidence that a pollution source or combination of sources (including moving sources) is presenting an imminent and substantial endangerment to the public health or welfare, or the environment." Section 303 also authorizes EPA broadly to initiate civil action or issue orders for the protection of the public health, or welfare, or the environment. This emergency authority is not pollutant specific. Thus, should EPA receive evidence that nanoparticulate emissions from a particular source pose such an "imminent and substantial" endangerment, EPA has emergency powers sufficient to cause such a source to cease and desist.

The CAA's citizen suit provision is available to members of the public who believe that the threat of litigation, or litigation itself and an order from a federal judge, are necessary to mobilize EPA to undertake a required task. Section 304 allows citizens to sue EPA where EPA allegedly has failed to perform any nondiscretionary duty or act under the CAA. Many individuals and organizations have filed suit against EPA under Section 304; at some point, should EPA fail to properly regulate nanoparticulate emissions, a good attorney may identify a nondiscretionary duty that EPA failed to perform and go to court to force EPA to act appropriately.

Section 320 provides EPA with authority to reconvene every three years to review its air quality modeling practices. If EPA finds itself in need of additional statutory authority for developing parameters to describe behavior of nanoparticulate in standard air models, it may turn to this provision for support.

Subchapter IV—Acid Deposition Control

Although nanoparticles often contain sulfur and nitrogen, the small overall mass contribution to the acid deposition issue that would seem to result from emissions of nanoparticles may render Title IV less of a priority in this chapter. Additionally, according to the literature, some sulfur is actually helpful in serving as a nucleation base for agglomerating nanoparticles. In view of these circumstances, at this point, Title IV seems less applicable than the CAA provisions discussed earlier.

Subchapter V—Permits

Should nanoparticles become regulated pursuant to other sections of the CAA, the operating permit provisions of Title V would apply accordingly. Implementation of Title V will be particularly affected by the timeline necessary to develop and adopt appropriate technology for the identification, capture, and monitoring of nanoparticles.

Subchapter VI—Stratospheric Ozone Protection, Sections 601 and 602

The science of nanoparticles is not yet sufficiently developed to know whether ambient levels of certain manufactured nanoparticles could cause a detrimental effect on stratospheric ozone. Insofar as Section 601 lists Class I and Class II substances in a chemical-specific manner similar to the listings of HAPs in Section 112, the discussion regarding Section 112 applies here as well. Pursuant to Section 602(c), EPA may add any substance to the list of Class I or Class II that the Administrator finds is known or may reasonably be anticipated to cause or contribute to harmful effects on the stratospheric ozone layer. If nanoparticle substances were to be added to the lists of Class I or Class II substances, then the remaining provisions of Section 602 would apply.

Conclusion

Based on the foregoing, EPA has clear authority under the CAA to address issues associated with nanoparticles. To do so effectively, however, EPA must (1) distinguish between types of nanoparticles, identifying nanoparticles posing actionable risk and determining appropriate regulatory approaches for each type of nanoparticle requiring regulatory control; (2) develop appropriate methods of sampling, analysis, and control sufficiently effective for nanoparticles; (3) recognize and adapt to a new form of "quantification" as number, rather than mass; and (4) avoid creating unnecessary delay in developing strategies to address nanoparticle emissions, because such delay could result in overregulation stifling this new industry.

Notes

1. This discussion addresses "engineered" nanoparticles, as opposed to other small particles that result from natural processes or simply a material's chemical and physical properties, such as by-products of the combustion process or materials in the vapor phase including fumes and aerosols. "Engineered" nanoparticles are those manufactured through construction at the molecular level.
2. *See* http://www.epa.gov/ttn/emc/tmethods.html.
3. Although EPA has long regulated air emissions of particulate matter, in 1997 it adopted for the first time National Ambient Air Quality Standards (NAAQS) specifically applicable to particulate matter with a diameter of 2.5 µm and smaller.
4. EPA, *Review of the National Ambient Air Quality Standards for Particulate Matter: Policy Assessment of Scientific and Technical Information* (OAQPS Staff Paper—First Draft, EPA-452/D-03-001, Aug. 2003), at tbl. 2-1, *available at* http://www.epa.gov/ttn/naaqs/standards/pm/data/pm_staff_paper_august2003_1stdraft.pdf.
5. *See also* 40 C.F.R. Part 50, Appendix L; 40 C.F.R. Part 53, Subpart F, Table F-3 (showing "fine" particulate as 0.85 µm).
6. *See* OAQPS Staff Paper, *supra* note 4, at Section 2.4.2.
7. P. A. Solomon & C. Sioutas, *Continuous and Semi-Continuous Methods for PM Mass and Composition*, EM (Air and Waste Management Association's magazine for environmental managers), April 2006, at 17–23.
8. OAQPS Staff Paper, *supra* note 4, at 2-4 and 2-5.
9. The largest number of ambient particles in a typical distribution is very small, below 0.1 µm in diameter. Most of the particle volume, and therefore most of the mass, is found in particles with diameters larger than 0.1 µm. Most of the surface area is between 0.1 and 1.0 µm, the distribution of which peaks around 0.2 µm.
10. Guidance on the Application of Refined Dispersion Models for Hazardous/Toxic Air Releases (May 1993), EPA-454/R-93-002, Revises EPA-450/4-91-007 (Radian Corporation, EPA Contract No. 68-D00125, WA51.
11. The term "criteria pollutant" derives from Section 108(a)(2), which requires EPA to publish air quality "criteria" for each of the listed pollutants that will "accurately reflect the latest scientific knowledge useful in indicating the kind and extent of all identifiable effects on public health or welfare that which may be expected from the presence of such pollutant in the ambient air."

12. CALVIN R. BRUNNER, HANDBOOK OF INCINERATION SYSTEMS ch. 22, fig. 22.1 (1991).
13. *Id*. at fig. 22.14.
14. The impacts on capture efficiency of greater particle size are limited to those that can be obtained without resort to operational parameters that are unrealistic in application, such as attempting extraordinarily high-pressure drops to achieve greater impacts.
15. C.-J. Tsai et al., *An Efficient Venturi Scrubber System to Remove Submicron Particles in Exhaust Gas*, 55 J. AIR & WASTE MGMT. ASS'N 319 (Mar. 2005).
16. *Id*. at 323.
17. P. Biswas & C.-Y. Wu, *Nanoparticles and the Environment*, 55 J. AIR & WASTE MGMT. ASS'N 708, 720 (June 2005).
18. Such substantial pressure drops can take their toll on the equipment, which must be run at maximum performance levels—consuming, in turn, a good deal of power.
19. Biswas & Wu, *supra* note 17, at 720.
20. *Id*. at 721.
21. *Id*.
22. CAA § 112(b)(2) (emphasis added).
23. CAA § 112(r)(3).
24. CAA § 112(r)(4).
25. *See* 40 C.F.R. § 68.130, Tables 1 through 4.
26. Since 112(b)(1) was enacted, the list of 188 chemicals has been modified only four times, removing methyl ethyl ketone, certain glycol ethers, caprolactum, and hydrogen sulfide. EPA has not added to the list. *See* http://www.epa.gov/ttn/atw/pollutants/atwsmod.html.
27. CAA § 112(r)(4); 40 C.F.R. § 68.120.
28. 40 C.F.R. § 68.120(g)(6).
29. Extremely hazardous substances are not limited to the list of regulated substances listed under Section 112(r), nor the extremely hazardous substances under EPCRA § 302 (40 C.F.R. Part 355, Appendices A and B). "Extremely hazardous substance" would include any agent "which may or may not be listed or otherwise identified by any Government agency which may as the result of short-term exposures associated with releases to the air cause death, injury or property damage due to its toxicity, reactivity, flammability, volatility, or corrosivity." Senate Committee on Environment and Public Works, Clean Air Act Amendments of 1989, Senate Report No. 228, 101st Congress, 1st Session (1989) at 211 (Senate Report). "The release of any substance which causes death or serious injury because of its acute toxic effect or as a result of an explosion or fire or which causes substantial property damage by blast, fire, corrosion or other reaction would create a presumption that such substance is extremely hazardous." *Id*.

30. *See, e.g.,* http://www.foresight.org/nanodot/?p=1930.
31. *See, e.g.,* http://www.azonano.com/details.asp?ArticleID=31.
32. *See, e.g.,* http://physchem.ox.ac.uk/MSDS/CE/cerium_IV_oxide.html.
33. ROBERT J. MARTINEAU & DAVID P. NOVELLO, *Regulation of Fuel and Fuel Additives,* in THE CLEAN AIR ACT HANDBOOK 300 (2004).
34. CAA § 302(g).
35. CAA § 302(h).

CHAPTER 5

Nanotechnology and the Endangered Species Act

Executive Summary

The Endangered Species Act (ESA) furnishes protections for species listed as "threatened species" or "endangered species" (listed species) and habitat designated as "critical habitat" by the Secretary of the Interior (through the U.S. Fish and Wildlife Service) or the Secretary of Commerce (through the National Marine Fisheries Service). Species listings and critical habitat designations occur through a rulemaking process, either on a Service's own initiative or in response to a citizen petition. The ESA's language is broad enough to apply to virtually any conduct or substance that affects listed species and critical habitat, including the development, use, and disposal of nanoscale materials.

The ESA's two main protective mechanisms are the "Interagency Cooperation" provisions for federal agency actions in Section 7(a)(2), and the "take" prohibition in Section 9. Section 7(a)(2) imposes the obligation on federal agencies, through consultation with one of the Services, to ensure that agency actions are not likely to "jeopardize" listed species or "result in the destruction or adverse modification" of critical habitat. Section 9 applies to the conduct of any private or public "person" and prohibits the take of listed wildlife species. Remedies for take include injunctions, civil penalties, and criminal sanctions.

Both of these protective statutory provisions can apply to the effects of nanoscale materials. As this chapter explains, however, Section 7(a)(2) may apply more effectively and fairly than Section 9 for now, until more becomes known about the environmental impact of nanotechnology. The

This chapter was prepared by Steven P. Quarles, Crowell & Moring LLP; J. Michael Klise, Crowell & Moring LLP; and Wm. Robert Irvin, Defenders of Wildlife.

Supreme Court's gloss on Section 9 in the leading ESA take case, *Babbitt v. Sweet Home Chapter of Communities for a Great Oregon*,[1] complicates, and creates uncertainties about, applying the take prohibition to nanoscale materials and other technologies on the frontiers of science. Under *Sweet Home*, establishing take from nanoscale materials may be difficult because Section 9 requires proof that a given material is a "proximate cause" of harm—that is, the material's effects were reasonably foreseeable and not a scientific unknown. *Sweet Home* also requires proof of actual injury to, or death of, an identifiable member of a listed wildlife species—a challenging evidentiary standard even if the adverse effects of activities or substances on listed wildlife species are clearly known and understood. Further, Section 9's breadth and the potentially harsh penalties for violations may give rise to use of prosecutorial discretion by the U.S. Department of Justice to refrain from prosecuting end users who in good faith are unaware of a nanoscale material's potential effects on wildlife. Nevertheless, fear of potential criminal and civil liability for take may also discourage companies from pursuing research and development of nanoscale technology, including its use for environmentally beneficial purposes.

By contrast, the protections afforded by ESA Section 7(a)(2) do not raise the same concerns or complications. Instead of imposing a tort-like prohibition, Section 7(a)(2) establishes a *process* for involving private stakeholders and the federal agencies that oversee nanoscale materials as part of their responsibilities under organic statutes such as the Toxic Substances Control Act and the Federal Insecticide, Fungicide, and Rodenticide Act. As is appropriate for emerging technologies, Section 7(a)(2) can trigger protections early in product development and marketing (when federal permits are needed) and high in the chain of commerce (at the preconsumer level), without the Section 9 demands of demonstrating proximate cause. Further, since Section 7(a)(2) contains built-in measures for minimizing take, as well as means to excuse liability should take occur in the course of otherwise legitimate activity, it can protect listed species and their habitat and still provide an incentive for exploring emerging areas such as nanotechnology without fear of legal sanctions should inadvertent take occur.

Introduction: The Endangered Species Act and Nanotechnology

Protection of imperiled wildlife and plants under the ESA[2] has evoked superlatives from many quarters. A National Academy of Sciences study referred to the ESA as "the broadest and most powerful wildlife-protection law in U.S. history."[3] Professor Coggins, in his public land law treatise, stated that the "[f]ederal endangered species law is the closest thing to an absolute legislative command in public natural resources law."[4] The Supreme Court in its first opinion on the ESA over a quarter century ago rendered effusive descriptions of the law's might: The "plain intent of Congress in enacting this statute was to halt and reverse the trend toward species extinction, whatever the cost"; the ESA "admits of no exception" and "reveals a conscious decision to give endangered species priority over the 'primary missions' of Federal agencies."[5] The statute reflects the judgment of Congress about how best to protect imperiled species and their habitats from the threats of endangerment and extinction arising from a variety of human actions.

Implementation of the ESA most often occurs and is most visible in the context of major land-disturbing activities, such as residential or commercial development, highway construction, energy and mining projects, and timber harvesting. But it also applies to new technologies, including, most recently, Navy sonar and wind energy turbines. Nanotechnology, in turn, will receive ESA attention, even when it may be the source of potential benefits to biodiversity by providing the means to remediate environmental contamination or to develop smaller, smarter medical or surveillance devices to protect threatened or endangered species. While nanotechnology may pose new questions to be examined under the ESA, the Act's broad language is sufficient to address this technology in the same manner it addresses others.

How Animal and Plant Species and Their Habitats Receive the ESA's Protection: Listing of Species and Designation of Critical Habitat

The ESA protects species at risk and the "ecosystems upon which [they] depend."[6] Nanotechnology has implications for both. ESA Section 4 provides the criteria and rulemaking procedures for the Services to list species as "endangered" or "threatened" species and designate those species' "critical habitat," thereby extending the ESA's protections to those species and habitats.[7]

The ESA identifies the criteria to be considered in determining whether to list a species:[8] "the present or threatened destruction, modification, or curtailment of [the species'] habitat"; "overutilization for commercial, recreational, scientific, or educational purposes"; "disease or predation"; "the inadequacy of existing regulatory mechanisms"; and "other natural or manmade factors affecting [the species'] continued existence."[9] Listing determinations must be made "solely on the basis of the best scientific and commercial data available."[10] The factors that lead to listing can include the effects of nanoscale materials, and may do so increasingly as the use and environmental presence of those materials expand and more is understood about their biological and ecological effects.

The criteria for designating "critical habitat" are contained in the ESA's definition of the term: areas within the geographical area occupied by the species at the time of listing that contain "physical or biological features essential to the conservation of the species" and "may require special management considerations or protection," and areas not occupied at the time of listing if the Secretary determines the entire "areas . . . are essential for the conservation of the species."[11] Once critical habitat is designated, impacts to it—including any impacts from nanoscale materials—are scrutinized under ESA Section 7.

Applying the ESA's Principal Protective Mechanisms to the Effects of Nanoscale Materials

The ESA contains two principal protective mechanisms for listed species that can apply to impacts from nanoscale materials: the take prohibition of ESA Section 9,[12] which protects individual members of a species, and the procedures for consultation between federal agencies and the Services on federal agency actions under ESA Section 7(a)(2),[13] which is aimed at avoiding "jeopardy" to entire species. The effects of nanoscale materials could be subject to either or both of these mechanisms. Each mechanism presents its own set of issues generally, as well as in the context of nanotechnology.

Protecting against Effects of Nanotechnology Using the ESA Section 9 Take Prohibition

Statutory and Regulatory Provisions

ESA Section 9(a)(1)(B)[14] prohibits the take of any endangered wildlife.[15] "Take" is defined broadly to encompass "harass, harm, pursue, hunt, shoot, wound, kill, trap, capture or collect" listed wildlife or any "attempt to engage in . . . such conduct."[16] By regulation, the Services define "harm" in the definition of take to include the concept that habitat disturbance, as might conceivably occur through the use or disposal of nanoscale materials, can be a cause of wildlife take—"significant habitat modification or degradation where it actually kills or injures wildlife by significantly impairing essential behavioral patterns, including breeding, feeding or sheltering."[17]

Several features make the take prohibition the ESA's preeminent wildlife protection mechanism:

- Section 9(a)(1)(B)'s take prohibition arguably prohibits any action that adversely affects a *single member* of a species. In contrast, as explained later, ESA Section 7(a)(2) bars actions that are likely to threaten the survival of an entire species, not its individual members, or that likely adversely modify habitat which is designated by rulemaking as critical habitat pursuant to ESA Section 4(b).
- The take prohibition has the broadest application to human actors. Private citizens—companies and individuals—are affected by Section 7(a)(2) only if they require a federal permit or other federal authorization and the issuance of that permit or authorization is deemed to be a federal "agency action." Otherwise, Section 7(a)(2) is applicable only to, and establishes obligations only for, *federal agencies*. In contrast, Section 9(a)(1) applies equally to any "person"—federal employees, state and local government officials, and private-sector companies and individual citizens.
- The take prohibition contains no *scienter* element—it applies to all conduct, whether inadvertent, negligent, or intentional.
- Penalties for take can be severe. Violations are subject to civil and criminal sanctions: civil penalties of not more than $25,000 if the take is done "knowingly" and $500 otherwise;[18] and a maximum criminal penalty of $50,000 and/or one year in jail for anyone who "knowingly" commits a take.[19]
- ESA Sections 11(e)(6) and (g)(1)[20] authorize the Department of Justice through enforcement actions, and private citizens through citizen suits, to seek injunctions to halt or bar any activity that causes a take or other violation of the ESA.

Potential Applicability of Take Prohibition to Nanotechnology

In some instances, the development and use of nanoscale materials could result in a take of a listed wildlife species. For example, use of a nanopesticide could be toxic to members of listed species, resulting in their death or injury.[21] Similarly, release of nanoscale materials into the environment resulting in the destruction of plants, insects, or other organisms that serve as food sources for listed species could constitute habitat destruction that results in actual death or injury to members of those species and, therefore, could be a prohibited take.

Protecting against Effects of Nanotechnology Using Federal Agency Consultation with the Services under ESA Section 7(a)(2)

ESA Section 7(a)(2)[22] requires federal agencies to carry out their actions in ways that are not likely to jeopardize the continued existence of listed species or destroy or adversely modify critical habitat. This provision may protect against nanoscale materials more handily than the take prohibition, especially until more is known about the properties and behavior of those materials. It better addresses scientific uncertainty, is fairer, and (unlike Section 9) also covers plants.

Statutory and Regulatory Provisions

ESA Section 7(a)(2) applies to all federal agencies and to private parties who seek federal permits or funding or whose activities have some other nexus to federal agency actions. The provision establishes a two-part standard by requiring each federal agency to "insure" through "consultation" with the pertinent Service that any agency action "authorized, funded, or carried out" by the agency "is not likely to jeopardize the continued existence of any" listed species "or result in the destruction or adverse modification of [any designated critical] habitat of such species."[23]

As with the initial listing of a species under the ESA, Section 7(a)(2) looks to the current state of knowledge: "In fulfilling the requirements of this paragraph each agency shall use the best scientific and commercial data available."[24] On its face, this standard does not contemplate the need for an exhaustive body of data proving that a new program or technology does not pose any risks of harm. It is a procedural requirement to consider the best science currently "available," not a substantive duty to conduct new studies.[25] The Supreme Court has interpreted the "best scientific and commercial data available" standard not only to "advance the ESA's overall goal of species preservation" but also to prevent the "haphazard" implementation of the ESA that could lead to "needless economic dislocation."[26] The standard balances competing interests of species preservation and the original intent of the triggering agency action.

The "best available data" requirement is not technology specific. While nanotechnology may pose new considerations of possible effects on listed species or habitat, it nevertheless fits into Section 7(a)(2)'s existing procedural paradigm and should be subject to the same requirements as other new technologies. Fundamentally, the ESA's consultation requirements function as a tool to ensure that federal agencies (and the public) are aware of their actions' effects on listed species and their critical habitats, and that the agencies consider and adopt alternatives or protective measures when appropriate. The consultation process will serve the same functions when the agency actions involve nanotechnology applications.

The Services have adopted joint regulations that establish a triage system for procedural compliance with ESA Section 7(a)(2).[27] The regulations require no consultation if the action agency determines that its action will have "no effect" on listed species or critical habitat; "informal consultation" if the action agency determines, and the relevant Service concurs, that the action is "not likely to adversely affect" a listed species/critical habitat; and the "formal consultation" described in Section 7(a)(2) and (b) if the "not likely to adversely affect" finding cannot be made. If formal consultation occurs, the Service prepares a biological opinion (BiOp) on the agency action's impacts.[28]

Under ESA Section 7(b)(4) and (o)(2), the Service submits to the action agency (and the applicant for a federal permit, license, grant, etc., if that is the agency action) in a BiOp an incidental take statement that provides immunity from prosecution for the action agency (and applicant) for any incidental take otherwise barred by Section 9 if the agency (and applicant) adopts the "reasonable and prudent measures" (RPM) the Service includes in the statement to "minimize" (but not mitigate for) the "impact" of the expected incidental take. The agency (and applicant) must also adhere to the "terms and conditions" the Service specifies for implementing the RPMs.[29] The RPMs are the increment above the Section 7(a)(2) minimum of avoiding "jeopard[y]" or "adverse modification" that the Service believes will minimize take and still allow the desired action to proceed. If the Service determines that the federal agency action would likely result in jeopardy or adverse modification, it must offer to the agency (and applicant) in the BiOp any possible "reasonable and prudent alternatives" (RPA) to the action (which, here, might include mitigation steps).[30] While the RPMs and RPAs are not mandatory, an agency that disregards the BiOp "does so at its own peril."[31]

Applicability of Section 7(a)(2) to Nanotechnology

ESA Section 7(a)(2) applies broadly to all federal agencies and to private parties who seek federal permits or funding or whose activities have some other nexus to federal agency actions, and this section covers listed plants as well as wildlife. Federal environmental statutes already reach many nanoscale materials. Thus, any number of federal actions regarding nanotechnology could trigger the Section 7(a)(2) analysis. Pesticide registration, drug approval, or federal approval of environmental remediation or issuance of a research grant involving nanotechnology could each create a need for this review.

While complete information regarding all aspects of the environmental impact of nanotechnology is not currently available, Section 7(a)(2) does not require that level of certainty. The consultation process encompasses societal decisionmaking at or beyond the bounds of scientific certainty. The ultimate fate of Pacific salmon, the northern spotted owl, and numerous other species cannot be known with certainty. To protect listed species and designated critical habitat, the relevant action agencies and the Services regularly employ cutting-edge scientific models, technologies, and strategies to protect these animals and lands—the "best available data"—without complete knowledge of their effectiveness. The same analysis can, and should, be applied in Section 7(a)(2) consultations involving nanotechnology.

Emerging and Future Directions

Using the Take Prohibition to Protect against Nanoscale Materials

Using the ESA's take prohibition to protect against the effects of nanoscale materials raises issues of effectiveness, fairness, and economic incentives. The first of these is primarily a legal concern, whereas the other two involve questions of policy.

Effectiveness

Considering how much muscle Congress gave the take provision as described above, ESA Section 9 would seem to be a highly effective means of policing against any adverse effects of nanoscale materials on ESA-listed wildlife. Yet, its effectiveness in this context is tempered by the reality that scientific understanding of many nanoscale materials is in its infancy. In *Sweet Home*, the Supreme Court upheld a challenge to the Services' regulation defining the "harm" form of take likely most applicable to nanotechnology, but identified three compulsory elements to establish harm and thus take: (1) there must be death or actual injury (2) to an identifiable member of a listed wildlife species (3) that is *proximately caused* by the conduct in question.[32]

Given the current limitations on scientific understanding, the need to demonstrate proximate cause may make it difficult to establish ESA take from nanoscale materials, even assuming there has been death of, or injury to, an identifiable member of a protected species. In *Sweet Home*, the Court stressed the foreseeability component of proximate cause. The majority opinion explained that ESA take violations incorporate "ordinary requirements of proximate causation and foreseeability"; and Justice

O'Connor specifically conditioned her concurrence on the understanding that the "ordinary principles of proximate causation, which introduce notions of foreseeability," apply.[33]

The novelty of many aspects of nanotechnology may compound the difficulty of demonstrating the foreseeability of its effects on wildlife. Even when adverse effects of a certain nanoscale material on listed species may be foreseeable, the nascent state of knowledge of the effects may render the task of proving that use of the material caused actual injury to, or death of, a member of a listed wildlife species virtually impossible. Thus, while the ESA's stringent take prohibition no doubt would apply to the effects of nanoscale materials, as a practical matter the prohibition may lack the punch it has in other contexts in which, for example, a conventional material's behavior is more fully understood and predictable.

Fairness

The take prohibition's broad scope, the potential harshness of penalties for violations, and the current state of scientific and public knowledge about the behavior of nanoscale materials also raise concerns about the fairness of using ESA take to police the effects of nanoscale materials on wildlife. For example, given the nature of some of the prohibited conduct ("hunt," "shoot," "wound," "kill"), it may not be equitable to impose take liability on a consumer if damage to wildlife results from nanoscale materials disposed of by a consumer who has no knowledge of the potential for damage, no role in placing the materials in the stream of commerce, and no economic stake in marketing or distributing the materials. Further, the ESA's principal take-avoidance mechanism for the private sector—to prepare a habitat conservation plan and obtain an incidental take permit, as discussed in the next section—has proven enormously costly and time-consuming.

Economic Incentives

The threat of Section 9 take liability without some sort of safe harbor for harm that occurs incidental to some otherwise lawful activity may also prove a disincentive for companies to invest in the emerging nanotechnology field. In 1982, Congress added provisions that enabled the Services to allow landowners to take listed species when that take is "incidental" to otherwise lawful land uses. This "incidental take" permission comes in the form of either an incidental take permit (ITP) when no other federal permit or authorization for the particular land use is sought[34] or an "incidental take statement" where such other federal permit or authorization is involved.[35] To obtain an ITP, a landowner must prepare, and secure the pertinent Service's approval of, a conservation plan (often called a habitat conservation plan, or HCP) for the affected listed species covering the contemplated land use.[36] To approve the HCP and issue an ITP, the Service must find that the "taking" identified in the ITP application "will be incidental"; "the applicant will, to the maximum extent practicable, minimize and mitigate the impacts" of the taking; "the applicant will ensure that adequate funding" will be provided for the HCP; and "the taking will not appreciably reduce the likelihood of the survival and recovery of the species in the wild."[37] The Service may add any "measures" that it "may require as being necessary or appropriate for purposes of the" HCP.[38] Meeting the substantive requirements for an HCP may prove difficult if not impossible given what little is known about the biological effects of many nanoscale materials.

Using ESA Section 7(a)(2) to Protect against Effects of Nanoscale Materials

ESA Section 7(a)(2) provides comparable protections to those available under Section 9, without the attendant drawbacks discussed earlier.

Effectiveness

Section 7(a)(2) protects against jeopardy to species as a whole, not against take of individual species members as such. But that seeming reduction in protection for individual species members is offset by other protections that are available under Section 7(a)(2) and unavailable in a Section 9 take prosecution.

The threshold for protection under Section 7(a)(2) is lower and more flexible than the showing required for take under Section 9 and therefore may be better suited for situations involving nanotechnology, where scientific understanding is in an emergent stage. There is no need to demonstrate death or injury to an identifiable member of a species under Section 7(a)(2), or to establish proximate cause, which could prove difficult if a nanoscale material's effects are unknown and therefore not foreseeable. Rather, Section 7(a)(2) is triggered any time an agency determines that an action it has authorized, funded, or carried out "may affect" a listed species or critical habitat; and formal consultation between the action agency and the Service must occur for any action that is "likely to adversely affect" the species or habitat.

These lower and more flexible thresholds will provide protections not available in a pure Section 9 enforcement action (which by its terms does not apply until take has occurred), as formal consultation produces a BiOp that, if followed by the action agency, will protect wildlife against jeopardy and take. A BiOp will contain recommended RPMs to protect the species against all but incidental take;[39] and a BiOp that finds a likelihood of species jeopardy will identify the RPAs to the proposed agency action that, if taken, would avoid jeopardy at the species level.[40]

Fairness

In situations involving emerging technologies, the Section 7(a)(2) consultation process enhances fairness by focusing appropriately on the upstream levels of the chain of commerce. At these levels are the manufacturers and marketers who are responsible for introducing—and have the greatest economic stake in the environmental consequences of—these new products, and whose need for federal permits or licenses, or other authorizations or federal funding, brings them within the purview of Section 7(a)(2).[41] The process would place the burden of complying with the RPMs or implementing RPAs jointly on the authorizing or funding agencies and on the appropriate economic interests that apply for the authorizations or funding. These parties are in the best position to determine (agencies) and implement (applicants) the RPMs to protect listed species and designated critical habitat and, by doing so, to "earn" the protection of the incidental take statement. Meanwhile, at the other end of the chain of commerce, end users (i.e., consumers) who may be unaware of, and likely are unable to address effectively, the species and habitat consequences would benefit from that incidental take statement acquired through the consultation process.

Economic Incentives

As already noted, the potential for take liability under ESA Section 9, and the costs and potential unavailability of an HCP and accompanying ITP, can provide disincentives for companies to do business in emerging areas of nanotechnology, where environmental effects are so unknown and could well be beneficial. Consultation under Section 7(a)(2) avoids that deterrent because it provides a means, based on *currently available* scientific and commercial data, to proceed with business in an emerging technology while still enjoying the protection from liability for incidental take of protected wildlife and habitat.

The ESA's Conservation Goal and Nanotechnology

The ESA's ultimate goal is the *conservation* of endangered and threatened species and the ecosystems on which they depend.[42] ESA Section 3(2) defines "conservation" to mean actions that permit eventual recovery of the listed species to the point that it no longer requires ESA protection.[43]

Protective measures such as the Section 7(a)(2) consultation process and the Section 9 take prohibition can help achieve conservation. Other ESA provisions address the conservation goal more directly but do so without the same force of law. For example, in recognition that "conservation" is the ultimate objective of the ESA and to enlist those who are most knowledgeable, Section 4(f) directs the Services to prepare "recovery plans" for most listed species and suggests the appointment of "recovery teams" to draft those documents.[44] But a recovery plan, while it could address the effects of nanotechnology, is not a legally binding document.[45] Similarly, Section 7(a)(1) requires that federal "agencies shall, in consultation with" the Services, "utilize their authorities in furtherance of the purposes of this Act by carrying out programs for the conservation of" listed species.[46] Although Section 7(a)(1) consultations have been found to be legally enforceable,[47] the level of generality of the provision (which addresses entire programs and not individual agency actions) and the degree of discretion it confers on agencies[48] limit its use as a tool for regulating a specific subject such as nanotechnology.

Conclusion

Nanotechnology intersects the ESA at many points, including the initial listing of species, protecting wildlife against harm at the individual and species levels, and safeguarding wildlife habitat. Both the take prohibition in ESA Section 9 and federal agency consultation with the Services under Section 7(a)(2) protect wildlife and habitat from adverse effects of nanotechnology. But given the difficulties of proving take, the nascent state of scientific understanding of the behavior and environmental impacts of nanoscale materials, and questions of fairness and commercial incentives, Section 7(a)(2) may be the more appropriate of these two approaches for addressing nanotechnology under the ESA until science and society achieve a fuller understanding of the biological effects of the use and presence of nanoscale materials in the environment.

Notes

1. 515 U.S. 687 (1995).
2. 16 U.S.C. § 1531 *et seq.*
3. COMMITTEE ON SCIENTIFIC ISSUES AND THE ENDANGERED SPECIES ACT, SCIENCE AND THE ENDANGERED SPECIES ACT 19 (National Academy Press 1995).

4. II Coggins & Glicksman, Public Natural Resources Law § 156.01[1].
5. TVA v. Hill, 437 U.S. 153, 184–85 (1978).
6. 16 U.S.C. § 1531(b).
7. 16 U.S.C. § 1533. An endangered species is "any species which is in danger of extinction throughout all or a significant portion of its range." *Id.* § 1532(6). A threatened species is one "which is likely to become an endangered species within the foreseeable future throughout all or a significant portion of its range." *Id.* § 1532(20).
8. Under the ESA, "species" includes "any subspecies of fish or wildlife or plants, and any distinct population segment [DPS] of any species of vertebrate fish or wildlife which interbreeds when mature." 16 U.S.C. § 1532(16). A species, subspecies, or DPS can be listed in only a portion of its range. *Id.* § 1532(6).
9. 16 U.S.C. § 1533(a)(1). The endangered and threatened species are "listed" in 50 C.F.R. § 17.11 (animals) and § 17.12 (plants).
10. 16 U.S.C. § 1533(B)(1)(A).
11. 16 U.S.C. § 1532(5). The critical habitats are mapped and described in 50 C.F.R. § 17.95 (animals) and § 17.96 (plants).
12. 16 U.S.C. § 1538.
13. 16 U.S.C. § 1536(a)(2).
14. 16 U.S.C. § 1538(a)(1)(B).
15. The Section 9 take prohibition applies only to *endangered* wildlife species, not to *threatened* wildlife species. Another ESA provision, Section 4(d), grants to the Services discretion to extend by regulations the take and/or any other Section 9 prohibitions to threatened wildlife species. 16 U.S.C. § 1533(d). The Services have adopted different approaches under this authority: the Fish and Wildlife Service fastened the take prohibition generically to almost all threatened wildlife species in a single rule (50 C.F.R. § 17.31(a)); whereas the National Marine Fisheries Service makes decisions on whether to apply the prohibition by specific rules addressed to individual threatened wildlife species or groups of such species. Take of listed *plant* species is not proscribed; other Section 9 prohibitions not likely to be relevant to the use of nanotechnology do apply to listed plant species. *See* 16 U.S.C. § 1538(a)(2).
16. 16 U.S.C. § 1532(19).
17. 50 C.F.R. §§ 17.3, 222.102.
18. 16 U.S.C. § 1540(a)(1).
19. 16 U.S.C. § 1540(b)(1). The maximum fines have been increased by general legislation to $100,000 for individuals, and $200,000 for corporate violators, per violation. 18 U.S.C. §§ 3559, 3571.
20. 16 U.S.C. §§ 1540(e)(6), (g)(1).
21. *See, e.g.,* Defenders of Wildlife v. Administrator, EPA, 882 F.2d 1294 (8th Cir. 1989) (finding ESA take when endangered species died after ingesting strychnine from agricultural pesticides that had been applied to crops).

22. 16 U.S.C. § 1536(a)(2).
23. *Id.*
24. *Id.*
25. *See* Southwest Ctr. for Biological Diversity v. Norton, 215 F.3d 58, 60-61 (D.C. Cir. 2000).
26. Bennett v. Spear, 520 U.S. 154, 169 (1997).
27. 50 C.F.R. §§ 402.13, 402.14.
28. 16 U.S.C. § 1536(b), (c).
29. 16 U.S.C. § 1536(b)(4), (o). The Services also have discretion to extend the coverage of the incidental take statement beyond the action agency and applicant to anyone involved in a related action whose impacts were fairly considered in a BiOp (here, e.g., a consumer or user of a product containing nanoscale material). Ramsey v. Kantor, 96 F.3d 434, 440, 440-42 (9th Cir. 1996).
30. 16 U.S.C. § 1536(b), (c), and (o).
31. Bennett v. Spear, 520 U.S. at 169–70.
32. 515 U.S. at 696–97 n.9, 700 n.13, 707–08.
33. 515 U.S. at 696 n.9, 700 n.13; *id.* at 709, 712–14 (O'Connor, J. concurring).
34. 16 U.S.C. § 1539(a)(1)(B).
35. 16 U.S.C. § 1536(b)(4), (o).
36. 16 U.S.C. § 1539(a)(2).
37. 16 U.S.C. § 1539(a)(2)(B).
38. 16 U.S.C. § 1539(b)(2).
39. 16 U.S.C. § 1536(b)(4)(C)(ii).
40. 16 U.S.C. § 1536(b)(3)(A).
41. *See* 16 U.S.C. § 1536(a)(3), (b)(1)(B) (describing permit or license applicant's role in consultation process).
42. 16 U.S.C. § 1531(b).
43. 16 U.S.C. § 1532(2).
44. 16 U.S.C. § 1533(f).
45. Fund for Animals v. Rice, 85 F.3d 535, 547 (11th Cir. 1996).
46. 16 U.S.C. § 1536(a)(1).
47. Sierra Club v. Glickman, 156 F.3d 606 (5th Cir. 1998).
48. *See, e.g.,* Defenders of Wildlife v. Babbitt, 130 F. Supp. 2d 121, 135 (D.D.C. 2001) ("[t]he case law is well settled that federal agencies are accorded discretion in determining how to fulfill their 16 U.S.C. § 1536(a)(1) obligations") (citing Coalition for Sustainable Resources v. U.S. Forest Serv., 48 F. Supp. 2d 1303, 1315-16 (D. Wyo. 1999) (and cases cited therein)).

CHAPTER 6

RCRA and Nanotechnology

Executive Summary

The booming growth of nanotechnology in the U.S. economy has already begun to create an expanding universe of wastes from the manufacture, use, and disposal of products containing nanomaterials.[1] Just as nanomaterial products offer useful novel properties, nanomaterial wastes may present regulators with unexpected and unique questions. Researchers are trying to assess how nanomaterials and nanoparticles released into the environment will migrate through groundwater, adhere to soil, move through air/water and water/sediment partitions, and become available for bio-uptake. For example, some scientists have raised concerns that the relatively large surface area presented by small amounts of nanoparticles may make such nanomaterials comparatively more toxic than similar amounts of larger-scale versions of the same materials.[2]

Nanomaterials will also offer new opportunities for cleaning up hazardous wastes and contamination. For example, nanoscale iron particles have proven effective at reducing concentrations of persistent chlorinated organic compounds in groundwater.[3] Nanomaterials may also play a vital role in creating environmental detectors and sensors that can quickly identify small concentrations of toxic compounds in the environment. Ironically, the use of these nanomaterials to solve environmental problems may collide with concerns that releasing these same nanomaterials into the environment raises unknown and unacceptable risks.[4]

The chapter expands upon the Section of Environment, Energy, and Resources' June 2006 paper entitled *RCRA Regulation of Wastes from the Production, Use, and Disposal of Nanomaterials*. The Team Leader on that paper was Tracy Hester, Bracewell & Giuliani LLP, with assistance from Christopher Bell, Sidley Austin Brown & Wood LLP; and Joseph Guida, Guida, Slavich & Flores, P.C. Revisions to this chapter are by Tracy Hester.

131

EPA has the authority under the Resource Conservation and Recovery Act (RCRA) to regulate the generation, transportation, management, and disposal of secondary materials that become solid or hazardous wastes.[5] EPA now shares some of that authority through delegation to states with hazardous waste regulatory programs that meet—or exceed—EPA's standards. Neither federal nor state waste management programs offer regulations or guidance that expressly address the management or disposal of nanoscale wastes. EPA has noted, however, that "[n]anomaterials that meet one or more of the definitions of a hazardous waste (i.e., a waste that is specifically listed in the regulations and/or that exhibits a defining characteristic) potentially would be subject to subtitle C regulations."[6]

This chapter assesses the potential application of current RCRA statutory and regulatory requirements to the burgeoning field of nanoscale materials.[7] It discusses whether current federal requirements can adequately address potential environmental concerns posed by nanoscale materials. EPA already has expansive authority under RCRA to regulate discarded wastes that might include nanoscale materials. EPA's current regulations governing the management of hazardous wastes will also likely apply broadly to solid and hazardous wastes containing nanoscale constituents. Despite EPA's sweeping powers to regulate hazardous waste management and its comprehensive regulatory framework, this chapter also identifies below several areas of potential interest where current regulations may have unintended consequences when applied to nanoscale waste materials.

RCRA Offers Broad Statutory Authority to EPA to Regulate Wastes Containing Nanoparticles

RCRA provides EPA with broad statutory and regulatory powers to control the management of hazardous wastes in the United States. For example, RCRA Section 3002 directs EPA to set out comprehensive regulatory standards for generators of hazardous wastes, and other provisions of RCRA empower EPA to set out detailed regulatory standards for all aspects of waste management and disposal.[8] Similar statutory provisions direct EPA to set out expansive regulatory standards for persons who generate or transport hazardous wastes.[9]

If nanomaterials are discarded or are included in other secondary materials managed as wastes, they will almost certainly fall under this sweeping statutory framework. To the extent that nanomaterials in wastes pose novel environmental risks unaddressed by EPA's current regulations, EPA likely has sufficient authority under RCRA to promulgate new regulations to address discarded secondary materials arising from the generation, use, treatment, or disposal of nanomaterials.

EPA's powers to promulgate new regulations to address environmental risks will allow it to respond to novel characteristics or hazards from discarded nanoscale materials. For example, if EPA's current regulatory definitions of hazardous characteristics (ignitability, corrosivity, reactivity, and toxicity) fail to encompass unexpected risks from nanoscale materials, EPA possesses ample statutory authority to promulgate regulations to define a new characteristic or listing aimed at certain troubling nanomaterials.

As an intermediate step before promulgating new regulations, EPA can also draw on its emergency authorities to address particular hazards posed by discarded nanomaterials. For example, EPA (and, to a lesser extent, private parties) can seek injunctive relief to address imminent and substantial endangerments posed by the release of hazardous constituents from solid or hazardous wastes.[10] It is likely that the conventionally sized versions of many nanomaterials will fall within the broad array of chemicals that qualify as "hazardous constituents" under EPA guidance,[11] and therefore EPA can rely on its emergency authority to address dangerous releases of these nanomaterials. EPA can also rely on other authorities to address releases of nanomaterials that might otherwise fall outside its regulatory ambit, including its permit omnibus authority for facilities that have (or should have had) permits to treat, store, and dispose of hazardous wastes.[12]

EPA's Regulatory Definitions of "Solid Waste" and "Hazardous Waste" Can Encompass Most Secondary Materials Containing Nanomaterials

Nanomaterials and the Definition of "Solid Waste"

EPA has expansive authority to regulate secondary materials once they are discarded and become "solid waste" within the RCRA universe. EPA has promulgated regulations that broadly interpret the types of discarding activities that can bring secondary materials into the category of solid waste. As a result, EPA's RCRA regulations should apply to wastes containing nanomaterials that are discarded onto land, burned, or recycled as a means of disposal.[13] These broad categories of "discard" should cover actions that would typically occur with wastes containing nanomaterials.

EPA's authority to regulate secondary materials containing nanomaterials is less clear, however, when manufacturers attempt to recycle or reuse those nanomaterials. Given the high value of specially manufactured nanomaterials (e.g., nanoscale metals such as platinum used in catalysts or gold in biomedical devices, or highly valuable configurations of single-walled carbon nanotubes), manufacturers and users may have a strong interest in recovering certain nanomaterials for reuse or recharging. While EPA's regulatory authority only extends to discarded secondary materials, it has set out detailed regulations for the management and handling of recycled materials that may become sufficiently waste-like to trigger RCRA requirements.

The issues related to recycling of nanomaterials in manufacturing and consumer products have received comparably less attention.[14] If off-specification nanomaterials retain valuable characteristics[15] and remain in commercial use, they may fall outside EPA's regulatory ambit under RCRA.[16] The long-term accumulation and storage of secondary nanomaterials destined for continuing commercial use also may potentially pose regulatory concerns.[17]

Nanomaterials and the Definition of "Hazardous Waste"

EPA regulations currently define solid wastes as "hazardous wastes" if they either display a hazardous characteristic or appear on a list of hazardous wastes from certain industrial activities or certain discarded commercial chemicals.

Characteristic Hazardous Wastes and Nanomaterials
If a solid waste containing nanomaterials exhibits a hazardous characteristic, the nanoscale dimensions of its constituent should not be relevant to the waste's classification as hazardous. For example, a waste that displays the hazardous characteristic of ignitability because it contains powdered aluminum will remain characteristically hazardous regardless of whether the aluminum is nanoscale. While smaller quantities of the nanomaterials may be required to create the characteristic in the solid waste, the characteristic itself (and the regulatory authority over the solid waste) remains unaffected.

While EPA clearly can regulate nanoscale materials under its current regulations, the management scenarios it uses for hazardous characteristic definitions do not currently reflect any special uses and characteristics of nanomaterials.[18] Given the lack of clear data at present, it is unclear whether any special concerns might arise over EPA's management scenarios or computer modeling for its current hazardous characteristic definitions.

EPA may also need to address concerns about the standard of knowledge required to adequately characterize a waste containing nanoscale materials relying on the generator's process knowledge. EPA's current regulations allow a generator to classify a waste as hazardous by "[a]pplying knowledge of the hazard characteristic of the waste in light of the materials or the processes used."[19] To the extent that manufacturing processes using nanoscale materials pose novel issues with comparatively less process knowledge, generators may need to assess carefully and document the extent to which they sample or test their nanoscale wastes rather than rely solely on process knowledge.

If nanoscale materials ultimately pose new qualities or risks not adequately captured by current hazardous characteristics, EPA has the statutory authority to define new hazardous characteristics to reflect these new risks. Current research, however, has not identified any particular novel hazard posed by nanomaterials generally that might require the development of such a new characteristic. As discussed earlier, however, EPA has broad statutory authority to define new hazardous characteristics as needed through the regulatory process if it feels that current hazardous characteristics fail to properly regulate risks posed by wastes containing nanoscale materials.

Listed Hazardous Wastes and Nanomaterials

EPA's listings for hazardous waste encompass wastes generated either by specific industrial activities and uses (F and K wastes) or by the discarding of commercial chemicals (U and P wastes). Neither category of listings expressly addresses wastes containing nanoscale materials or wastes from nanomaterials manufacturing.[20]

F and K listings include categories of industrial activities that will likely use or generate nanoscale materials. For example, K-listed wastes from the organic chemical, inorganic chemical, pesticides, explosives, and ink formulation industries may soon include nanoscale materials as these industries increasingly formulate new nanoscale products or adopt nanoscale materials to produce existing chemicals in more efficient ways.[21] F-listed wastes may also soon include nanomaterials. EPA's regulations will impose hazardous waste management standards on these listed wastes without regard to the use of nanomaterials as an ingredient or production process.

While EPA has broad and sufficient authority to regulate listed hazardous wastes that might contain nanomaterials, EPA's current framework might yield unintended consequences. For example, a nanoscale formulation of a commercial chemical may lack the hazardous effects that led EPA to list it (despite the presence of the same hazardous constituents).[22] The derived-from rule and the mixture rule might also lead to the designation of a large quantity of mixed wastes as hazardous because it contains extraordinarily small amounts of a listed hazardous nanomaterial waste. Given special efforts to formulate nanoscale versions of commercial chemical products that would offer comparative environmental benefits, retaining nanoscale versions of listed wastes as hazardous without regard to their actual environmental risks may discourage efforts to harness nanotechnology for green chemistry or other environmentally beneficial uses.[23]

Nanoscale materials may also affect the process that EPA uses to list or delist solid wastes as hazardous. EPA currently adds solid wastes to the hazardous waste listings based on whether they (1) exhibit a hazardous characteristic; (2) display acute toxic effects on humans or rats; or (3) pose a substantial present or potential hazard to human health or the environment when improperly managed.[24] EPA uses similar factors to weigh whether to delist a hazardous waste upon a showing the waste does not pose an environmental hazard based on its actual management and disposal. To the extent that wastes containing nanomaterials display unique characteristics that EPA's current regulatory factors or computer models would not accurately predict, the listing process and delisting procedures may inappropriately over- or under-predict environmental risks.

Nanomaterials and Exemptions from the Definitions of "Solid Waste" and "Hazardous Waste"

The regulatory definitions of "solid waste" and "hazardous waste" include numerous exemptions for several types of secondary wastes. EPA included these exemptions for a broad array of reasons, including (1) other regulatory programs already address risks posed by the materials (e.g., exemptions for discharges pursuant to National Pollutant Discharge Elimination System permits); (2) the materials pose relatively little environmental risk (e.g., de minimis releases to wastewater treatment systems); (3) RCRA includes statutory exemptions for certain activities (e.g., Bevill amendment wastes or wastes resulting from oil and gas exploration and production activities); or (4) a need to provide flexibility for production activities that may include some wastes at an intermediate stage (e.g., exemptions for in-process recycling or product storage tank bottoms before removal).

Notably, the exemption from the definition of "hazardous waste" given to household hazardous wastes may pose the most immediate forum for EPA to address these issues.[25] A large array of consumer items purporting to contain nanomaterials have already entered the marketplace.[26] One potential avenue for the uncontrolled release of nanomaterials into the environment will be the discarding of consumer goods that qualify as household hazardous wastes. While EPA can address some of these releases, if necessary, through its emergency authorities under RCRA and the Comprehensive Environmental Response, Compensation, and Liability Act,[27] this approach would allow mitigation of environmental damages only after they occur rather than prevent the release in the first place.

Given the large array of exemptions and the separate policy rationales underlying each of them, the application of these exemptions to specific uses of nanomaterials will likely be resolved on a case-by-case basis. Unfortunately, the large variety of nanomaterials and the significant difference in their properties based on small, incremental differences in particle size or structure make it difficult to craft modifications to these exemptions on broad-based principles.

EPA's Current Regulatory Framework Allows It to Regulate Generators of Solid and Hazardous Wastes Containing Nanoscale Materials

RCRA regulations set out several requirements for generators of hazardous wastes. Depending on the quantity of hazardous waste produced at its facility, a generator may need to satisfy notification, recordkeeping, storage, and management requirements. Facilities that generate waste containing nanomaterials will face the same requirements regardless of the dimensions of the underlying constituents of their hazardous waste.

Wastes containing nanomaterials may nonetheless pose challenges to EPA's current framework to regulate generators. Most notably, RCRA requirements for generators vary based on the amount of hazardous waste they generate in a calendar year. Large quantity generators of hazardous waste must notify EPA of their activities, establish contingency plans, and store their wastes in certain units generally for 90 days or less.[28] By contrast, small quantity generators (SQG) and conditionally exempt small quantity generators (CESQG) need to meet only a subset of these requirements and have more flexible time limits for storing waste on-site. Because nanoscale materials may present novel properties at comparatively small quantities, the current 100-kilogram annual threshold to qualify as a CESQG may allow the on-site storage and management of nanomaterials for extensive periods of time.[29]

Numerous regulatory exemptions allow generators to stay outside the full panoply of hazardous waste regulatory management standards.[30] While these exemptions also serve numerous policy objectives, they generally assume that larger quantities of hazardous waste stored for a longer period at a generator's facility will pose a larger risk to human health and the environment. To the extent that nanomaterials may change the degree of risk posed by equivalent volumes of waste, or may have qualities that make standard tank and container storage inappropriate for them, the suitability of standard regulatory standards applicable to generators managing hazardous nanomaterials under exemptions from RCRA permitting may come under challenge.

The exemption of on-site storage of nanoscale wastes in certain types of management units may pose one of the most immediate and significant questions for waste management. It is likely that many nanoscale materials or wastes may be handled under existing exemptions for 90-day storage in tanks and containers, treatment in elementary neutralization units and totally enclosed treatment facilities, in-loop recycling, and other exempt storage and treatment options. To the extent that nanoscale materials display unusual qualities or respond differently to standard treatment technologies, these exemptions may not adequately address those unique aspects. Alternatively, the special qualities of nanoscale materials may make it very difficult for generators to manage their wastes in certain types of units and create regulatory uncertainty and dislocation for existing operations.[31]

Last, novel issues may arise from the application of universal waste management standards to wastes that may now begin to contain nanomaterials. For example, EPA has promulgated universal waste standards that provide reduced management burdens on certain types of large-volume, low-risk wastes such as discarded batteries and lamps. Some of the most promising applications for nanomaterials will likely arise in exactly these areas, and discarded universal wastes in these categories may begin to contain nanoscale components. If universal waste management standards for these items allow their co-disposal into municipal solid waste landfills, this current regulatory framework could create unanticipated waste management and regulatory issues for wastes containing nanomaterials.[32]

EPA's Current Regulations Allow It to Regulate Transporters of Solid and Hazardous Wastes That Contain Nanomaterials

EPA's current regulations provide a comprehensive framework for persons who transport hazardous wastes. These rules require generators to provide manifests to allow tracking of hazardous waste shipments, establish management standards for the transporters themselves, and impose obligations on the ultimate receivers of hazardous waste to report discrepancies between the shipped wastes and the manifest information. These rules do not address any specific risk or management practice that expressly affects nanoscale materials, but the current regulatory scheme effectively addresses any larger environmental risks posed by the transport of solid and hazardous wastes containing nanomaterials.

As burgeoning nanomaterial production leads to the generation of growing amounts of hazardous nanomaterial wastes that require shipping for off-site treatment or disposal, generators will have to consider how certain EPA requirements for transporters might apply to their waste shipments. For example, the pending uniform hazardous waste manifest provides a block for special handling instructions and additional information. Given that many nanomaterials may not contain clear handling instructions or spill response information in the material safety data sheets that accompany them, generators and transporters may wish to assure that the nanowaste's manifest includes any special measures needed to respond to a release or spill. To the extent that transporters may also temporarily store hazardous wastes containing nanomaterials during transport for periods up to ten days, some of the same concerns outlined below for on-site accumulation by generators may also apply to transporters operating or using transfer facilities.

EPA's Current Rules for Treatment, Storage, and Disposal Facilities Allow It to Regulate These Facilities' Management and Disposal of Nanoscale Wastes

RCRA bestows EPA with broad authority to regulate facilities that treat, store, and dispose of hazardous wastes (treatment, storage, and disposal facilities, or TSDFs), and the statute sets out numerous specific requirements that EPA must implement for certain types of waste disposal methods (e.g., minimum technology standards for certain land-based units used to store or treat hazardous wastes).[33] This sweeping statutory grant of authority appears unaffected by the nanoscale dimensions of wastes that might be managed at the TSDF, and EPA should have the ability to promulgate regulations as needed to address novel environmental risks posed by the disposal of hazardous wastes containing nanoscale materials.

While EPA has extensive statutory authority to address hazardous wastes containing nanoscale materials, some of its existing TSDF regulatory standards may prove problematic for nanomaterials. For example, some land disposal restriction (LDR) treatment standards for certain waste codes arguably may not—when applied to wastes containing nanoscale materials—meet the statutory standard of substantially reducing the underlying hazardous constituents in the waste[34] so as to minimize any risk it poses to human health and the environment.[35]

Facilities that treat, store, or dispose of nanoscale waste materials must assure that they have adequate plans in place for closure and post-closure activities. To the extent that nanoscale materials exhibit unexpected or qualitatively different properties in groundwater, soils, or wastewaters, current standards for corrective action may also need to expressly account for these factors when selecting an appropriate response action. For example, to the extent that EPA or delegated states rely on conservative default values to select a response action threshold, those default values will almost certainly not include any adjustments for potentially different risks posed by nanomaterials.

Several aspects of nanomaterial management remain relatively unexplored. For example, rigorous tests have not been performed or published on the efficacy of incineration or combustion as a control strategy for nanoscale versions of either hazardous constituents or wastes typically handled in incinerators, boilers, or industrial furnaces. While it is unclear whether any anticipated chemical aspect of these nanomaterials would affect the suitability of combustion or other control strategies, research has already begun to focus on these issues.[36]

Delegated State Waste Programs May Also Set Out Their Own Management Requirements for Nanomaterial Wastes, But None Have Yet Done So

Pursuant to RCRA's provisions that allow states to assume primary responsibility to administer their own hazardous waste programs that are at least as stringent as federal requirements, EPA has delegated authority to most states to implement their own hazardous waste programs. None of these state programs have any regulations, guidances, or policies that expressly address any special risks posed by solid or hazardous wastes that contain nanomaterials. While several states are investigating nanomaterials, none of them have announced plans to proceed with any regulatory initiatives at this time.[37]

States, however, also have the ability to impose more stringent hazardous waste management requirements within their delegated programs under certain circumstances.[38] Some states may choose at a future date to regulate nanoscale waste materials expressly under standards that differ from EPA's regulatory framework. For example, some states may wish to designate certain nanoscale wastes as listed hazardous wastes even if EPA has chosen not to impose such a listing. Alternatively, other states may face regulatory barriers to the use of nanoscale materials in a dispersive fashion into the environment (e.g., as an environmental remediation technology) if EPA considers the placement of larger-scale versions of the same material as placement onto land.

RCRA Requirements Should Not Discourage the Environmentally Beneficial Use of Nanomaterials

This chapter has focused on the ramifications of applying RCRA regulatory standards to the wastes that contain nanomaterials. RCRA, however, may also affect the use of nanotechnology in environmentally beneficial ways. For example, nanomaterials offer innovative means to treat intractable soil and groundwater contamination.[39] It is unclear, however, how RCRA regulations will deal with the intentional placement of these nanoscale materials onto land in a manner that arguably constitutes disposal. These uses do not currently enjoy any express clarification from EPA on their use similar to existing policies for the application to land of agricultural chemicals or military munitions in their intended use.[40]

At the least, current EPA regulations do not provide a clear path for TSDFs that wish to use innovative nanotechnology in corrective actions to address groundwater or soil contamination. Other potential nanotechnologies that may apply to RCRA waste management options include the use of nanoscale filters for groundwater remediation and environmental sensors that use nanomaterials for inexpensive and speedy sample analysis or release detection.

Conclusion

EPA already has expansive authority under RCRA to regulate discarded wastes that might include nanoscale materials. EPA's current regulations governing the management of hazardous wastes will also likely apply broadly to solid and hazardous wastes containing nanoscale constituents. Despite EPA's sweeping powers to regulate hazardous waste management and its comprehensive regulatory framework, EPA may wish to determine whether its current regulations will have unintended consequences when applied to nanoscale waste materials.

Notes

1. The Woodrow Wilson Institute's Project on Emerging Nanotechnology has assembled a database listing over 1,000 consumer products that claim to include nanomaterial components. This database can be accessed at http://www.nanotechproject.org/inventories/consumer/. The market for single-walled carbon nanotube products alone is projected to approach $5 billion within the next five years, and the National Science Foundation has predicted that nanotechnology will have a $1 trillion impact on the world's economy a decade from now. Nanomaterials will likely become ubiquitous parts of consumer products, chemical and metals manufacturing processes, biomedical services and devices, power sources, and military weaponry and systems.
2. *Getting Nanotechnology Right the First Time*, Statement to the National Research Council, Dr. Richard Denison, Environmental Defense (Mar. 25, 2005), at 2.
3. *See, e.g.*, W. Zhang, *Nanoscale iron particles for environmental remediation: An overview*, 5 J. NANOPARTICLE RES., 323–32 (2003).
4. The Royal Society & The Royal Academy of Engineering, *Nanoscience and Nanotechnologies: Opportunities and Uncertainties* (Final Report, July 2004) at 9 ("[s]pecifically, we recommend as a precautionary measure that . . . the use of free nanoparticles in environmental applications such as remediation of groundwater be prohibited"), *available at* http://www.nanotec.org.uk/finalReport.htm.
5. Regulations implementing Subtitle C of RCRA for hazardous waste management appear in 40 C.F.R. Parts 260–279.
6. U.S. Environmental Protection Agency (EPA), *Nanotechnology White Paper* (Feb. 2007) at 68, http://www.epa.gov/osa/pdfs/nanotech/epa-nanotechnology-whitepaper-0207.pdf.
7. This chapter uses the terms "nanomaterials" and "nanoparticles" in a generic sense. The precise definitions of nanoscale materials, however, remains a topic of active open discussion, and several associations (including the International Standards Organization and the ASTM International) are developing multiple standards that will define these materials.
8. 42 U.S.C. § 6921 *et seq.*
9. *Id.*

10. 42 U.S.C. §§ 7002, 7003.
11. *See* 40 C.F.R. Part 261, App. VIII (listing of hazardous constituents); 40 C.F.R. Part 264, App. IX (groundwater monitoring list of hazardous constituents); 55 Fed. Reg. 30798, 30874 (July 27, 1990) (proposal to define "hazardous waste" or "hazard constituent" for corrective action purposes to include items listed in these two Appendices). To the extent that RCRA arguably grants EPA corrective action authorities only over "hazardous wastes" at interim status treatment, storage, and disposal facilities, EPA has interpreted "hazardous waste" under Section 3008(h) of RCRA to encompass any kind of waste within the broad statutory definition of the term. Under this interpretation, EPA can order corrective action for releases of nanomaterials that qualify as "hazardous wastes" under 42 U.S.C. § 6903(5) even if they do not constitute "hazardous waste" under EPA's current regulatory definition. 55 Fed. Reg. at 30809.
12. 42 U.S.C. § 3005(c)(3) (authorizing Administrator to include terms and conditions "necessary to protect human health and the environment" in permits for hazardous waste treatment, storage, and disposal facilities). As discussed below, EPA can also order permit holders to take similar actions to address releases of hazardous constituents from solid waste management units at facilities that manage hazardous wastes. 42 U.S.C. §§ 3004(u)–(v), 3008(h).
13. 40 C.F.R. Part 240 *et seq.*
14. *See, e.g.*, Letter from David Wagger, Institute of Scrap Recycling Industries, Inc., to William Farland, U.S. EPA (Jan. 24, 2006) (commenting that EPA's draft White Paper on Nanotechnology failed to adequately address issues posed by the prospective recycling of nanoscale materials and products). These comments are available at http://www.isri.org/AM/Template.cfm?Section=Home&CONTENTFILEID=2589&TEMPLATE=/CM/ContentDisplay.cfm.
15. For example, a batch of nanoscale silver may lack a sufficient concentration of a specific size of nanoparticles needed for use as a medical antibacterial salve, but it may nonetheless remain useful as a general antifungal surface coating.
16. Of course, some of these issues involving conventionally sized materials have been addressed in EPA's final rule revising the regulatory definition of solid waste. 73 Fed. Reg. 64668 (Oct. 30, 2008).
17. *See* 40 C.F.R. § 261.2(c)(4) (discarding secondary materials through recycling via speculative accumulation). This regulatory provision, however, does not categorize commercial chemicals listed in 40 C.F.R. § 261.33 as solid wastes even if they are speculatively accumulated. *Id.*
18. For example, the current toxicity characteristic relies on the toxicity characteristic leaching procedures (TCLP) to determine whether a waste is characteristically toxic. EPA originally designed this test to yield extracts from waste samples that would reflect the releases expected to occur if

the hazardous wastes were co-managed in an unlined municipal solid waste landfill. EPA then set levels of constituents allowed to leach from the waste so that such releases would not migrate through groundwater in sufficient concentrations to exceed maximum concentration limits for persons relying on the aquifer for drinking water. To the extent that nanoparticles adhere to soils, transport in groundwater, or infiltrate into drinking water in significantly different ways from larger-scale particles, EPA's current assumptions for the toxicity characteristic may not fully assess how characteristically toxic wastes with nanomaterials might affect groundwater. The presence of nanomaterials in a waste sample might arguably also affect the waste's behavior in a Pensky-Martens Closed Cup test for ignitability, the waste's classification as a "liquid" under the paint filter test for purposes of the ignitability characteristic, and the waste's status as "aqueous" for purposes of the corrosivity characteristic.

19.   40 C.F.R. § 262.11(c)(2).

20.   While these industries are still adapting to nanotechnologies, many potential examples could quickly arise. For example, the use of nano-scale aluminum in high-grade military explosives might yield wastewater treatment sludges that qualify as K044 listed wastes.

21.   Given the likely ubiquitous use of nanomaterials and nanotechnology, other K-listed industrial sectors may generate wastes containing nanomaterials. For example, petroleum refineries may look to nanoscale catalysts to increase production efficiency, and many printing operations will likely adapt inking formulations that rely on precise application of inks in nanoscale amounts.

22.   This situation may pose tricky questions of statutory interpretation. For example, petitioners may request that EPA classify nanoscale materials as fundamentally different and consequently a "new chemical" under the Toxic Substances Control Act. At the same time, however, those same petitioners may ask EPA to designate nanoscale versions of currently listed hazardous wastes as the same material within the hazardous waste listing description.

23.   While the mixture rule has always posed this policy difficulty, the growing use of nanomaterials will sharpen the issue because extraordinarily small quantities of nanomaterials may still have useful properties and effects. If the nanomaterial constitutes a listed hazardous waste, a mixture of solid waste and the discarded nanomaterial may carry the waste listing code even if the mixture contains only a minute quantity of nanomaterials.

24.   40 C.F.R. § 261.11(a).

25.   40 C.F.R. § 261.4(b)(1).

26.   Some products marketed as "nanotechnology" may not actually contain nanomaterials. A. von Bubnoff, *Study Shows No Nano in Magic Nano,*

the German Product Recalled for Breathing Problems, SMALL TIMES (May 26, 2006), *available at* http://www.smalltimes.com/document_display .cfm?document_id=11586.

27. *See* Chapter 7, CERCLA and Nanotechnology. EPA can address releases of constituents of solid or hazardous wastes that pose an imminent risk to human health and the environment under RCRA Section 7003. While the household hazardous waste exemption removes such materials from the definition of hazardous wastes, they nonetheless remain solid wastes and therefore releases of hazardous constituents from them should be subject to EPA's emergency order authority.

28. 40 C.F.R. Part 262 *et seq.*

29. As EPA has already recognized, wastes that pose a greater toxic risk in relatively smaller doses may merit different classification and treatment. Acute hazardous waste, for example, remains subject to different thresholds for accumulation and temporary storage at generator facilities.

30. Perhaps the most notable exemptions allow generators to store and (in limited circumstances) treat hazardous waste in Subpart J tanks and Subpart I containers for less than 90 days without triggering full permitting requirements under 40 C.F.R. Parts 264 or 265. EPA also exempts satellite accumulation areas from permitting requirements, and as a result facility operators may store and manage nanoscale waste materials for an unlimited time as long as they satisfy labeling and minimal storage requirements and they do not exceed 55 gallons (or 1 quart for acute wastes). 40 C.F.R. § 262.34(c).

31. For example, it may prove problematic for a generator to demonstrate that a totally enclosed treatment facility (TETF) has prevented all possible releases of nanoscale materials treated in the TETF when current monitoring and detection technologies may not reliably detect low-level releases of nanoscale materials. Current regulatory standards require that a TETF be "constructed and operated in a manner which prevents the release of hazardous waste or any constituent thereof into the environment during treatment." 40 C.F.R. §§ 260.10 (definition of TETF), 264.1(g) (5) (exemption from permitting for treatment occurring in a TETF).

32. Generators must certify on the Uniform Hazardous Waste manifest that they have a waste minimization program in place, and (for large generators) that they selected the "practicable method of treatment, storage, or disposal currently available" that "minimizes the present and future threat to human health and the environment." 40 C.F.R. Part 262 Appendix (uniform hazardous waste manifest).

33. 42 U.S.C. § 6924(o) (minimum technological requirements).

34. K. Kulinowski et al., Draft report from *Advancing the Eco-Responsible Design and Disposal of Engineered Nanomaterials: An International Workshop* (dated May 19, 2009) at part 7 ("Emerging Issues for Environmental Protection Infrastructure").

35. While some treatment methods will likely address any likely novel characteristics of nanoscale materials within their waste code (e.g., thermal retorting for solid wastes containing nanoscale metals), other technologies that rely on fixation or chemical bonding may need review.
36. EPA has already actively and expansively supported research into the environmental uses and aspects of nanomaterials, and some of its research may already encompass these issues.
37. California, for example, has already taken initial steps to require reporting of testing information on nanomaterials. S. Lockard & M. Boyd, *Regulatory Developments in California & Canada Continue Trend Toward Increasing Oversight of Nanotechnology Risks*, 248 THE ENVIRONMENTAL COUNSELOR, 2009, at 10–11; L. Bergeson, *Nanotechnology: Opportunities and Challenges for EPA*, EPA Millennium Lecture Series, Frontiers in Nanotechnology (May 9, 2005).
38. 40 C.F.R. § 270.1 *et seq.*
39. Zhang, *supra* note 3; A. Gavaskar, L. Tatar, & W. Condit, *Cost and Performance Report—Nanoscale Zero-Valent Iron Technologies for Source Remediation*, Presentation to Naval Facilities Engineering Command (Sept. 2005); PARS Environmental, Inc., *In situ Groundwater Treatment Using Nanoiron: A Case Study* (2005).
40. 40 C.F.R. § 261.2(c)(1)(ii).

CHAPTER 7

CERCLA and Nanotechnology

Executive Summary

The Comprehensive Environmental Response, Compensation and Liability Act (CERCLA), 42 U.S.C. § 9601 *et seq.*, addresses risks to human health and the environment posed by uncontrolled releases of hazardous materials.

In the context of a rapidly emerging nanotechnology and nanomaterials sector, existing CERCLA mechanisms would be useful primarily to provide response and liability authority if releases of nanoscale materials prove hazardous to human health or the environment, particularly if their risk becomes known only after production and release. Unlike the prospective authority of the Toxic Substances Control Act (TSCA) or the current disposal authority of the Resource Conservation and Recovery Act (RCRA), the CERCLA liability framework is intrinsically retrospective. It thus can serve as a backup tool to deal with adverse consequences that emerge in the future but that are unanticipated or otherwise elude environmental regulation. Certain provisions of the statute may also operate prospectively to regulate current use and disposal of nanomaterials that may in the future be classified as hazardous, extremely hazardous, or toxic.

The functional core of the statute is the "hazardous substance" definition, which serves as the gateway to the substantive response, liability, funding, and reporting mechanisms. The single greatest challenge for applying CERCLA to nanomaterials is deciding whether they fall within this definition. None has been formally so classified, although

This chapter expands upon the Section of Environment, Energy, and Resources' June 2006 paper entitled *CERCLA Nanotechnology Issues*. The Team Leader on that paper was Christopher P. McCormack, Pullman & Comley, LLC. Revisions are by Christopher P. McCormack.

the potential for nanoscale substances to manifest hazardous properties continues to receive serious attention. To evaluate the application and operation of CERCLA, this chapter assumes that nanomaterials exist or can be created that will have adverse effects on human health or the environment and therefore can be classified as "hazardous." Because of the unique properties of nanomaterials, it is further assumed that such adverse effects may manifest themselves upon low-level exposure or release. The means of validating these assumptions and their applicability to different classes and uses of nanomaterials are beyond the scope of this chapter.

Despite the practical challenges posed by this threshold definitional question, it is possible to conclude that the existing statutory framework is readily adaptable to nanomaterials that are identified, now or in the future, as "hazardous substances." The following discussion focuses on the major elements of the statute and the challenges posed by their application to nanomaterials. It also comments on elements of CERCLA for which nanomaterials present special considerations.

Triggering the Statute: "Hazardous Substances" and Release Reporting

Designation of Hazardous Substances

Virtually all of CERCLA's substantive liabilities and enforcement authorities turn on the statutory definition of "hazardous substances." Release, use, or detection of materials within this category serves to bring the statute to bear on facilities, their owners and operators, and a variety of activities and events.

CERCLA defines "hazardous substances" in the broadest possible terms. In addition to a CERCLA-specific list, the category includes listed or characteristic "hazardous waste" under RCRA, and materials designated as hazardous or toxic under numerous other statutes.[1] Under CERCLA Section 102(a), the U.S. Environmental Protection Agency (EPA) has omnibus authority to list substances "which, when released into the environment may present substantial danger to the public health or welfare or the environment."[2]

Before considering how these concepts may apply to nanotechnology, it is useful to recall their origin. CERCLA cast a wide net to assure that government would have the authority to react to events and conditions that endanger human health and the environment, and that responsible parties would shoulder a fair share of costs. The broad-spectrum approach to hazardous substances reflects legislative intent to leave no room for jurisdictional hairsplitting. This fundamental philosophy is a hallmark of the statute.

Upon enactment and in the decades since, CERCLA has built on a broad foundation of received knowledge to define what should qualify as a hazardous substance. Chemicals of concern were and have been defined by reference to extant medical and epidemiological knowledge. Incorporation of regulatory decisions under media-specific programs such as RCRA, the Clean Water Act, the Clean Air Act, and the Occupational Safety and Health Act (OSH Act) brings into the net materials identified as appropriate for regulatory control because of their environmental and human health effects. Those programs also provide conceptual frameworks for risk assessment. CERCLA draws these diverse elements into a comprehensive, flexible mechanism for dealing with environmental harms not regulated under other programs.

When it comes to nanomaterials, no comparable base of knowledge exists today, so there is no foundation for designating one or more nanoscale substances as hazardous. Yet paradoxically, the CERCLA hazardous substance definition can readily accommodate the fluid and evolving nature of the nanotechnology sector: it was originally enacted only after information emerged concerning materials not formerly considered hazardous. That same profile applies to any materials, nanoscale or otherwise, that may in the future be identified as hazardous.

Considering the diversity of nanomaterials and the pace and breadth of nanotechnology innovation, the gap between the sector and the environmental knowledge necessary to regulate it seems likely to persist and even expand. These problems are compounded by the fact that nanoscale forms of some elements or compounds may present concerns not normally associated with conventional forms of the same materials. Carbon 64 fullerenes and carbon nanotubes, for example, appear to behave differently than bulk elemental carbon; nanoscale aluminum particles may present an explosion hazard not normally associated with metallic aluminum. But nanomaterials may also behave differently in the sense that "hazardous" properties may not persist in the natural environment. Small particles that present exposure concerns in pure form may agglomerate, disperse, or react, for example, and thus may not pose the kind of "substantial danger" that the hazardous substance definition requires "when released into the environment." Issues like these seem likely to pose ongoing challenges for classification of nanoscale materials. The power under CERCLA Section 102 to list new hazardous substances provides EPA ample authority to meet such challenges: EPA can classify nanomaterials as hazardous if it concludes that they present "substantial danger to the public health or welfare or the environment." This definition is flexible enough to permit EPA to define "danger" as appropriate for a given material. The built-in cross-references to other statutes moreover operate to extend CERCLA's reach in parallel with other regulatory decisions about specific nanomaterials.

Once a material is designated a hazardous substance, it and actors associated with it are subject to the statute regardless of regulatory status at the time of production, use, or disposal. In other words, should adverse effects of a nanomaterial become apparent after release and exposure, the decision to classify it as a hazardous substance would operate, as it did upon enactment in 1980, to trigger the portions of the statute oriented toward remedying past mistakes.

Release Reporting and "Reportable Quantities"

The reporting requirement of CERCLA Section 103 operates in conjunction with the hazardous substance definition to bring the statute into play when a release to the environment occurs. Section 103 requires reporting of hazardous substance releases that exceed "reportable quantity" thresholds defined pursuant to Section 102. EPA's authority to promulgate regulations defining reportable quantities[3] goes with the hazardous substance listing authority and provides ample power to set reportable quantities for nanomaterials deemed hazardous.

For nanomaterials, the concept of a reportable quantity runs up against much the same knowledge gap as does the hazardous substance definition. Since CERCLA was enacted, it has typically been possible not only to identify materials that should be deemed hazardous but also to define a threshold level of regulatory concern that could be translated into a CERCLA reportable quantity. For nanomaterials, both questions turn on information yet to be developed.

The concept of a reportable quantity also highlights a conceptual problem distinct from the state of current knowledge. It has long been a fundamental assumption of environmental regulation that larger quantities of regulated material pose greater risk.[4] This relation may not hold for a nanomaterial that causes toxic or hazardous effects at low volumes or weights. For this reason, it is not clear that the seemingly conservative default quantity threshold of 1 pound[5] would be adequate for all nanoscale materials.

Response/Remediation

Federal Authority to Respond

CERCLA authorizes direct governmental action to address environmental contamination upon discovery, regardless of the passage of time since the act or omission giving rise to it, and regardless of whether such acts or omissions were lawful at the time. These powers include authority to conduct and fund removal and remedial action and to coordinate action by state and tribal authorities,[6] to compel disclosure of information from private parties,[7] and to acquire property needed to conduct remedial action.[8] Complementary authorities include funding for response actions and "peripheral matters,"[9] and for brownfields evaluation.[10]

For nanomaterials, these powers are important for two reasons. The first harks back to the statute's origins—EPA could respond to a hazardous nanomaterial release or condition under the statute just as it has for hundreds of sites over the last quarter-century. There is nothing unique about nanoscale "hazardous substances" that would constrain this authority or impair the statute's operation.

The second is crucial in light of the limited knowledge currently available about the environmental fate and transport of nanoscale materials. Nothing in the statute would prevent EPA from deciding *in the future* to classify a nanomaterial as hazardous and then invoking its response authority to address conditions arising from preceding releases or actions. In such a scenario, CERCLA would operate precisely as it did upon enactment to impose "retroactive" liability for historic practices.

After-the-fact responses would be no more desirable for future problems associated with nanoscale materials than they were for the drum dumps uncovered in the 1980s. The immediate question, however, is whether the statutory authorities under CERCLA would be available in that eventuality. The answer is that they would be. The sole qualification is again technical rather than legal—as discussed earlier, the threshold question is whether a given nanomaterial should be treated as a hazardous substance. For nanomaterials deemed to fall within that category, the statutory response authorities could operate without modification.

Risk Assessment

Within the CERCLA framework, risk assessment operates at two levels. One is the threshold determination of whether a substance warrants regulatory concern. The other is whether a given site warrants response or remediation.

As to the first of these, CERCLA expressly provides for coordination between EPA and the Agency for Toxic Substances and Disease Registry (ATSDR).[11] It also contemplates that research on materials or substances should be coordinated with similar programs of toxicological testing under TSCA and the Federal Insecticide, Fungicide, and Rodenticide Act (FIFRA).[12] There is nothing unique to nanomaterials that would require modification of this basic structure. Considering the scope of research already in progress and the existing level of interagency coordination, there is no evident reason to think that the framework defined by the statute cannot be effective in developing information necessary to make regulatory decisions about nanomaterials.

As to the second, evaluation of releases and sites proceeds under the authority of CERCLA Section 105, which authorizes the National Contingency Plan (NCP) and the National Priorities List (NPL),[13] the Hazard Ranking System,[14] and coordination with state-led response actions.[15] Conditions associated with nanomaterials can be addressed within these authorities. Their application is again constrained only by the current state of knowledge, in this context the lack of information about the environmental fate and effects of nanomaterials.

Mechanics/Standards of Response and Remediation

CERCLA response actions proceed under criteria stated in the NCP, and remedial actions are selected in accordance with Section 121. The general rules applicable to remedial actions include the preference for permanent remedies that reduce the volume, toxicity, or mobility of hazardous substances.[16] The degree of cleanup is defined by reference to the general concept of assuring protection of human health and the environment.[17] Implementation includes state and public involvement under CERCLA Sections 121(f) and 117, respectively.[18]

EPA has authority under these provisions to define remediation objectives and select remedies for releases of hazardous nanoscale materials. No general or site-specific standards, criteria, or best practices yet exist for such releases. But their development falls within the existing mandates of EPA's Office of Solid Waste and Emergency Response and Office of Site Remediation and Enforcement; complementary research may be conducted under the aegis of the Office of Research and Development. These authorities and structures seem capable of serving without modification as vehicles for developing information necessary to define response and remediation objectives for hazardous nanomaterial releases.

In this context, nanomaterials present an interesting dichotomy—their potential adverse effects must be balanced against their potential utility as remediation tools. EPA's National Center for Environmental Research lists remediation among possible "applications"[19]—for example, nanomaterials may promote degradation of chlorinated hydrocarbons. The idea of using nanomaterials to mitigate known risks of "conventional" hazardous substances is in tension with concerns about the environmental and health effects of the nanomaterials themselves. This tension has prompted the U.K.'s Royal Society and Royal Academy of Engineering to argue that the use of free nanoparticles in environmental applications such as remediation should be prohibited until appropriate research has demonstrated that benefits outweigh risks.[20] Presumably, risks posed by nanoscale materials in a remediation context will be evaluated in light of the risks they pose given the usual considerations of environmental setting, fate and transport, and potential receptors as well as in light of their benefits in reducing the hazards posed by other pollutants.

For present purposes, it is sufficient to note that the existing statutory authorities provide ample latitude to explore the positives of nanomaterials as well as the negatives.

Compensation/Liability/Enforcement Mechanisms
Core Section 107—"Polluter Pays" Concept

CERCLA's liability provisions provide means to impose and allocate responsibility for releases of hazardous nanomaterials. CERCLA Section 107 expresses the central liability concept—persons standing in certain well-defined relationships to "hazardous substances" are jointly and severally responsible for response costs. These potentially responsible parties (PRP) may be the owners of facilities where hazardous substances are now located, the owners or operators at the time of disposal, or generators, transporters, or disposers of hazardous substances. These familiar PRP categories can apply to facilities and operations involving nanomaterials that fall within the hazardous substance definition.

It would of course be preferable to anticipate and avoid adverse effects of nanomaterials through regulation under other programs. Given the rapid pace of nanotechnology and nanomaterial development and marketing, however, regulatory decision making may have difficulty keeping up. If we assume that nanomaterials may warrant classification as hazardous substances, it seems prudent to assume as well that unanticipated problems will arise after releases have occurred.

The CERCLA liability framework can be expected to function perfectly well in the latter scenario, serving as a backstop for consequences that other programs fail to anticipate or avoid. Its ability to do so reflects its historic origin as a reaction to discovery of hazardous materials at uncontrolled disposal sites—sites created, in many instances, in violation of no contemporaneous legal requirements. CERCLA embodies a legislative policy judgment that the need to protect human health and the environment warrants the imposition of strict joint and several liability, even if the conduct in question was lawful at the time and the liability is in effect retroactive. The statute is intrinsically backward looking. It provides a means of second-guessing risk assessment judgments and of assuring that persons within the statutory categories of PRPs bear the costs of late-emerging external costs.

These concepts can readily be adapted to evolving knowledge about the fate and environmental effects of nanomaterials. Perhaps more importantly, the statute's notorious burdensomeness can be a significant deterrent in a sector where rapid change taxes the capacities of prospective regulatory tools. The specter of retroactive CERCLA liability, with all it implies, provides a powerful incentive for developers and manufacturers to assure that their nanomaterials are produced, used, and disposed of safely.

In the context of nanomaterials, it is particularly appropriate that CERCLA Section 107 imposes no minimum or quantity threshold. It is axiomatic that liability attaches upon the release of any amount of hazardous substance.[21] Thus, although certain other portions of the statute tie affirmative reporting and disclosure obligations to mass triggers—for example, the release reporting, reportable quantity, emergency planning, and toxic release disclosure authorities discussed later155—release of any amount of a hazardous substance can give rise to Section 107 liability. The *de micromis* exemption of Section 107(o) does not materially alter this conclusion. Although it defines presumptive thresholds below which persons in the "arranger" or "transporter" categories[22] are not liable, it is subject to an exception for situations in which materials disposed of contribute significantly to costs of response or natural resource restoration.[23] The *de micromis* exemption does not apply at all to current owners of CERCLA "facilities," or to persons who owned such facilities when hazardous substances were released. In those important categories, the rule remains unqualifiedly that any release triggers liability.

Complementary liability provisions address natural resource damages,[24] the federal superlien for response costs,[25] and authority to settle claims and grant covenants not to sue and contribution protection.[26] Like the core liability principles, all could function without modification in the context of hazardous nanomaterial releases.

Collateral Enforcement Tools

There is nothing unique to nanomaterials that would affect the operation of the CERCLA enforcement mechanisms and collateral authorities that complement the core liability provisions of Section 107.

Enforcement authorities begin with the power to compel disclosure of information pursuant to Section 104(e).[27] The statute also authorizes enforcement action or the issuance of unilateral administrative orders under Section 106(a),[28] as well as the imposition of fines for noncompliance pursuant to Section 106(b).[29] The special notice procedures of Section 122(e)[30] would be available to provide PRPs with an opportunity to settle their liability. Incentives to settlement could include the covenant not to sue pursuant to Section 122(f).[31]

The financial responsibility obligations of Sections 108(a) and 108(b) could be applied to vessels and facilities that handle nanoscale substances determined to be hazardous. Guarantors of such obligations could be subject to direct action pursuant to Section 108(c).[32]

The "whistle-blower" protections of Section 110(a)[33] would be available against any person who retaliated against an employee who disclosed information about nanomaterials determined to be hazardous substances.

For nanomaterials denominated hazardous substances, for sites warranting attention consistent with the NCP, and with respect to persons within the categories of responsible parties under Section 107, these CERCLA liability provisions can be expected to operate with respect to nanoscale materials as they have with respect to conventional hazardous substances.

Contribution and Related Issues

CERCLA Section 113(f)(1) provides a right of contribution among liable parties and authorizes allocation of proportional responsibility on equitable terms. Section 113(f)(2) limits this right by affording settling parties protection against contribution claims.

These mechanisms complement the basic liability framework and similarly can be expected to operate as they stand with respect to liability for nanomaterial releases.

Incidental Liability Provisions: Exemptions, Safe Harbors, Defenses

Since 1980, several categories of liability exemptions and qualifications have been engrafted onto the basic CERCLA liability framework. These involve fiduciaries,[34] secured creditors,[35] *de micromis* parties,[36] disposers of municipal solid waste,[37] de minimis parties,[38] certain categories of landowners (contiguous property owner,[39] innocent landowner,[40] bona fide prospective purchaser[41]), and parties who send waste for recycling rather than disposal.[42] These provisions do not pose any unique problems as applied to nanomaterials.

The technical question of quantity thresholds arises in several of these categories. The de minimis category is expressed in relative terms, as a comparison with the danger posed by other hazardous substances at a facility, so there is no problem with a numerical threshold. The *de micromis* category is defined by a quantity threshold (110 gallons of liquid, 200 pounds of solid) that might be problematic for nanomaterials, but at least part of the disposal must have occurred before April 1, 2001, so it is unlikely disposal of nanomaterials will fit within the definition in any event.

A similar question may arise as to the municipal solid waste (MSW) exemption of Section 107(p), which applies to "waste generated by a household" or waste generated by certain other entities that is "essentially the same as" household waste and that contains hazardous substances in relatively the same proportion. As nanomaterials come into more widespread use, residual quantities may be expected to show up in MSW. It is unclear whether these materials would appear in forms, amounts, or concentrations that would call into question the continued appropriateness for the MSW exemption. This possibility should be noted, however, as another manifestation of the larger question about whether existing quantity thresholds are adequate to deal with nanomaterials. If so, however, Section 107(p)(2) already provides that the exemption shall not apply if EPA determines that the MSW "has contributed significantly or could contribute significantly, either individually or in the aggregate, to the cost of the response action or natural resource restoration."[43] That determination is not judicially reviewable.[44] The statute is thus again flexible enough to cope with any special concerns that might arise in connection with nanomaterials in the municipal solid waste stream.(*See* discussion in RCRA, Chapter 6.)

Collateral and Incidental Elements/Subprograms

Among the changes made by the Superfund Amendments and Reauthorization Act of 1986 were new requirements for reporting and disclosure concerning hazardous and toxic materials.[45] These include emergency planning[46] and inventory[47] requirements primarily for the benefit of first responders, and notice requirements relating to toxic chemical releases[48] and emergency release notification.[49] These requirements share the fundamental premise that emergency planners, employees, and members of the public need information about the presence and release of materials that are hazardous, extremely hazardous, or toxic. For nanomaterials that may be determined to fall within these categories, the same premise applies.

Aside from the subcategory of extremely hazardous substances, these programs rely on well-settled CERCLA definitions. Unsurprisingly, the major question would appear again to be whether the default mass-based thresholds for these programs are valid for nanoscale materials that are classified as hazardous substances. For extremely hazardous substances in general, for example, the default EPCRA Threshold Planning Quantity (TPQ) is 10,000 pounds, but 500 pounds "if the solid exists in a powdered form and has a particle size less than 100 microns."[50] The minimum threshold level for inventory reporting is 500 pounds for the TPQ for extremely hazardous substances and 10,000 pounds for all other hazardous chemicals. There is no statutory restriction, however, on EPA's authority to set these values lower if warranted; the Extremely Hazardous Substance lists appended to 40 C.F.R. Part 355 identify numerous materials with TPQs of 1 pound. This conclusion would have to be reconsidered, however, if continuing research and development revealed that the weight and risk of nanomaterials or classes of nanomaterials are wholly independent. As the nanotechnology sector continues its rapid change and growth, the adequacy of these threshold levels will require continuing attention.

If a Material Safety Data Sheet must be maintained on premises pursuant to the OSH Act, then the Tier 1 and Tier 2 inventory requirements of 42 U.S.C. § 11022 automatically apply. As a practical matter, the SARA Title III obligations follow automatically from the OSH Act determination—subject again to the distinct question of whether the default weight thresholds are adequate in light of the type and degree of risk posed by a given nanoscale material.

Conclusion

The current state of knowledge concerning the environmental and health effects of nanomaterials poses practical difficulties in applying CERCLA. It is probably correct to say that most of the scientific and technical predicates for applying the statute to nanomaterials do not yet exist.

This knowledge gap is not as problematic under CERCLA as it is for environmental statutes that focus on current activities. Indeed, CERCLA was purpose-built to cope with the unanticipated adverse consequences of previously accepted practices. It expanded existing law by creating a totally new concept—liability for conditions that exist today, no matter when the conduct giving rise to them occurred. This concept fits the paradigm of adverse consequences that may arise in the future from as yet unknown properties of nanomaterials.

Only technical input is needed to apply the statutory authorities to nanomaterials. When we can answer the questions of whether nanomaterials are hazardous—and if so, in what ways and in what amounts—the CERCLA machinery will be available to address adverse consequences.

Notes

1. *See* CERCLA § 101(14), 42 U.S.C. § 9601(14).
2. 42 U.S.C. § 9602(a).
3. CERCLA § 102(a), 42 U.S.C. § 9602(a).
4. *See* Hester, "Small Stuff, Big Challenges: RCRA and CERCLA in the New World of Nanoscale Materials" (ELI/Woodrow Wilson Institute presentation, May 25, 2005).
5. *See* CERCLA § 102(b), 42 U.S.C. § 9602(b).
6. CERCLA § 104(a)–(d), 42 U.S.C. § 9604(a)–(d).
7. CERCLA § 104(e), 42 U.S.C. § 9604(e).
8. CERCLA § 104(j), 42 U.S.C. § 9604(j).
9. CERCLA §§ 111, 112, 42 U.S.C. §§ 9611, 9612.
10. CERCLA § 104(k), 42 U.S.C. § 9604(k).
11. CERCLA § 104(i), 42 U.S.C. § 9604(i).159
12. CERCLA § 104(i)(5)(C), 42 U.S.C. § 9604(i)(5)(C).
13. CERCLA § 105(a), 42 U.S.C. § 9605(a).
14. CERCLA § 105(c), 42 U.S.C. § 9605(c).
15. CERCLA § 105(h), 42 U.S.C. § 9605(h).
16. CERCLA § 121(b)(1), 42 U.S.C. § 9621(b)(1).
17. CERCLA § 121(d), 42 U.S.C. § 9621(d).
18. 42 U.S.C. §§ 9621(f), 9617.
19. *See* "Nanotechnology: Research Projects," http://es.epa.gov/ncer/nano/research/index.html.

20. *See* The Royal Society and Royal Academy of Engineering, "Nanoscience and nanotechnologies: opportunities and uncertainties" (2004) at 46–47, Section 5.4, Paragraph 44, *available at* http://www.nanotec.org.uk/finalReport.htm.

21. *See, e.g.*, Goodrich Corp. v. Town of Middlebury, 311 F.3d 154, 161 (2d Cir. 2002), *cert. denied*, 537 U.S. 937 (2003); A&W Smelter and Refiners, Inc. v. Clinton, 146 F.3d 1107, 1110–11 (9th Cir. 1998).

22. CERCLA § 107(a)(3) and (4), 42 U.S.C. § 9607(a)(3) and (4).

23. CERCLA § 107(o)(2), 42 U.S.C. § 9607(o)(2).

24. CERCLA § 107(f), 42 U.S.C. § 9607(f).

25. CERCLA § 107(l), 42 U.S.C. § 9607(l).

26. CERCLA § 122, 42 U.S.C. § 9622.

27. 42 U.S.C. § 9604(e).

28. 42 U.S.C. § 9606(a).

29. 42 U.S.C. § 9606(b).

30. 42 U.S.C. § 9622(e).

31. 42 U.S.C. § 9622(f).

32. 42 U.S.C. § 9608(a)–(c).

33. 42 U.S.C. § 9611(a).

34. 42 U.S.C. § 9607(n).

35. 42 U.S.C. § 9601(20).

36. 42 U.S.C. § 9607(o).

37. 42 U.S.C. § 9607(p).

38. 42 U.S.C. § 9622(g).

39. 42 U.S.C. § 9607(q).

40. 42 U.S.C. § 9601(35).

41. 42 U.S.C. § 9601(40).

42. 42 U.S.C. § 9627.

43. 42 U.S.C. § 9607(p)(2).

44. CERCLA § 107(p)(3), 42 U.S.C. § 9607(p)(3).

45. Pub. L. 99–499, Title III, codified at 42 U.S.C. § 11001 *et seq.* (known as SARA Title III or EPCRA, the Emergency Planning and Community Right-to-Know Act).

46. 42 U.S.C. § 11003.

47. 42 U.S.C. § 11022.

48. 42 U.S.C. § 11023.

49. 42 U.S.C. § 11004.

50. 40 C.F.R. § 355.30(e)(2)(i).

CHAPTER 8

Clean Water Act

Executive Summary

This chapter evaluates the existing statutory authority under the Clean Water Act (CWA or Act) to regulate nanotechnology and nanoparticles. One of the stated national goals of the CWA is the elimination of the discharge of pollutants into navigable waters. Accordingly, the CWA generally provides the U.S. Environmental Protection Agency (EPA) with authority to regulate the discharge of "pollutants" consistent with this national goal. The term "pollutant" is defined broadly so that nanoparticles discharged into navigable water likely would be subject to regulation under the Act as a discharge of a pollutant. Thus, there appears to be adequate existing authority under the CWA that would allow EPA to regulate nanoparticles.

Although EPA has the authority to regulate nanoparticles, it likely would be necessary for EPA first to demonstrate that certain nanoparticles (e.g., specific chemicals or a class or category of nanoparticles) have a potential adverse effect on human health or the environment, thus making CWA regulation necessary and appropriate. To this end, further research and study likely will plainly be necessary. In addition, before any meaningful regulation could be promulgated and implemented, the technology that would allow nanoparticles to be monitored, measured, and controlled must be developed.

In light of the above, and by way of illustration, this chapter evaluates specific sections of the CWA that have some readily apparent relevance

This chapter expands upon the Section of Environment, Energy, and Resources' June 2006 paper entitled *Nanotechnology Briefing Paper Clean Water Act*. The Team Leader on that paper was Pamela E. Barker, Godfrey & Kahn, S.C. Revisions are by Alicia J. Edwards, Doerner, Saunders, Daniel & Anderson, LLP; with assistance from Lynn L. Bergeson, Bergeson & Campbell, P.C.

to the potential regulation of nanoparticles and generally considers the following four questions:

1. Does the section have any applicability to the regulation of nano-particles? In other words, is the section of any use to EPA if it were to find that regulation was necessary and appropriate?
2. If so, does the section provide EPA the authority to regulate nanoparticles?
3. What are the technical, legal, or other problems involved in the application of this section to nanotechnology due to the unique nature of nanoparticles?
4. What are the options for dealing with such problems?

Nanoparticles may enter the wastewater stream in multiple ways. First, releases to the environment may occur as nanoparticles, or prod-ucts containing them, are manufactured, processed, or transported to the point of use. Second, the intended use of certain products may result in nanoparticles either becoming a contaminant in a water body or part of the influent being treated at a publicly owned treatment works (POTW). For example, nano-sunscreen lotions may be rinsed off in ponds, lakes, rivers, swimming pools, and showers. Nanoparticles also may be released into the environment when treated fabrics are laundered or as certain antifouling coatings for vessels and offshore structures degrade over time. In the future, fertilizers and pesticides designed to reduce runoff of nitrogen, phosphorous, and toxic substances may incorporate nanotech-nology, creating the potential for widespread exposure to aquatic life and humans. Finally, nanoparticles may be released into the environment when products containing them are discarded.

Nanoparticle-containing products that may result in releases of nano-particles to receiving waters or POTWs are already being actively sold and marketed. For example, several manufacturers are marketing socks that reportedly contain nanosilver particles as an antibacterial agent.[1] A recent study demonstrates that when the socks are washed, some of the silver nanoparticles may be released into the water.[2]

A more controversial example is Samsung's SilverCare option on sev-eral models of washing machine. Samsung advertised the generation of silver nanoparticles in the rinse cycle as a benefit to consumers because of silver's antibacterial effects and because the option allowed clothes to be washed in cooler water, resulting in energy and cost savings.[3] Consumers and POTW owners and operators, however, expressed concern about the potential consequences of using SilverCare products, and the machines were even taken off the market briefly in Sweden due to concerns over the potential toxic effects of discharging silver nanoparticles from these machines to wastewater treatment plants.[4] In the United States, EPA ultimately determined that the washing machines required registration as pesticides under the Federal Insecticide, Fungicide, and Rodenticide Act, perhaps in part due to concerns expressed by the National Association of Clean Water Agencies (NACWA) and an organization representing POTWs in California.[5]

Ultimately, the concentration of nanoparticles in wastewater depends on several factors: (1) the amount of nanoparticles produced or used locally; (2) whether the nanoparticles are fixed in a matrix or free; (3) the concentration of the free nanoparticle in the commercial product; (4) the fraction that is washed down the drain; (5) the degree of agglomeration or adsorption that occurs in aqueous solution and changes the form of the nanoparticle or removes it from solution; and (6) the extent of dilution.[6]

Effluent Guidelines and Toxic and Pretreatment Standards

EPA may include nanoparticles as a regulated pollutant pursuant to Sections 301(g)(4) and 307(a). In doing so, EPA will have to place nanoparticles in a particular class of pollutants—conventional, toxic, or nonconventional. CWA Section 301 requires EPA to set technology-based effluent limitations for point source discharges; CWA Section 307 requires the establishment of toxic and pretreatment effluent standards. EPA, under these sections, has the authority to establish technology-based effluent limitation guidelines and standards for nanoparticles discharged from a point source. EPA also has the authority, pursuant to CWA Section 307(b), to establish pretreatment standards for those facilities that discharge to a POTW.

A key challenge EPA will face in addressing nanoparticles will be determining the best available technology that is economically feasible for regulated entities. Nanotechnology is still in the evolutionary stage, and the availability of technology to control nanoparticles in wastewater streams is evolving. EPA should consider research projects, including collaborative efforts with regulated entities, and the use of technology-forcing regulations to ensure the development of appropriate control technologies.

Water-Quality-Related Effluent Limitations

CWA Section 502(6) defines the term "pollutant" so broadly as to include virtually any material added to a watercourse. Accordingly, for purposes of analyzing the application of the water quality provisions of the CWA to nanoparticles, it can be assumed that all the provisions of the Act dealing with the creation of and implementation of water quality standards will apply to the discharge of any form of nanoparticles to any water of the United States covered by the Act.

Section 302 of the CWA allows EPA to create and modify water-quality-related effluent limitations whenever EPA determines that the technology-based effluent limits created under CWA Section 304 are not sufficient to protect the affected waters to the degree required under the Act. The section further allows EPA to modify such water-quality-based effluent limitations on economic or technical grounds, with certain special considerations in the case of toxic pollutants.

In the case of nanoparticles, a necessary prerequisite for application of Section 302 will be the existence of a reasonably accurate scientific basis on which to make a judgment that the quality of the affected water is adversely affected by the addition of nanoparticles to the water body. While any detailed description of the process is beyond the scope of this chapter, the general outlines of the analysis can be described.

First, unless there is a determination that nanoparticles are per se harmful, the toxicity or degree of pollution will probably be extrapolated based on the known toxicity of the same materials in non-nano quantities as conventional chemical substances. So, for example, since lead is harmful as a pollutant in some quantity, EPA may assume it is harmful in smaller quantities and act accordingly by prescribing some form of pollution abatement based on best available technology. If, on the other hand, an assumption of harm is not appropriate, EPA will be required to develop data to show that the nanoparticles do in fact cause harm to the water body before it can invoke CWA Section 302 jurisdiction.

Water Quality Standards, Implementation Plans, and Revised Water Quality Standards

CWA Section 303 provides for the adoption of state water quality standards by EPA and for the periodic revision of such standards on a three-year cycle. The objective of the section is to ensure that the state standards as approved by EPA are consistent with federal guidelines established by EPA under those provisions dealing with technology-based water quality standards, toxic effluent limitations, and water-quality-based effluent limitations. The section also provides for the identification of water bodies not meeting federal/state criteria, and the creation of Total Maximum Daily Load (TMDL) programs for such water bodies.

Since there are no existing state or federal criteria for nanoparticles as such, the application of CWA Section 303 and 33 U.S.C. Section 1313a to these materials necessarily must await the development of such criteria. It is possible, however, that there may be some materials already regulated by EPA for which the applicable criteria may apply to such materials in nano form. For example, if nanoparticle X is discharged to a water body in such amounts as to be measurable at levels in excess of some existing criterion value for material X, that discharge would be subject to the provisions of CWA Section 303.

Information and Guidelines

CWA Section 304 provides in pertinent part that EPA shall develop water quality standards for all waters of the United States for any and all pollutants, establish technology-based effluent limitations to be imposed under the National Pollutant Discharge Elimination System (NPDES) program, and establish individual control strategies for toxic pollutants. The section also provides for the evaluation and control of nonpoint source pollutants.

With respect to nanoparticles, this element of EPA's statutory authority likely will be the most challenging. To develop applicable water quality standards, EPA will be required to assemble a reasonable database covering all known effects of specified nanoparticles in water bodies. Such information will necessarily include toxicity studies, biological and chemical effect studies, transport/deposition data, uptake and bioaccumulation information, and a host of other data to evaluate the possible adverse effects of specific nanoparticles on biological organisms, including humans.

As one example, there is a study of buckyballs (i.e., carbon fullerenes) and their effect on two aquatic species, largemouth bass and water fleas.[7] The data show an adverse effect on brain tissue. Such studies must be collected and peer reviewed before they can be used to create water quality standards that can be relied upon to develop applicable discharge criteria. Likewise, EPA will have to evaluate appropriate discharge control mechanisms to determine if they are technologically viable and economically achievable. As suggested earlier, it is possible that EPA can use data previously gathered on known pollutants (i.e., lead, cadmium) to extrapolate effects of such materials in nanoparticle form. Such extrapolation must be scientifically defensible in light of critical differences between conventional and nanoscale chemical substances and the relevance of these differences to quantifying hazard and risk potential.

State Reports on Water Quality

CWA Section 305 provides for the reporting of the states' progress in implementing the provisions of the CWA to Congress. Given the state of knowledge concerning nanoparticles, it is unlikely that the states will have much to report until the scientific database expands and EPA has created applicable water quality standards and criteria, including effluent limitations. Once the requisite data are collected and are implemented in the form of state/federal regulations, effluent limitations, and applicable permit conditions, states will be required to include data on nanoparticles as part of their biennial reports.

National Standards of Performance

CWA Section 306 pertains to national standards of performance as a means to control the discharge of pollutants. National standards of performance are based on best available demonstrated control technology, processes, or operating methods for sources within a list of categories (e.g., pulp and paper mills, organic chemicals manufacturing). The list of categories may be revised by EPA from time to time to incorporate the pertinent category of sources discharging nanoparticles, if those sources are not already within the listed categories. CWA Section 306 allows EPA to consider other factors such as the cost of achieving the reduction of nanoparticles in effluent, as well as any non-water-quality, environmental impact, and energy requirements in establishing national standards. The existence of such technology or other demonstrated control alternatives for nanoparticles is a prerequisite to regulation under Section 306, and the standards are subject to change by EPA as technology and alternatives concerning nanoparticles change.

As with CWA Sections 301 and 307, advancements in science and technology are key to the establishment of appropriate standards for regulating nanoparticles and achieving a reduction of nanoparticles in effluent. Additional research is required to determine whether nanoparticle performance standards should be added to existing point source categories or whether the nanotechnology industry itself will require the creation of its own category.

Records and Reports; Inspections

CWA Section 308 may be EPA's best regulatory tool to gather data on nanoparticles that may be discharged to waters of the United States. Congress and other regulatory agencies are currently in an information-gathering mode with respect to nanotechnology and its effects on the environment, and the most effective way EPA can participate in that effort is to invoke Section 308 to gather data and require monitoring from nanoparticle users and manufacturers. This section grants EPA broad authority to require the owner or operator of a point source to maintain records, make reports, perform monitoring and sampling, and provide such information to EPA as is "reasonably" required to carry out the purposes of the Act. Section 308 also authorizes EPA to enter and inspect facilities of an "effluent source," along with facility records.

The power to gather information does not need to be exercised in anticipation of an enforcement action, as courts have interpreted Section 308 broadly. As one court has stated, "[t]he breadth of this statutory grant of authority is obvious. In our view, the statute's sweep is sufficient to justify broad information disclosure requirements relating to the Administrator's duties, as long as the disclosure demands which he imposes are 'reasonable.' "[8] In *NRDC*, the D.C. Circuit upheld EPA's ability under Section 308 to require NPDES permit applicants to list all toxic pollutants currently used or manufactured as an intermediate or final product or by-product. Thus, EPA was not limited to information related to toxic pollutants in a facility's effluent discharge—it could obtain information under Section 308 on *all* toxic pollutants at a facility because they *could* be discharged from the facility. Therefore, if a facility that uses or manufactures nanoparticles is discharging to waters of the United States, EPA could utilize Section 308 to inspect the facility, obtain records, require discharge monitoring, and require reporting to EPA to gain more information on the nature of nanoparticle discharges.

While EPA has legal authority to collect data, technical challenges in monitoring and measuring nanoparticles in an effluent discharge may render Section 308 less effective than it might otherwise appear. EPA cannot impose unreasonable requirements under Section 308 (i.e., a high-cost experimental monitoring system), so until reasonable and effective monitoring technology is developed for nanoparticles, EPA may be limited to obtaining operational data from a nanoparticle facility. Due to the current difficulty of quantifying and measuring nanoparticles in water, EPA's first steps under Section 308 could be to gather data from nanoparticle use and production facilities on (1) the use and manufacture of nanoparticles and (2) the frequency and volume of any discharges to waters of the United States. EPA should work with the scientific community to develop feasible monitoring technologies for nanoparticles, which could then be used for requiring nanoparticle users and manufacturers to install and use Section 308 monitoring and reporting programs.

Enforcement

CWA Section 309 governs enforcement of the CWA's provisions for regulating pollutants. If nanoparticles are added as a pollutant under Section 309(c)(7), EPA could use this section to enforce nanoparticle standards and limitations. Nanoparticle listings and the ability to enforce whatever standards EPA may set require an appropriate, measurable, and well-defined limit. Continued research into technologies that may effectively measure and capture nanoparticles from discharge effluent is required before EPA begins any enforcement activities.

Oil and Hazardous Substance Liability

CWA Section 311 regulates discharges of oil and "hazardous substances," defined under Section 311(b)(2)(A), to the waters of the United States from vessels and onshore and offshore facilities. EPA could conceivably designate particular nanoparticles, or specific groups of nanoparticles, as "hazardous substances" under Section 311. These materials, however, currently defy description, classification, and characterization in terms of what impacts they might have on human health and the environment. If future scientific and political support exists to characterize such materials as hazardous, Section 311 may serve to require cleanup of nanoparticle discharges.

Federal Facilities' Pollution Control

CWA Section 313 reaffirms that federal facilities are subject to and must comply with all federal, state, interstate, and local requirements relating to the control and abatement of water pollution. While this section may not serve to add any substantive limitations, federal research, military, and production facilities may be significant sources of potential nanoparticle emissions. Should EPA regulate these discharges, enforcement initiatives involving federal facilities could set significant precedents for nanotechnology management.

Nonpoint Source Management Programs

Unlike with point sources, nonpoint source pollution derives from varied and often unidentifiable sources. Rainwater transports a variety of potentially harmful substances, such as sediment, fertilizer, pesticides, agricultural nutrients, motor oil, or salts, into surface and groundwater. There is no formal definition of nonpoint source pollution. CWA Section

319 is structured to accommodate the watershed-to-watershed variability of nonpoint source pollution by vesting most of the responsibility for investigation and control with the states. Among these responsibilities are (1) a state assessment report identifying waters failing to attain water quality standards and significant nonpoint source contributors; and (2) a state management program utilizing best management practices or other methods to control nonpoint source pollution for each watershed. These reports and programs are subject to approval by the Administrator. The remainder of the section discusses funding and federal cooperation to aid the states in carrying out the listed goals.

The effect of nanoparticles on aquatic life remains largely unknown. Should evidence showing an adverse impact on surface water ecosystems appear, however, states will be obligated to evaluate the extent of water quality impairment caused by nanoparticles added through nonpoint sources. Due to their size, nanoparticles originating from industrial processes, consumer products, or an unknown number of other sources could be easily transported by rain and runoff to water bodies. Deposition of suspended, airborne nanoparticles via raindrops is also a potential source adding to nonpoint source impairment. It is possible that surface waters could become laden with nanoparticles originating from somewhere other than a point source. Should this occur, the statutory structure already in place could adequately track and potentially reduce nonpoint nanoparticle pollution, provided that certain prerequisites are met. First, common to all nanoparticle pollution issues, effective measurement technologies and methods must be developed. Second, potential sources of nanoparticle diffusion must be identified. This may include everything from residential property to smokestacks, automobile tailpipes, and agricultural operations. Finally, state agencies must have enough of an understanding of nanoparticles to effectively create and enforce best management practices that prevent nanoparticles from eventually draining into surface waters, whether through runoff or aerial deposition.

Should nanoparticle impairment become a serious concern, the scientific and technical issues unique to nanoparticles may require some centralization to manage nonpoint source pollution. Best management practices might best be developed at the federal level in the form of product assembly guidelines. Examples could be the requirement of certain types of bonding to prevent nanoparticle deterioration and dispersion over time. Other requirements under the Clean Air Act to limit nanoparticle emissions could prevent suspended nanoparticle deposition in surface waters, similar to the formation of acid rain. Best management practices, however, most likely will require a reactive approach as it is unlikely that they may be designed and implemented until after EPA better understands nanotechnology uses and the fate and transport of nanoparticles in water runoff.

Certification

Applicants for a federal license or permit to conduct any activity that may result in a discharge into navigable waters must obtain certification from the state or an interstate water pollution control agency that the proposed discharge will comply with applicable water quality standards. Under Section 401, this would include any future water quality standards for nanoparticles.

The Section 401 certification process depends greatly on the content of the state's water quality standards. Most state water quality rules contain provisions prohibiting the degradation of water quality and the impairment of beneficial uses. Given the uncertain state of scientific knowledge regarding the environmental and health effects of nanoparticle discharges, some states might assert that any level of nanoparticle discharge violates state water quality standards and should be prohibited or restricted. EPA could begin developing guidance for states to use in establishing water quality standards for nanoparticles. This approach, however, may be complicated by the fact that each state could decide to develop its own response to this issue pending completion of any EPA guidance.

NPDES

The basic features of the NPDES program are (1) the issuance of point source discharge permits with pollutant-specific numeric effluent limitations based on either technology-forcing standards or water quality protection standards; (2) the measurement of compliance against those effluent limitations by routine and frequent monitoring of effluent quality using standardized sampling and analytical methods; and (3) the routine and frequent reporting of the effluent quality measurements through discharge monitoring reports that are readily available to and understandable by the public as well as regulators.

In the formative years of the NPDES permit program, the effluent limits tended to be based on technology rather than water quality. Before the development of industry-specific effluent limitation guidelines, NPDES permits tended to be based on the permit writer's "best professional judgment."

As the program matured, it became more standardized. For example, the NPDES program now includes prescribed analytical methods,[9] industry-specific effluent limitation guidelines,[10] specific toxic pollutant standards,[11] and national recommended water quality criteria for 128 pollutants issued pursuant to CWA Section 304. Following the 1987 amendments to the CWA, renewed emphasis was placed on water quality issues (including contributions from stormwater-related sources and nonpoint sources) and water-quality-based effluent limitations. Where water-quality-based effluent limitations are unattainable through the application of treatment technology, source-specific "best management practices" are often prescribed in addition to or in lieu of numeric effluent limitations. Best management practices are included as "special conditions" in the NPDES permit. Other special conditions that have been employed to address unusual situations include the collection of additional source-specific data and information above and beyond routine effluent quality monitoring, as well as the performance of special studies such as ambient stream studies, toxicity reduction evaluations, sediment studies, mixing zone studies, and bioaccumulation studies, all for the purpose of acquiring data and information for future NPDES permit modifications or renewals.

Generally speaking, the discharge of any pollutant from a point source is unlawful unless the discharge is authorized by a NPDES permit.[12] Presuming the nanoparticle in question is determined to be within the CWA's broad definition of "pollutant," the NPDES permit program is applicable to point source discharges of the nanoparticle. To fit neatly within the NPDES permit program, the nanoparticle in question must be detectable and measurable through reasonably reliable and feasible sampling and analytical methods. In addition, the nanoparticle must be amenable to treatment by available treatment technology.

To the extent that the nanoparticle in question is detectable and measurable, the NPDES permit application process should be able to determine anticipated concentration and mass loading values for the regulated discharge. Similarly, the effluent quality of the permitted discharge will be amenable to measurement for discharge monitoring and compliance purposes. To the extent that the nanoparticle in question is treatable through available technology, there will be a basis for the establishment of technology-based effluent limitations. The establishment of water-quality-based effluent limitations may lag in time pending the performance of research on effects of the nanoparticle on various surface water receptors and designated uses.

It is conceivable, perhaps even likely, that the regulation of nanoparticles covered by the NPDES program will follow the same evolutionary curve described at the outset of this section. In the early years, NPDES permits will be based upon the "best professional judgment" of the permit writer. As nanotechnology sectors emerge and develop, sector-specific effluent limitation guidelines can be promulgated to standardize the regulatory outcomes of the NPDES permit application and renewal processes. In addition, water quality criteria can be derived as the field research database develops.

To the extent the nanoparticle in question is not detectable and/or reliably measurable and/or treatable, the NPDES permit program may still be able to provide some degree of regulation through the development of source-specific special conditions. The NPDES permit program enables the permit writer to employ "special conditions" to deal with atypical situations such as the emerging scientific and regulatory issues presented by nanoparticles. For example, a NPDES permit covering the discharge of nanoparticles could require the collection of "effects" data relating to ambient stream parameters, sediment, bioaccumulation in receptors, and other factors of potential concern. A NPDES permit also could require the performance of toxic reduction evaluation studies or treatability studies. If the establishment of numeric effluent limitations is not technically feasible, the permit writer is authorized to specify best management practices as a means of regulating discharges through source control pending the development of a basis for specifying numeric effluent limitations.

National Pretreatment Program

40 C.F.R. Part 403 establishes the national pretreatment program, which applies to all nondomestic sources that discharge wastewater to POTWs rather than directly to receiving waters. The pretreatment program is designed to (1) prevent the introduction into POTWs of pollutants that will interfere[13] with POTW operations, including the use and disposal of municipal sludge; (2) prevent the introduction into POTWs of pollutants that will pass through[14] the treatment works or otherwise be incompatible with such works; and (3) improve opportunities to recycle and reclaim municipal and industrial wastewaters and sludges.[15] Pretreatment programs generally are implemented and enforced at the local level with oversight by the state environmental protection agency or EPA.

Three types of pretreatment standards may apply to industrial users. First, all industrial users are subject to the general and specific discharge prohibitions in 40 C.F.R. Section 403.5. In particular, the discharge of any pollutant that may cause pass through or interference is prohibited. Second, categorical pretreatment standards are technology-based standards that apply to discharges to POTWs in specific industrial categories. Like technology-based effluent limitations for point sources, categorical pre-treatment standards are intended to ensure a consistent level of minimum treatment throughout the United States. Third, an individual POTW may develop local limits, based on the POTW's treatment capabilities and/or receiving water quality standards, for pollutants that may cause interference, pass-through, sludge contamination, or health and safety concerns for its employees.[16]

EPA's White Paper on nanotechnology acknowledges that the fate of nanoparticles in POTWs is "not well characterized."[17] Potential concerns regarding nanoparticles exist at all stages of the pretreatment process. First, nanoparticles may simply pass through the POTW's treatment system and, depending upon their quantity and characteristics, cause violations of the POTW's NPDES permit limits.[18] Second, nanoparticles may interfere with conventional treatment processes. For example, biocides like silver nanoparticles may inhibit biological degradation, making it impossible for the POTW to effectively treat wastewater. As another example, nanoparticles that settle out with the sludge during primary treatment could adversely affect microorganisms that aid in sludge stabilization and digestion. Finally, sludges containing large quantities of nanoparticles may be unsuitable for land application or other conventional methods of disposal.[19]

EPA's White Paper also identifies the "interactions of nanomaterials with microbes in sewage treatment plants in sewage effluent and natural communities of microbes in natural soil and natural water" as an area where research is critically needed.[20] The development of pretreatment standards for nanoparticles will probably follow the path as described for point source effluent limitations and have the same needs for reliable measurement and effective treatment methods.[21] Thus, initial standards are likely to be based on the best professional judgment of the POTW and will make a gradual transition to categorical pretreatment standards for specific industrial sectors. As sufficient site-specific information becomes available, local limits can be developed to address the needs of individual treatment plants and receiving waters.

Administration

CWA Section 501 allows the Administrator to recognize achievements in innovation related to waste treatment and pollution abatement programs. The Administrator may award a certificate or plaque to a regulated entity to recognize an outstanding "technological achievement or an innovative process, method, or device in their waste treatment and pollution abatement programs."[22] Regional Administrators may also provide awards to eligible nominees.[23] This recognition includes an announcement in the *Federal Register* and notification to the President, the Governor of the State or the Tribal leader of the jurisdiction where the recipient is located, the Speaker of the House, and the President pro tempore of the Senate.[24] The award does not allow for monetary awards or grants.[25]

The Administrator may use these powers to promote or recognize any regulated entity that takes substantial steps towards solving many of the problems related to nanotechnology in wastewater, including the detection and filtration of nanoparticles or, conversely, the use of nanotechnology as an innovative solution to current problems involving wastewater treatment. Few, if any, government-owned wastewater treatment plants could afford the research and development required to produce this type of novel technology. The powers of this statute and their attendant regulations could best be used to promote and recognize research and development by other entities eligible for the award, such as privately owned corporations and universities.[26]

Definitions

CWA Section 502 provides definitions of the various terms used in subchapter II of the Clean Water Act. As these terms are currently defined, nanoparticles could already be considered a "pollutant," "toxic pollutant," or "medical waste" under the Act.

The term "pollutant" is defined to include, inter alia, chemical wastes and "industrial, municipal, and agricultural waste discharged into water."[27]

The term "toxic pollutant" is defined to include

[T]hose pollutants, or combination of pollutants . . . which after discharge and upon exposure, ingestion, inhalation or assimilation into any organism, either directly from the environment or indirectly by ingestion through food chains, will, on the basis of information available to the Administrator, cause death, disease, behavioral abnormalities, cancer, genetic mutations, physiological malfunctions (including malfunctions in reproduction) or physical deformations, in such organisms or their offspring.[28]

The definition is notably broad enough to include materials known to harm aquatic life, but not human beings. Provided that the Administrator is satisfied with information showing harm to human or aquatic life, EPA may issue regulations for nanoparticles under 40 C.F.R. Part 129.

The term "medical waste" includes, inter alia, "such additional medical items as the Administrator shall prescribe by regulation."[29] Considering the planned use of nanotechnology in drug delivery, if adequate information exists to warrant regulation, nanoparticles could be regulated under this narrower definition.

Considering that nanoparticles conceivably fit under three separate definitions of pollutants, the Administrator may wish to consider an exclusion of nanoparticles from these sections (either through a requested congressional amendment or amendment to the Code of Federal Regulations), if they are to either be regulated in some other manner or left unregulated.

Water Pollution Control Advisory Board

CWA Section 503 creates an advisory board whose members are appointed by the President. Unlike the Effluent Standards and Water Quality Information Advisory Committee established under CWA Section 515, the scope of the Section 503 Board's advisory role is not specifically defined. Since the Board exists to "advise, consult with, and make recommendations to the Administrator on matters of policy,"[30] it is authorized to study and make recommendations on the issue of nanoparticle regulation.

Conclusion

Although EPA has the authority to regulate nanoparticles, it likely is necessary for EPA to demonstrate that certain nanoparticles (e.g., specific compounds or a class or category of nanoparticles) have a potential adverse effect on human health or the environment, thus making regulation of the nanoparticle necessary and appropriate under the CWA. To this end, further research and study likely would be required. In addition, before any meaningful regulation could be implemented, technology must be developed that would allow nanoparticles to be accurately monitored, measured, and controlled.

Notes

1. K. Sellers & L. L. Bergeson, *Nanomaterials Down the Drain: Perception and Reality*, poster presented at the Nano Science and Technology Institute (NSTI) Nanotech 2008 conference held June 1–5, 2008.

2. T. M. Benn & P. Westerhoff, *Nanoparticle Silver Released into Water from Commercially Available Sock Fabrics*, 42 ENVTL. SCI. & TECH. 4133 (2008), *available at* http://pubs.acs.org/cgi-bin/abstract.cgi/esthag/2008/42/i11/abs/es7032718.html.

3. Nanowerk News, *Concerns About Nanotechnology Washing Machine* (Nov. 16, 2006), *available at* http://www.nanowerk.com/news/newsid=1037.php.

4. R. Senjen, *Nanosilver—A Threat to Soil, Water, and Human Health?* Friends of the Earth Australia (Mar. 2007), *available at* http://nano.foe.org.au/node/189.

5. Sellers & Bergeson, *supra* note 1.

6. *Id.*

7. E. Oberdörster, *Manufactured Nanomaterials (Fullerenes, C60) Induce Oxidative Stress in the Brain of Juvenile Largemouth Bass*, 112 ENVTL. HEALTH PERSP. 1058 (2004), *available at* http://www.ehponline.org/members/2004/7021/7021.html; E. Oberdörster, *Toxicity of nC60 Fullerenes to Two Aquatic Species: Daphnia and Largemouth Bass Abstract IEC21*, 227th American Chemical Society National Meeting (Mar. 27–Apr. 1, 2004), Anaheim, CA.

8. NRDC v. EPA, 822 F.2d 104, 119 (D.C. Cir. 1987).

9. 40 C.F.R. §§ 136.1–136.6.

10. 40 C.F.R. §§ 401.10–471.106.

11. 40 C.F.R. §§ 129.1–129.105.

12. CWA §§ 301(a) and 402(a), 33 U.S.C. §§ 1311(a) and 1342(a).

13. "Interference" is defined as a discharge that, alone or in conjunction with a discharge or discharges from other sources, both (1) inhibits or disrupts the POTW, its treatment processes or operations, or its sludge processes, use, or disposal; and (2) therefore is a cause of a violation of any requirement of the POTW's NPDES permit (including an increase in the magnitude or duration of a violation) or of the prevention of sewage sludge use or disposal in compliance with applicable requirements. 40 C.F.R. § 403.3(k).

14. "Pass-through" is defined as a discharge that exits the POTW into waters of the United States in quantities or concentrations that, alone or in conjunction with a discharge or discharges from other sources, is a cause of a violation of any requirement of the POTW's NPDES permit (including an increase in the magnitude or duration of a violation). 40 C.F.R. § 403.3(p).

15. 40 C.F.R. § 403.2.

16. 40 C.F.R. §§ 403.5(c), 403.8(f)(4).

17. U.S. Environmental Protection Agency, *Nanotechnology White Paper* (White Paper) (Feb. 2007) at 35, *available at* http://www.epa.gov/osa/pdfs/nanotech/epa-nanotechnology-whitepaper-0207.pdf.

18. A study in Europe on cerium oxide nanoparticles found that while most of the nanoparticles were captured through adhesion to sludge, a significant fraction escaped the wastewater treatment plant's clearing system and was discharged in the plant's effluent. *See* L. Limbach et al., *Removal of Oxide Nanoparticles in a Model Wastewater Treatment Plant: Influence of Agglomeration and Surfactants on Clearing Efficiency*, 42 ENVTL. SCI. & TECH. 5828 (2008), *available at* http://pubs.acs.org/cgi-bin/abstract.cgi/esthag/2008/42/i15/abs/es800091f.html; *see also* P. Rizzuto, *Facilities Said to Lack Standard Methods to Test for Nanoparticles in Water, Sludge*, Env't Rep. (BNA) A-1 (Aug. 13, 2008) (contending that some nanoparticles could cause a POTW to fail the whole effluent toxicity test).

19. Benn & Westerhoff, *supra* note 2 (although POTWs may be able to remove sufficient amounts of nanosilver such that the POTW's effluent would comply with water quality criteria, the remaining activated sludge may contain levels of silver that render the sludge hazardous waste, thereby limiting the sludge's use as agricultural fertilizer).

20. White Paper at 88.

21. *See* Rizzuto, *supra* note 18, at A-1.

22. CWA § 501(e)(1), 33 U.S.C. § 1361(e)(1).

23. 40 C.F.R. § 105.1.

24. CWA § 501(e)(3), 33 U.S.C. § 1361(e)(3); 40 C.F.R. § 105.15.

25. CWA § 501(e)(2), 33 U.S.C. § 1361(e)(2).

26. *See* 40 C.F.R. § 105.5.

27. CWA § 502(6), 33 U.S.C. § 1362(6).

28. CWA § 502(13), 33 U.S.C. § 1362(13).

29. CWA § 502(20), 33 U.S.C. § 1362(20).

30. CWA § 503(b), 33 U.S.C. § 1363(b).

CHAPTER 9

Keeping Pace with Nanotechnology: The Need for a Diverse Set of Governance Mechanisms

Executive Summary

Among the many unique aspects of nanotechnology are its rapid evolution, the anticipated industry growth rate, the massive investments in research and development, and the almost visceral sense that no university, no company, no state, and no country wants to be left behind in the nanotechnology revolution. These characteristics, along with the facts that it is still not possible to routinely monitor releases of nanoscale materials and that health and environmental research funding remains a small fraction of overall nanotechnology research budgets, create serious challenges in designing an environmental governance system. An effective governance system must be capable of identifying and avoiding adverse consequences of a rapidly advancing industry; maintaining public confidence in the industry; and facilitating, or at least not unnecessarily inhibiting, the growth of potentially transformative technologies.

Part of the answer to this dilemma is reliance on a much broader set of management tools embedded in a new system of environmental governance. This new governance system should include traditional regulatory tools, but with more focus on products and pollution prevention. It also

This chapter was prepared by Lee Paddock, Associate Dean for Environmental Law Studies, The George Washington University Law School; Vice Chair, ABA SEER Committee on Innovation, Management Systems and Trading (2008–2009). The chapter is an updated version of an earlier article written by the author, *Keeping Pace with Nanotechnology: A Proposal for a New Approach to Environmental Accountability*, 36 Envtl. L. Rep. (Envtl. L. Inst.) 10943–10952 (Dec. 2006). Copyright © 2006 The Environmental Law Institute, Washington, D.C. Reprinted by permission.

must rely on a series of less traditional management tools, including robust public involvement and public dialogue, expanded information disclosure, government and industry voluntary and leadership programs, a liability system that checks irresponsible behavior, effective self-regulatory mechanisms, and adherence to clear and effective industry codes.

Background

Nanotechnologies include a broad array of materials with diverse characteristics, only the first generation of which has reached the market.[1] The International Risk Governance Council (IRGC) observed that

> [n]anoscience is the result of interdisciplinary cooperation between physics, chemistry, biology, biotechnology, material sciences and engineering in studying assemblies of atoms and molecules. . . . Applications of nanotechnology will penetrate and permeate through nearly all sectors and spheres of life (e.g. communication, health, labour, mobility, housing, relaxation, energy and food) and will be accompanied by changes in the social, economic, ethical and ecological spheres. . . .[2]

The IRGC recognizes four generations of nanotechnologies:

- First-generation *passive nanostructures* have stable behavior and quasi-consistent properties during their use and include intermediary system components such as particles, wires, and nanotubes. These nanostructures have been in existence since about the year 2000.
- Second-generation *active nanostructures* have properties that are expected to change during operation, so behavior is variable and potentially unstable. These nanostructures are beginning to emerge.
- Third-generation *integrated nanosystems* are systems in which passive or active nanostructures are integrated into systems using nanoscale synthesis and assembling techniques. These systems will develop based on the convergence of nanotechnology, biotechnology, information technology, and the cognitive sciences and could include artificial organs. Nanosystems are expected to be in use after 2010.
- Fourth-generation *heterogeneous molecular nanosystems* allow engineered nanosystems and architectures to be created

from individual molecules or supramolecular components, each of which have a specific structure and are designed to play a particular role. Fundamentally new functions and processes begin to emerge with the behavior of applications being based on that of biological systems and could include nanoscale genetic therapies. Heterogeneous systems are anticipated after 2015.[3]

The IRGC groups these four generations of nanotechnologies into two frames of reference: Frame One "passive" nanostructures and Frame Two "active" nanostructures. The IRGC notes that Frame One nanostructures include "developments" of existing products or products that will be developed in the future which contain relatively simpler nanostructures, which exhibit stable behavior during their use and which, in our view, do not present consumers or society with excessive novelty."[4] In marked contrast, for Frame Two nanostructures "new capabilities are expected to be developed to both create new molecules by design and change the structure of the existing molecules; together with their increased complexity and dynamic behaviour, this could directly increase the risks associated with these active nanomaterials and nanodevices. The active and more complex nanotechnology applications of Frame Two may, therefore, require a far greater level of knowledge and ability to control nanostructure behaviour and to assess potential risks. Additionally, a large number of the potential Frame Two applications involve genuinely new products and the social, economic and political consequences are expected to be more transformative. This greater level of novelty could, IRGC has concluded, heighten the potential for social concern."[5]

In less than ten years, nanomaterials are expected to evolve from today's stain-resistant fabric treatment, carbon fibers that strengthen golf clubs and tennis rackets, and titanium oxide particles in sunscreens to providing nanoscale genetic therapies and molecules designed to self-assemble. The anticipated scale of the nanotechnology industry is exceptional. This 2001 *Science* magazine "breakthrough of the year" technology may produce $1 trillion in goods and services by 2015.[6] The IRGC notes that

[n]anotechnology has the potential to become one of the defining technologies of the 21st century. Based on the ability to measure, manipulate and organise material on the nanoscale—it is set to have significant implications—envisaged breakthroughs for nanotechnology include order-of-magnitude increases in computer

efficiency, advanced pharmaceuticals, bio-compatible materials, nerve and tissue repair, surface coatings, catalysts, sensors, telecommunications and pollution control.[7]

Not surprisingly, governments and companies have invested heavily in nanotechnology research and development. More than 30 countries have nanotechnology initiatives, including many traditional industrial powers as well as less likely candidates such as Ukraine and Mexico. Research and development investments by industry worldwide are currently at about the same level as government investment, but these private investments are increasing at a higher annual rate.[8]

The United Kingdom's Strategy for Nanotechnology concluded "the field of nanotechnology and its applications is crucial to the future competitiveness and productivity of the UK economy, and to the well being and prosperity of its people."[9] The U.S.-based Nanotechnology Alliance observed

> [T]he countries that demonstrate the highest level of innovation and capture the most value from nanotech progress will exert a very significant level of influence on the global geopolitical landscape. For us to maintain our quality of life and global leadership position, the U.S. must play, not just to participate in, but to win the international nanotechnology race.[10]

State after state has enacted legislation trying to secure a competitive advantage in the industry through tax credits,[11] emerging technology funds,[12] direct appropriation to university research centers,[13] authorizing access to funding from Economic Development Banks,[14] or creating cabinet-level positions to help the state cultivate and expand growth industries such as nanotechnology.[15]

The breadth of nanotechnologies, the rate of development, and the race to be first with the next nano breakthrough present government with a significant challenge. In its study on *Managing the Effects of Nanotechnology*, the Woodrow Wilson International Institute for Scholars pointed out that

> [t]he rapid development of [nanotechnology] also means that government managers always will be operating with outdated information, and data on [nanotechnology] effects will lag behind commercial applications. Priorities for research and for regulation will need to shift constantly. We have moved into a world

which is, as David Rejeski states, "dominated by rapid improvements in products, processes, and organizations, all moving at rates that exceed the ability of our traditional governing institutions to adapt or shape outcomes." He warns, "If you think that any existing regulatory framework can keep pace with this rate of change, think again."[16]

The IRGC found that "innovation in the field of nanotechnology development is far ahead of the policy and regulatory environment."[17] It seems clear that the regulatory system alone cannot be relied upon to manage the environmental and public health consequences of nanotechnology.

Industry, too, faces a significant problem. Regulatory systems not only punish wrongdoing; they help build public confidence in an industry, especially an industry that may involve significant risks. Over the last decade, a number of industries have faced public confidence challenges with varying results. In the United States, the use of bovine growth hormones (BGH) became a significant issue in the 1990s. While the controversy has largely subsided, a number of milk products are now labeled "BGH Free" to address concerns of some consumers.[18] Genetically modified organisms (GMO), including such products as seed that can tolerate certain herbicides, have been similarly controversial. Concerns range from GMO "outcrossing"—in which GMOs cross breed with non-GMOs, changing the non-GMO plant's characteristics—to fears about the potential effect of GMO foods on health to the impact that patented GMO seeds may have on the cost of seed for farmers in developing countries.[19] Although GMO companies have overcome these concerns in the United States, political concerns driven by the public reaction in the European Union resulted in a long delay in introducing GMO seeds in Europe.[20] Problems of public acceptance can arise even in the absence of scientific facts substantiating the fears.[21]

Nanotechnologies face a similar risk, in significant part because so little is known about the effects of these technologies.[22] The IRGC noted: "Soliciting and integrating the social concerns of all stakeholders, especially civil society, is central . . . to risk governance and crucial for improving risk management and gaining public confidence."[23] Issues have been raised in several quarters about the potential impact of nanotechnologies. The Natural Resources Defense Council and Environmental Defense Fund staff observed that the novel properties of nanotechnologies

pose new risks to workers, consumers, the public, and the environment. The few data now available give cause for concern:

Some materials appear to have the potential to damage skin, brain, and lung tissue, to be mobile or persistent in the environment, or to kill microorganisms (potentially including ones that constitute the base of the food web). The trickle of data highlights how little is known about the environmental and health effects of engineered nanomaterials.[24]

The President of the Consumers Union noted: "[C]oncerns abound that nanoparticles can behave in unpredictable ways: They go places in the body previously off-limits to their clunky cousins; they might have altered magnetic properties; they might be able to move from package to person in a way we just don't yet understand."[25]

While a biotechnology-type backlash has not yet affected nano manufacturers, the level of uncertainty about effects, the dearth of public understanding, the lack of a clear management approach, and the potential health and environmental effects of some nanomaterials all create the setting for a nano backlash.[26] It certainly appears to be in the best interest of the industry to work quickly with governments, nongovernmental organizations (NGOs), and others to create and implement a credible environmental management system that can build and maintain public confidence in the industry. The challenge for policymakers, as the IRGC noted, is "to develop a flexible and adaptive approach to risk governance that supports responsible development of the technology while minimizing harm."[27]

A Systems Approach

For the last decade, government agencies have recognized the need for a systems approach to achieve broader compliance with environmental laws. From the beginning of the modern environmental era until the late 1980s, regulatory agencies tended to rely on permitting, inspections, and enforcement to achieve environmental objectives. As the number of organizations subject to environmental regulation rapidly expanded in the late 1980s and early 1990s to include tens of thousands of new smaller businesses, it became clear that additional tools would be needed to drive compliance. Agencies created compliance management systems that incorporate compliance assistance, auditing, and environmental management systems as well as enforcement mechanisms to produce desired environmental outcomes to better leverage their limited resources.[28] The concept of environmental accountability extends the compliance management systems approach to a still larger set of tools designed to produce better environmental results by subjecting the environmental behavior of organizations to public scrutiny.[29] These mechanisms include

- traditional regulatory, compliance, and enforcement tools;
- new approaches to regulation incorporating more flexible performance-based standards, economic instruments, and product standards;
- stakeholder dialogues supported by better information and new public education strategies;
- voluntary industry leadership programs and public reporting protocols;
- the possibility of liability in circumstances where products are prematurely or inappropriately introduced into the market place; and
- corporate self-regulation and social responsibility programs.

Instead of relying solely or even primarily upon government-imposed, post-production regulations, these accountability mechanisms take advantage of a variety of behavioral motivators, including requirements imposed through the regulatory system and activities encouraged by economics and values. Some mechanisms would be voluntarily adopted (or acquiesced to) by affected organizations based on self-interest or individual or organizational values; some may be based on economic pressure from customers, investors, the public, or economic opportunity created by incentives; and still others will continue to rely on government mandates and enforcement.[30]

While each of these mechanisms can enhance public accountability for environmental outcomes, it is critical that they be deployed in a systematic way. Each of these accountability mechanisms, much like each of our major environmental statutes, has been developed independently, rather than as an element of a comprehensive strategy to enhance public accountability and maximize environmental outcomes.

Using the full range of accountability tools more systematically— creating an environmental accountability system similar to, but much broader than, the compliance management system now used by the U.S. Environmental Protection Agency (EPA)—could significantly improve the effectiveness of environmental programs and improve environmental results. This will require government agencies, environmental organizations, and others concerned with environmental progress to analyze more carefully how the various mechanisms can be linked in a strategic fashion.

A Proposed Accountability System for Nanotechnology

Because of the speed at which the industry is growing and the range of materials and technologies that are part of the nano revolution, a systematic approach to environmental accountability is particularly important. If traditional government mechanisms cannot keep up with the industry, the environment and public health must be protected and public confidence must be created through a more comprehensive approach. This approach, whether implemented through government regulation, voluntary programs, or self-regulation, should be based on several basic principles including precaution, life-cycle review, sustainability, transparency, and public engagement.

Several organizations have urged that a precautionary approach be taken in nanotechnology development.[31] For most organizations that advocate a precautionary approach, this does not mean that nanotechnology research and development should be halted until each technology is proven to be safe. For example, the Commission of the European Communities in its proposed nanotechnology research code of conduct provides that research activities should be "conducted with the precautionary principle, anticipating potential environmental, health and safety impacts of N & N [nanoscience and nanotechnology] outcomes and taking due precautions, proportional to the level of protection, while encouraging progress for the benefit of society and the environment."[32]

Life-cycle analysis has become more common over the past decade in assessing the full environmental impact of products. Because of the dearth of information about the impacts of nanomaterials, life-cycle analysis is particularly important. The Environmental Defense–DuPont Nano Partnership recognizes this fact and incorporates life-cycle analysis as a critical step in their Nano Risk Framework.[33] The IRGC has pointed out that one of the shortcomings of current regulatory measures as applied to nanotechnologies is that they do not address the full life cycle of materials: "Current regulatory measures deal mostly with cause-and-effect of single events, and not the impact of a technology over its life cycle, or its secondary or interactive effects."[34] The Woodrow Wilson International Center for Scholars Project on Emerging Nanotechnologies pointed out: "In the field of nanotechnology, the broad framework of Life Cycle Thinking and the international standardized method of LCA can substantially help identify opportunities for pollution prevention and reductions in resource consumption while taking the entire life cycle of nanoproducts and the respective technologies into consideration."[35]

Companies and governments have increasingly embraced the concept of sustainability. This concept has particular relevance to nanotechnologies since projections indicate that these technologies may contribute in profound ways to energy efficiency, dematerialization, environmental remediation, and other areas critical to sustainability but may also create new problems that would undermine sustainability efforts. The Commission of the European Communities suggests that nanotechnology research should "be safe and contribute to sustainable development serving the sustainability objectives of the Community as well as contributing to the United Nation's Millenium Development Goals. They should not harm or create a biological or moral threat to people, animals, plants or the environment, at present or in the future."[36]

Transparency and public engagement is essential to good governance and to public acceptance of new technology. The IRGC notes: "Soliciting and integrating the social concerns of all stakeholders, especially civil society, is central to the IRGC approach to risk governance and crucial for improving risk management and gaining public confidence."[37] Similarly, the Commission for the European Communities observed: "Governance of N & N research activities should be guided by the principles of openness to all stakeholders, transparency and respect for the legitimate right of access to information. It should allow the participation in decision-making processes of all stakeholders involved in or concerned by N & N research activities."[38]

Government Regulation

Government regulation must be part of the accountability system both to assure that the environment and public health are protected and to build and maintain public confidence in the industry. Given the political stalemates that have occurred on environmental issues over the past few years, it is unlikely that major new legislation addressing nanotechnology will be adopted in the United States in the foreseeable future absent a dramatic incident involving nanomaterials.[39] Nonetheless, a 2009 report released by the Woodrow Wilson Center for Scholars Project on Emerging Nanotechnologies calls for the creation of a new Department of Environmental and Consumer Protection that would combine six existing federal agencies, including EPA and OSHA, with a strong oversight component and an integrated approach to research, technology assessment, pollution control, and product regulation.[40] A number of public interest groups have asserted that new nano-specific regulations are needed because, in their view, voluntary initiatives are "wholly inadequate to oversee nanotechnology."[41]

Much of this book discusses the application of existing regulatory programs to nanotechnologies. The ABA-SEER analysis of existing environmental statutes, as well as analyses by other organizations such the Environmental Law Institute,[42] indicates that these statutes are useful but imprecise mechanisms for dealing with various aspects of nanotechnologies. Regulation of nanotechnology, given the rapid changes within the industry, is likely to be an ongoing process with approaches evolving over time.[43] The IRGC concluded that governments worldwide "are not able to set up or modify comprehensive regulatory structures quickly enough to match the pace of innovation and product introduction. Nor, for nanotechnology, is the evidence base adequate to support an appropriate regulatory approach."[44]

EPA, in its White Paper on Nanotechology,[45] suggests a more product-oriented rather than emissions-related approach to managing the potential impacts of nanotechnologies:

> Opportunities exist to advance pollution prevention as nano-technology industries form and develop. EPA has the capability to support research into nanotechnology applications of pollution prevention and environmental stewardship principles that have been developed for green energy, green chemistry, green engineering, and environmentally benign manufacturing. EPA is well-positioned to work with stakeholders on pollution prevention and product stewardship approaches for producing nanomaterials in a green manner, as well as for identifying areas where nanomaterials may be cleaner alternatives to existing industrial inputs.[46]

States have increasingly turned to product legislation to control environmental hazards. For example, states have banned the use of metals such as cadmium, lead, mercury, and hexavalent chromium in packaging[47] and have required the manufacturers of electronic waste to take back a variety of products at the end of their useful life.[48] Product legislation may need to play a role in managing the risks related to nanotechnology over the long term.

Flexible Permitting

Given the limitations on the ability to detect and monitor nanoscale materials and the questions about the health effects of these materials, initial efforts must be directed at preventing releases into the environment. Still, at least some manufacturing operations are likely to need traditional EPA permits for environmental releases. Typically, changes in industrial operations that result in changes in type or quantity of emissions require a new permit. In the context of a rapidly evolving industry, this requirement is likely to be seen as stifling innovation and hindering competitiveness. At the same time, industry regulations must be stringent enough to reasonably protect human health and the environment.

This dichotomy may require stakeholders to consider more flexible regulatory approaches based on performance and transparency.[49] These types of regulatory approaches could be developed through a collaborative process involving government, industry representatives, and advocacy organizations to build confidence in the regulatory framework. One readily available model for flexibility is the "plant-wide applicable limits" approach developed under the Clean Air Act (CAA) and used in EPA's Project XL program. Under this program, Intel, working with its local stakeholders and EPA, was able to design a new permit that allowed its microchip production facilities to change their product mix without new permits so long as umbrella emissions limits for entire facilities were met. With a product life cycle that can be as short as eight months, the ability to change product lines without having to modify a permit was essential for Intel to remain competitive.

Two elements were vital to the success of the more flexible approach used in the Intel situation: enhanced monitoring and public reporting, and earlier, more substantial stakeholder involvement. Because flexible permits are designed to reduce delays arising from government reviews and approvals (particularly given increasingly limited government budgets), alternative accountability mechanisms must be included to ensure that the public is adequately informed and protected. These mechanisms include government and public access to additional information that could help track facility performance and identify problems, and more stakeholder influence at the front end of the approval process over the structure of the regulatory mechanisms. Just as it has worked for the microchip industry, a more flexible approach to permitting designed with broad stakeholder involvement and relying on enhanced monitoring and public reporting may allow the nanotechnology industry to continue its rapid growth while adequately protecting public health and the environment.[50]

Public Involvement and Dialogue

If the nanotechnology industry does not address issues of public confidence in the technology, it may suffer the same fate as that of genetically modified seed crops in the European Union—rejection of the crops as unsafe by the public and by public officials even though the scientific consensus identified little risk from the use of GMO seeds.[51] While regulatory schemes play a role in engendering public confidence, confidence is primarily an issue of values. If opinion leaders view a product as antipathetic to the values they hold, products may either be banned or may not survive in the market, regardless of the actual risk involved. The specter of unfounded public rejection suggests that accountability tools must be identified that create public confidence in the industry.

The risk of public rejection is especially acute in situations where scientific uncertainty is significant and where interest groups are likely to stake out strongly held positions early in the development of the technology. As Professor Gregory Mandel noted in his study of responses to risks posed by biotechnology and by nuclear power production, "individuals and interest groups do not revise their technology preferences in response to scientific and empirical information in the manner that such information appears to indicate."[52] Rather, a wide range of cultural factors drive and reinforce polarization. These factors include biased assimilation of new data—Mandel notes that "individual beliefs are remarkably resilient to the introduction of new data that challenges the beliefs";[53] the tendency of individuals to rapidly and automatically have a positive or negative feeling when confronted with certain ideas or concepts; cognitive dissonance avoidance, which leads individuals to discount information that conflicts with their perception of risks; and group dynamics that tend to perpetuate and reinforce polarization among individuals who socialize with those holding similar views.[54] The polarization phenomenon is aggravated by the fact that moderate voices tend to be underrepresented in debates involving technological risk because moderate voices typically do not inspire a "moderate movement."

A systematic approach to environmental accountability requires constructive contact among the industry, government, advocacy organizations, and other public stakeholders. Mandel espouses a concept he calls "dialogue and deliberation," in which representatives of all of the interest groups (including moderates) engage in a culture-conscious dialogue that focuses on values, not just competing scientific claims about benefits and risks. "The goal of the dialogue would be to help different groups learn about each other and each other's views, with a goal of cultural accommodation and understanding. Once these objectives have been achieved, a substantive policy deliberation can begin, aimed at developing widely-acceptable policy solutions."[55]

The Royal Society and Royal Academy of Engineering issued a similar call for public dialogue and debate on nanotechnology issues in its groundbreaking 2004 study of the industry.

The general case for wider societal dialogue about novel technologies, and with its greater openness about science policy, rests on three broad sets of argument. . . . The normative argument proposes that dialogue is a good thing in and of itself and as such forms a part of the wider democratic processes through which controversial decisions are made. . . . The instrumental argument suggests that dialogue, as one means of rendering decision-making more open and transparent, will increase the legitimacy of decisions and through this generate secondary effects such as greater trust in the policy-making process. . . . Finally, the substantive argument is that dialogue will help generate better quality outcomes. In the field of environmental risk, non-technical assessments and knowledge have been shown to provide useful commentary on the validity or otherwise of the assumption made in expert assessments.[56]

The Royal Society noted that with many mature technologies, public dialogue has often happened too little and too late to be effective.[57] With nanotechnology, there is a unique opportunity to avoid the problem of too little, too late.

Both the Meridian Institute and the Environmental Law Institute have convened policy dialogues related to nanotechnology, but a much more robust dialogue involving many more stakeholders and more approaches to assure environmental accountability will be needed as the industry continues to evolve.[58] A helpful example of the value of dialogue is the Environmental Defense–DuPont Nano Risk Framework, which utilized a very robust public consultation process in developing the Framework.[59] The Natural Resources Defense Council and the Environmental Defense Fund have called upon both government and industry to do a better job of "engaging the broad array of stakeholders outside government and industry—labor, health organizations, consumer advocates and environmental NGOs—whose constituencies stand to be both beneficiaries of this new technology and those most likely to bear any risks that arise."[60]

EPA, industry organizations, and interested NGOs should act with a sense of urgency in creating new forums for public dialogue and debate on nanotechnology. Several types of dialogue may contribute to the rationale and safe development of the industry. One model is a company-by-company dialogue, similar to the collaboration between the Environmental Defense Fund and DuPont, designed to create a framework for the responsible development, production, use, and disposal of nanoscale materials.[61] Another approach is a government-convened, ongoing dialogue among major stakeholders similar to the process EPA used in its Common Sense Initiative in the mid-1990s.[62] The lessons learned about how to conduct an effective, industry-focused, multi-stakeholder dialogue through the Common Sense Initiative, taken together with advances in understanding multi-stakeholder dialogues over the past decade and the fact that the nanotechnology industry is still in its infancy, could make a Common Sense type of dialogue far more effective today than it was ten years ago. A third approach is a dialogue convened by a well-regarded neutral facilitation organization, perhaps funded by a combination of government, industry, and foundation support.

Dialogues engage surrogates for the general public, but it is also important to find ways to engage interested members of the general public directly. Better public education is an important element of a new public dialogue on nanotechnology. Education in this context cannot simply be a one-way effort to convince the public that nanotechnology has important societal benefits and is safe. Instead, the education process must be part of the dialogue requiring "innovative approaches to information provision, ones that involve a genuine two-way engagement between scientists, stakeholders and the public."[63]

Engaging a broad public in an esoteric issue like nanotechnology is difficult. Still, the Internet offers intriguing possibilities for a new form of two-way dialogue with the broader public. Such a dialogue could start with a website on which the best and most credible information on the developments in nanotechnology is regularly posted. This should include up-to-date information on the risks and benefits of nanotechnologies, information about developments in government regulations, and information about industry standards and self-regulation approaches. The broader public could then use the site to comment on proposed regulations or on issues that could be addressed by members of the industry.[64]

Credibility and responsiveness are key issues for this idea to succeed. A government-managed site is one option; but given the role governments are playing in supporting nanotechnology development and the skepticism among many about government credibility, this may not be the best option. Other options include a neutral organization with experience in nanotechnology, such as the Meridian Institute, or a combination of well-regarded NGOs and broadly representative industry groups working together. One small-scale model of the latter type of arrangement can be found in the innovative website jointly maintained by the Minnesota Center for Environmental Advocacy (MCEA) and Flint Hills Resources, a large oil refiner. The website makes emissions data available to the public, which has an opportunity to comment directly to both MCEA and Flint Hills.[65]

Finally, a successful dialogue will require better information on the risks and benefits of nanotechnology. To date, most nanotechnology funding has been spent on technology development rather than on environmental, health, and safety (EHS) research or on detection and monitoring technology.[66] One estimate by environmental organizations indicated that of the roughly $1.5 billion that the federal government spent on nanotechnology, environmental, and health research in 2006, only about $68 million was spent for EHS research—a little over 4 percent. While EHS research has been increasing, it still is a small percentage of overall nanotechnology spending.[67] Assuring that adequate information is developed and disseminated on the health and environmental impacts of nanotechnology is critical to public credibility and an essential element of environmental accountability, as is better detection and monitoring technology.

Voluntary Programs

Industry leadership programs can play an important part in environmental accountability. Recognizing that environmental behavior is driven by factors beyond command-and-control regulations, EPA and many states have developed voluntary environmental leadership programs. The incentives for participating in these programs may include public recognition, improved working relationships with government agencies, penalty avoidance through auditing and self-reporting, and regulatory flexibility. As an emerging industry, it may be useful for EPA, industry leaders, and NGOs to consider the role that leadership programs could play in motivating desired environmental behavior.

Many voluntary leadership programs have included threshold entry requirements, such as

- a good compliance record;
- the existence of a company environmental management system that sets goals for environmental performance, maintains careful records, establishes employee training programs, requires periodic audits, provides for management review of the audits, and encourages continuous improvement in operations based on the management review; and
- reporting and prompt correction of violations that are identified through the environmental audits.

The goals established through leadership programs are often expected to go beyond mere compliance with the law to address unregulated matters, commit to emissions reductions that could not be required under existing regulations, or adopt preventive approaches that are not required by law.

Programs such as the Occupational Safety and Health Administration's (OSHA) Star Program,[68] EPA's Performance Track,[69] the Green Tier[70] in Wisconsin, and the Clean Corporate Citizen[71] program in Michigan are examples of well-developed leadership programs. EPA's Energy Star[72] program is another example of a leadership program, although one that exists in an area entirely unregulated by EPA.

While these programs generally have broad support, some NGOs have expressed concerns that leadership programs can be resource intensive, diverting government resources away from other important efforts such as strengthening inspection and enforcement efforts. In addition, some NGOs feel that leadership programs do not focus on priority environmental problems. Yet another concern raised by some NGOs is that some companies have been allowed to remain in EPA's Performance Track program despite what the organizations see as a poor compliance record.

Voluntary programs for nanotechnology may take a somewhat different form. For example, EPA's Nanoscale Materials Stewardship Program is designed to encourage companies developing nanotechnologies to voluntarily provide EPA with additional information about the technologies to provide EPA with "a firmer scientific foundation for regulatory decisions by encouraging submission and development of information including risk management practices for nanoscale materials."[73]

The IRGC has called upon industry, governments, and other stakeholders to collaborate now to lay the foundation for later regulatory action and to assess the potential for international voluntary agreements. Voluntary risk governance systems should include

- Development of standards and good practice guidelines in all areas, from basic research to product testing and tracking. Methods for assessing hazards and exposures should be a priority.
- Development of occupational safety guidelines and information disclosure programs for consumers.
- Establishment of transparent reporting schemes, especially of data and events that have a bearing on risk management.[74]

In addition to tracking the success of its Nanoscale Materials Stewardship Program, EPA should consider working with stakeholders to provide them with a direct role in overseeing the success of the Steward-ship Program or other voluntary programs related to the production of nanoscale materials. Participation by a broad range of stakeholders in the consideration and design of leadership programs may help to limit future concerns with this approach to environmental accountability.[75]

Liability

Nanotechnologies will face the threat of legal liability under nuisance, neg-ligence, or strict liability theories if their use causes harm to public health or the environment. The potential for civil liability is a key element of accountability because government resources to deal with environmental problems are shrinking while environmental threats are increasing. The civil liability system plays a critical role in tempering corporate decisions to introduce potentially risky products into the market prematurely.

Companies should be able to mitigate their liability exposure by incorporating aspects of environmental accountability into the way they do business.[76] Liability can be mitigated by a robust regulatory regime that will encourage courts to view compliance with the regula-tory scheme as establishing reasonable care on the part of the industry. The risks of civil liability can also be minimized by increased transpar-ency. The worst-case scenario for companies is demonstrated by the fate of the asbestos industry and, more recently, by litigation related to anti-inflammatory drugs. A key factor in both liability situations is that infor-mation about the adverse impact of asbestos and the drugs was available to the manufacturer but was not disclosed to the public or regulatory authorities. Prompt disclosure of information about adverse impacts of a product does not immunize a company from legal liability. It can reduce the potential of legal liability in several ways, however.

First, the prospect of disclosure can provide the impetus for a com-pany to modify its product, withhold, or temporarily remove it from the market until the impact can be better understood or the public can be more clearly warned. Second, disclosure can prompt regulatory action, including additional studies, product warnings, or market restrictions. Third, disclosure allows consumers to make more informed choices in the use of a product. Finally, wider stakeholder involvement with access to more complete information early in the approval process may raise issues or problems that could be resolved before a product reaches the market, avoiding potential mishaps.

The prospect of liability for harm to public health or the environment will be an important accountability tool for the nanotechnology industry.

Of equal importance is industry's opportunity to minimize that liability by employing accountability mechanisms such as public reporting and early public involvement.

Industry Codes and Self-Regulation

Industries have increasingly turned to codes of conduct and industry self-regulation as means of assuring compliance with environmental laws, maintaining their reputation, reducing the risk of legal liability, enhancing relationships with government agencies, minimizing exposure to penalties, and building public confidence. These codes and self-regulatory mechanisms are important accountability tools, especially if the codes or self-regulatory mechanisms contribute to transparency and public engagement by increasing the amount of information available to the public. Modern industry environmental codes trace their origin to the Coalition for Environmentally Responsible Economies (CERES) and its CERES Principles adopted in response to the *Exxon Valdez* disaster.[77] The American Chemistry Council (ACC, then the Chemical Manufacturers Association) adopted its Responsible Care[78] program in part to deal with increasing public concern about the role of discarded chemicals in groundwater contamination during the late 1980s. Responsible Care is a mandatory program for all ACC members and is practiced in 53 countries.[79] The Forest Stewardship Council, an NGO, developed a code for sustainable forestry practices and certifies compliance with its code to deal with the fact that forest management practices were rarely regulated.[80]

In the mid-1990s, the International Organization for Standardization (ISO) began work on a standard for what constitutes a quality environmental management program based on its early quality management standard.[81] The environmental management standard—ISO 14001, now in wide use around the world—provides a template for identifying the environmental aspects of an organization, setting goals for reducing those impacts, monitoring the goals, reporting results to management, and adjusting business practices based on the information—often referred to as the "plan, do, check, act" model. The most recent ISO 14001 survey shows that at the end of 2006, a total of 129,199 facilities held ISO 14001 certificates (up from 36,464 in 2001) in 140 countries.[82] A significant number of companies use the ISO 14001 management standard but do not take the additional steps necessary to qualify for formal certification.

Broad adoption of ISO 14001 by companies in the nanotechnology industry could help to identify and deal with potential adverse environmental and public health impacts of nanomaterials, even in the absence of government regulations. An enhanced environmental monitoring system (EMS) advocated by the Multi-State Working Group on Environmental Performance[83] (MSWG) could be an even better approach to self-regulation. The "External Value EMS" developed by the MSWG addresses three issues that many in government and NGOs see as major gaps in an ISO 14001 EMS. ISO 14001 does not require a company to demonstrate compliance with environmental requirements, involve stakeholders in the EMS process, or disclose information developed through the EMS to the public. The External Value EMS includes these additional requirements[84] and could be more effective than a standard EMS in building and maintaining public confidence.

Given the likely limitations on the government's ability to respond to nanotechnology, self-regulation is important to avoiding potential adverse impacts from nanotechnology and to build public confidence in the industry. Forms of self-regulation such as the External Value EMS, which enhance public access to information, may be particularly valuable. Both the Natural Resources Defense Council and Environmental Defense have recognized the importance of corporate standards of care.

> Even under the most optimistic scenario, it appears unlikely that federal agencies will put into place adequate provisions for nanomaterials quickly enough to address the materials now entering or poised to enter the market. Out of enlightened self-interest, industry must take the lead in evaluating and managing nanomaterial risks for the near term, working with other stakeholders to quickly establish and implement life cycle-based "standards of care" for nanomaterials.
>
> These standards should include a framework and a process by which to identify and manage nanomaterials' risks across a product's full life cycle, taking into account worker safety, manufacturing releases and wastes, product use, and product disposal. Standards of care should also include and be responsive to feedback mechanisms, including environmental and health monitoring programs to check the accuracy of the assumptions about a material's risks and the effectiveness of risk management practices. Such standards should be developed and implemented in a transparent and accountable manner, including by publicly disclosing the assumptions, processes, and results of the risk identification and risk management systems.[85]

Nanotechnology industries should act now through organizations such as ACC, the NanoBusiness Alliance, and other business entities to advance the dialogue on self-regulation in consultation with NGOs and government. Mediation organizations such as the Meridian Institute can play an important role in facilitating this dialogue.

In addition, the industry should consider labeling of products that contain nanoscale materials. Since the public still has a generally positive view of nanotechnology (even though the overall percentage of the public that is aware of nanotechnology is still low),[86] labeling a product as containing nanomaterials is not likely to adversely affect its marketability. Based on a recommendation from the Royal Society and the Royal Academy of Engineering, British Standards has issued a guidance document on labeling of products that incorporate nanoscale materials finding that: "Openness and transparency should accompany the responsible introduction of new technologies to the marketplace. Labelling, as part of this approach, helps consumers to make informed choices and should facilitate traceability and the monitoring of health and environmental impacts."[87]

Creating an Accountability System

Traditional regulatory systems are complex to develop and manage; a more inclusive environmental accountability system is likely to be even more difficult to oversee. Government controls the regulatory system, but can only influence many of the other accountability tools. Environmental accountability, especially in the context of nanotechnology, will require a new governance approach. The approach must incorporate government and its critical role in accountability but must also engage industry and the public in a new management partnership.

A multi-stakeholder Nanotechnology Council could serve this function. The Council could be independently chartered or could be organized by government under the Federal Advisory Committee Act (FACA). The Council should utilize facilitated dialogue provided by a highly credible mediation/facilitation organization to identify the parties that should be at the table, the issues that are discussed by the Council, the form of deliberation, and communication links to relevant stakeholders. Among the issues that the Council should address are public education, additional mechanisms for public dialogue, research priorities, risk/benefit identification, and regulatory approaches. It should analyze how the various accountability mechanisms—the regulatory system, dialogue and information, voluntary programs, liability, and self-regulation—can be organized in a systematic way to support appropriate growth of the industry.

The Council should not be a short-term project; rather, it should remain in existence as the major stages in nanotechnology reach the market and until it is clear there are no remaining major public policy issues related to nanotechnology.

Conclusion

Nanotechnology presents a daunting challenge to government, industry, and the public in building a credible system of environmental governance. Stakeholders from all sectors have recognized that a new system of governance that includes and reaches beyond reliance on government agencies will be needed. To ensure that public health and the environment are protected while facilitating the development of potentially transformative products and services, businesses, governments, and NGOs must act with a sense of urgency to develop and co-manage a new system of environmental governance that can keep pace with nanotechnology.

Notes

1. *New Dimensions for Manufacturing, A UK Strategy for Nanotechnology,* Dep't of Trade and Industry, 17, fig. 1 (June 2002).
2. International Risk Governance Council, *Nanotechnology Risk Governance* 19–20 (June 2006) (hereinafter IRGC 1).
3. *Id.* at 14; International Risk Governance Council, Policy Brief, *Nanotechnology Risk Governance: Recommendations for a global coordinated approach to the governance of potential risks,* 7 (2007) (hereinafter IRGC 2).
4. IRGC 2, *supra* note 3, at 8.
5. *Id.*
6. J. Clarence Davies, Woodrow Wilson Int'l Ctr. for Scholars, Project on Emerging Nanotechnologies, *Managing the Effects of Nanotechnology,* 8 (2006).
7. IRGC 1, *supra* note 2, at 21.
8. *Id.*
9. New Dimensions for Manufacturing, *supra* note 1, at 11.
10. Nanobusiness Alliance, *Nanotechnology: A Roadmap to Leadership,* 2 (Feb. 2006).
11. Ark. Code Ann. § 15-4-2104(a).
12. Mass. Gen. Laws Ann. ch. 23G, § 27(a), (c).
13. 2003 Or. Laws 725 (§ 11(4)(b)).
14. Tex. Gov't Code Ann § 489.0296(a).
15. Va. Code Ann. §§ 2.2–225.
16. Davies, *supra* note 6, at 9.
17. IRGC 2, *supra* note 3, at 13.

18. *See, e.g.,* http://www.biotech.iastate.edu/biotech_info_series/bio3.html #anchor346047.

19. *See, e.g.,* http://www.ovpr.uga.edu/researchnews/winter2000/viewpoint .html.

20. Sylvie Bonny, *Why are Most Europeans Opposed to GMOs? Factors Explaining Rejection in France and Europe,* 6 ELECTRONIC J. OF BIOTECH. 50, 53 (2003).

21. Gregory N. Mandel, *Technology Wars: The Failure of Democratic Discourse,* 11 MICH. TELECOMM. & TECH. L. REV. 117, 119–120 (2005).

22. *Id.* at 119.

23. IRGC 2, *supra* note 3, at 14.

24. John Balbus, Richard Denison, Karen Florini, & Scott Walsh, *Getting Nanotechnology Right the First Time,* ISSUES IN SCI. & TECH. 65 (Summer 2005).

25. Jim Guest, *A Small Matter of Great Concern,* CONSUMER REPORTS (Oct. 2006) at 5.

26. The Royal Society and the Royal Academy of Engineering, *Nanoscience and Nanotechnologies: Opportunities and Uncertainties* 61 (July 29, 2004).

27. IRGC 2, *supra* note 3, at 15.

28. *See* SUELLEN KEINER & LEROY PADDOCK, *Mixing Management Metaphors: The Complexities of Introducing a Performance-based State/EPA Partnership into an Activities-based Management Culture, in* ENVIRONMENT.GOV: TRANSFORMING ENVIRONMENTAL PROTECTION FOR THE 21st CENTURY, 11.51, 11.51–11.52 (2000).

29. LeRoy Paddock, *Environmental Accountability and Public Involvement,* 21 PACE ENVTL. L. REV. 243 (2004).

30. American Bar Association, Section on Environment, Energy, and Resources, *Briefing Paper on EMS/Innovative Regulatory Approaches* (June 2006) at 4–5, *available at* http://www.abanet.org/environ/nanotech/pdf/ EMS.pdf.

31. *See Principles for the Oversight of Nanotechnologies and Nanomaterials, available at* http://www.icta.org/doc/Principles%20for%20the%20Over sight%20of%20Nanotechnologies%20and%20Nanomaterials_final.pdf; IRGC 2, *supra* note 3, at 16; Commission of the European Communities, COMMISSION RECOMMENDATION of 07/02/2008 on a code of conduct for responsible nanosciences and nanotechnologies research, General Principles 3.3.

32. *Id.*

33. Environmental Defense and DuPont, *Nano Risk Framework* 8 (June 2007), *available at* http://www.nanoriskframework.com.

34. IRGC 2, *supra* note 3, at 13.

35. Woodrow Wilson International Center for Scholars, Project on Emerging Nanotechnologies, *Nanotechnology and Life Cycle Assessment,* 13 (March 2007), http://www.nanotechproject.org/ (last visited July 27, 2009).

36. Commission of the European Communities, *supra* note 31, at 6.

37. IRGC 2, *supra* note 3, at 18.
38. Commission of the European Communities, *supra* note 31, at 6.
39. Linda K. Breggin, *Securing the Promise of Nanotechnology: Is U.S. Environmental Law Up to the Job?* 8 ENVTL. LAW INST. ed. (Oct. 2005).
40. J. Clarence Davies, Ph.D., *Oversight of Next Generation Nanotechnology*, Woodrow Wilson Center for Scholars Project on Emerging Nanotechnologies (Apr. 2009) at 24–26. The other federal agencies to be brought into the new department would be the U.S. Geological Survey (USGS), the National Oceanic and Atmospheric Administration (NOAA), the National Institute of Occupational Safety and Health (NIOSH), and the Consumer Product Safety Commission (CPSC). *Id.* at 26.
41. Principles for the Oversight of Nanotechnologies, *supra* note 31, at 3.
42. Breggin, *supra* note 39, at 8–16.
43. Glenn Harlan Reynolds, *Environmental Regulation of Nanotechnology: Some Preliminary Observations*, 31 ENVTL. L. REV. 10681, 10685 (2001).
44. IRGC 2, *supra* note 3, at 16.
45. U.S. EPA, *Nanotechnology White Paper* (Feb. 2007), *available at* http://www.epa.gov/osa/pdfs/nanotech/epa-nanotechnology-whitepaper-0207.pdf.
46. *Id.* at 89.
47. *See, e.g.*, Minn. Stat. § 115A.965 (2007).
48. *See, e.g.*, Minn. Stat. §§ 115A.1310–1330 (2007).
49. The Royal Society and the Royal Academy of Engineering, *supra* note 26, at 82.
50. Lee Paddock, *A New Environmental Accountability System for the Nanotechnology Industry*, Nanotech, Technical Proceedings of the 2006 NSTI Nanotechnology Conference and Trade Show ch. 8, § 2.1 (2006).
51. Malcolm Grant, *2005 Kerlin Lecture*, 9 GREENLAW 7 (Spring 2006).
52. Mandel, *supra* note 21, at 141.
53. *Id.* at 159.
54. *Id.* at 159–63.
55. *Id.* at 178.
56. The Royal Society and the Royal Academy of Engineering, *supra* note 26, at 63.
57. *Id.* at 64.
58. Meridian Institute, *Dialogue Series on Nanotechnology and Federal Regulations*, http://www.merid.org/showproject.php?ProjectID=9233.0; Environmental Law Institute, *Securing the Promise of Nanotechnology: Is U.S. Environmental Law Up to the Job?* (2005).
59. Nano Risk Framework, *supra* note 33, at 11–12.
60. Balbus et al., *supra* note 24, at 70.
61. *See* Environmental Defense Fund, *Getting Nanotech Right: Partnership with DuPont to ensure the responsible development of nanotechnology* (posted Oct. 11, 2005; updated July 17, 2007), *available at* http://www.environmentaldefense.org/article.cfm?contentID=4821.

62. *See* U.S. EPA, *Lessons Learned About Protecting the Environment in Common Sense, Cost Effective Ways* (Dec. 1998), *available at* http://www.epa.gov/sectors/pdf/pubs_lessons.pdf.

63. The Royal Society and the Royal Academy of Engineering, *supra* note 26, at 66.

64. American Bar Association, *supra* note 30, at 16.

65. *See* Flint Hill Resources and Minnesota Center for Environmental Advocacy, *Environmental Reporting Made Easy*, http://www.fhrpinebend.com/.

66. *See* Davies, *supra* note 6, at 29.

67. National Nanotechnology Initiative, *Strategy for Nanotechnology-related Environmental, Health and Safety Research* 1 (February 2008), *available at* http://www.nano.gov/NNI_EHS_Research_Strategy.pdf.

68. *See* U.S. Dep't of Labor, *OSHA Voluntary Protection Program*, http://www.osha.gov/dcsp/vpp/index.html.

69. *See* U.S. EPA, *National Environmental Performance Track*, http://www.epa.gov/performancetrack. EPA canceled the Performance Track Program in a March 16, 2009, memorandum; *available at* http://www.epa.gov/performancetrack/.

70. *See* Wis. Dep't of Natural Res., *Green Tier*, http://www.dnr.state.wi.us/org/caer/cea/environmental.

71. *See* Mich. Dep't of Envtl. Quality, *Clean Corporate Citizen*, http://www.michigan.gov/deq/0,1607,7-135-3307_3666_4134---,00.html.

72. *See* Energy Star, http://www.energystar.gov.

73. U.S. Environmental Protection Agency, *Nanoscale Materials Stewardship Program*, http://www.epa.gov/oppt/nano/stewardship.htm.

74. IRGC 2, *supra* note 3, at 17.

75. American Bar Association, *supra* note 30, at 6–7.

76. Mark Stallworthy, *Environmental Liability and the Impact of Statutory Authority*, 15 J. Envtl. L. 3 (2003).

77. *See* Ceres, http://www.ceres.org.

78. *See* Responsible Care, http://www.americanchemistry.com/s_responsiblecare/sec.asp?CID=1298&DID=4841.

79. *Id.*

80. *See* Forest Stewardship Council, http://www.fscus.org.

81. *See* International Organization for Standardization, *ISO 9000 and ISO 14000—in brief*, *available at* http://www.iso.org/iso/en/iso9000-14000/understand/inbrief.html.

82. International Organization for Standardization, *The ISO Survey—2006* (2006) at 25, *available at* http://www.iso.org/iso/survey2006.pdf; International Organization for Standardization, *The ISO Survey—2005* (2005) at 25, *available at* http://www.iso.org/iso/en/iso9000-14000/pdf/survey2005.pdf.

83. *See* Multi-State Working Group, *Welcome to the Multi-State Working Group on Environmental Performance*, *available at* http://www.mswg.org.

84. Multi-State Working Group, *The External Value Environmental Management System Voluntary Guidance* (March 2004), *available at* http://www .mswg.org/documents/guidance04.pdf.
85. Balbus et al., *supra* note 24, at 70.
86. *See* The Woodrow Wilson International Center for Scholars, *Project on Emerging Nanotechnologies, Awareness of and Attitudes Toward Nanotechnology and Federal Regulatory Agencies* 1 (September 25, 2007), *available at* http://www.nanotechproject.org/.
87. British Standards, Guidance on the labeling of manufactured nanoparticles and products containing manufactured nanoparticles 1 (PAS 130:2007, December 2007).

CHAPTER 10

Risk Management and Product Stewardship Strategies

Executive Summary

Given the somewhat limited availability of legal and regulatory standards specific to nano manufacturing operations, nanotech businesses and other stakeholders have devoted considerable effort to developing alternatives to traditional "command and control" regulation to identify and manage risk. These strategies are discussed in the next section, grouped in these categories: key industry standard-setting initiatives, key government-led initiatives, and key private sector stewardship initiatives.

Key Industry Standard-Setting Initiatives

Several major efforts are under way to develop standards involving nanotechnology. The International Organization for Standardization (ISO) Technical Committee 229 is preparing international consensus standards on several aspects of nanotechnology, including vocabulary, terms, and definitions; measurement and metrology; and environmental, health, and safety (EHS).[1]

ASTM International is working on a similar set of standards. ASTM International Committee E56 on Nanotechnology is developing standards and guidelines for nanotechnology, specifically including terminology and nomenclature; characterization, environmental and occupational safety and health; international law and intellectual property; liaison and international cooperation; and standards of care and product stewardship.[2]

This chapter was prepared by Lynn L. Bergeson, Bergeson & Campbell, P.C.

Key Government-Led Initiatives

Key among the U.S. Environmental Protection Agency's (EPA) governance responses to nanotechnology is the Office of Pollution Prevention and Toxics (OPPT) voluntary Nanoscale Materials Stewardship Program (NMSP),[3] which OPPT rolled out in January 2008. First announced by EPA's OPPT in 2005, the NMSP reflects EPA's interest in obtaining quickly much-needed information on existing engineered nanoscale materials to facilitate EPA's ongoing review of potential risks posed by these materials.[4]

After some initial public discussions about the concept of a voluntary program, on October 18, 2006, then EPA Assistant Administrator James Gulliford sent a letter to stakeholders formally announcing the development of the NMSP and inviting their participation.[5] Several months later, EPA simultaneously published three *Federal Register* notices related to the NMSP.[6]

The January 2008 notice announced the NMSP, which consists of two parts: (1) a basic program, where participants report all known or reasonably ascertainable information regarding specific nanoscale materials, including risk management practices; and (2) an in-depth program, where participants commit to develop data. Under the basic program, participants forwarded to EPA available data on nanoscale materials to EPA within six months, or by July 29, 2008. EPA used data received within the six-month period to prepare an interim report on the NMSP. Participants in the basic program may continue to submit new data that become available on any nanoscale material reported to EPA during the initial six-month period.

Under the in-depth program, participants develop a plan and submit data over a longer period of time yet to be determined. EPA expressed its intention to conduct both the basic and in-depth programs until early 2010, "although it may make adjustments or decide on future steps or direction of the program at an earlier point as sufficient experience is gained." To avoid duplication of testing, EPA will coordinate the in-depth program with its research program, other federal testing and research programs, and internationally through the Organization for Economic Cooperation and Development's (OECD) Working Party on Manufactured Nanomaterials (WPMN). EPA will also coordinate with the Canadian government to encourage participation of Canadian companies in the in-depth program or participation of American companies in Canadian data development activities, which will allow joint development and sharing of data by both countries.

EPA also invited each participant in the basic program to submit available data on risk management practices for nanoscale materials it manufactures, imports, processes, or uses. EPA invites participants who have already developed a risk management plan to include the plan as part of their submission under the basic program. EPA encouraged participants who do not have a risk management plan to "consider developing one."

On January 12, 2009, EPA released its interim report on the NMSP.[7] EPA stated that based on the current interim results, "the NMSP can be considered successful." EPA noted that a number of the environmental health and safety data gaps still exist, however, and "EPA is considering how to best use testing and information gathering authorities under the Toxic Substances Control Act to help address those gaps." EPA stated that it will continue to review new chemical nanoscale materials submitted under TSCA Sections 5(a) and 5(h)(4) and apply, as appropriate, testing requirements and exposure controls under Section 5(e) and significant new use rules under Section 5(a)(2). EPA will issue a detailed final report on the NMSP in early 2010.

In addition to the NMSP and related voluntary initiatives sprouting up around the world, the OECD is engaged in a robust nanotechnology program. OECD includes 30 member countries, including the United States, and 70 others with OECD relationships.[8]

Two OECD group activities are relevant. In September 2006, OECD established the WPMN, noted earlier. The chemicals sector is the principal focus of the WPMN, and EPA and the Food and Drug Administration (FDA) are engaged in the WPMN.

In 2007, the WPMN initiated work on eight projects, each managed by a Steering Group (SG). The projects are SG1, "Development of an OECD Database on EHS Research"; SG2, "EHS Research Strategies on Manufactured Nanomaterials"; SG3, "Safety Testing of Representative Set of Manufactured Nanomaterials"; SG4, "Manufactured Nanomaterials and Test Guidelines"; SG5, "Co-operation on Voluntary Schemes and Regulatory Programmes"; SG6, "Cooperation on Risk Assessment and Exposure Assessment"; SG7, "Alternative Test Methods"; and SG8, "Exposure Measurement and Mitigation." These projects, which have commanded the international cooperation of an unprecedented number of OECD participants and others, are rapidly advancing the goals of each SG. The output is expected to be historic at several levels, not the least of which is the international cooperation exhibited to complete the eight projects.

In March 2007, the OECD created the Committee on Scientific and Technological Policy (CSTP), which focuses on considering applications of nanotechnologies. CSTP's primary objective is to promote international cooperation that facilitates the research, development, and responsible commercialization of nanotechnology in member countries.

The WPMN also launched in 2008 a Sponsorship Program for Testing Manufactured Nanomaterials. The OECD will act as a clearinghouse for the sponsorship program and will prepare a guidance manual for sponsors. EPA is sponsoring environmental effects and fate testing of fullerenes, single-walled carbon nanotubes (CNT), multi-walled CNTs, and cerium oxide.

Key Private Sector Stewardship Initiatives

In June 2007, Environmental Defense Fund (EDF) and DuPont formally announced the release of their joint effort, the *Nano Risk Framework*. The Framework is rapidly becoming the standard for measuring best management practice in the nano industry. The Framework defines "a systematic and disciplined process for identifying, managing, and reducing potential environmental, health, and safety risks of engineered nanomaterials across all stages of a product's 'lifecycle'—its full life from initial sourcing through manufacture, use, disposal or recycling, and ultimate fate."[9]

EDF and DuPont began their collaborative effort to develop the *Framework* in September 2005. They released a draft version to the public on February 26, 2007, and received comments from a diverse array of stakeholders—government, academia, public interest groups, and both large and small companies. In addition to considering the various comments, EDF and DuPont conducted pilot testing on surface-treated, high-rutile-phase titanium dioxide (TiO2), single- and multi-walled CNTs, and nano-sized, zero-valent iron (nano-FeO) "to ensure that [the *Framework*] is flexible, practical, affordable, and effective." The final document "offers guidance on the key questions an organization should consider in developing applications of nanomaterials, and on the information needed to make sound risk evaluations and risk-management decisions." The *Framework* is intended to support ongoing regulatory initiatives, not replace them.

EDF and DuPont believe that the *Framework*—aimed primarily at organizations, both private and public, that are actively working with nanomaterials and developing associated products and applications—will help users organize and evaluate currently available information; assess, prioritize, and address data needs; and communicate clearly how risks are being mitigated. Ultimately, EDF and DuPont "believe that the adoption of the *Framework* can promote responsible development of nanotechnology products, facilitate public acceptance, and support the formulation of a practical model for reasonable government policy on nanotechnology safety."

The *Framework* consists of six distinct steps and is intended to be used iteratively as stages of development advance and new information becomes available. The six steps are as follows:

Step 1: Describe Material and Application. The first step is to develop a general description of the nanomaterial and its intended uses, based on information in the possession of the developer or in the literature. The user also identifies analogous materials and applications that may help fill data gaps in this and other steps.

Step 2: Profile Lifecycle(s). Step 2 defines a process to develop three sets of profiles—the nanomaterial's properties, its inherent hazards, and associated exposures throughout the life cycle. The user considers the nanomaterial's full life cycle from material sourcing, through production and use, to end-of-life disposal or recycling. The user considers how the material's properties, hazards, and exposures may change during that life cycle.

Step 3: Evaluate Risks. In this step, all of the information generated in the profiles is reviewed to identify and characterize the nature, magnitude, and probability of risks presented by the nanomaterial and its anticipated application. The user considers gaps in the life-cycle profiles, prioritizes those gaps, and determines how to address them—either by generating data or by using, in place of such data, "reasonable worst case" assumptions or values.

Step 4: Assess Risk Management. In the fourth step, the user evaluates the available options for managing the risks identified in Step 3 and recommends a course of action. Options include engineering controls, personal protective equipment, risk communication, and product or process modifications.

Step 5: Decide, Document, and Act. In Step 5, the user consults with the appropriate review team and decides whether or in what capacity to continue development and production. Consistent with transparent decision making, the user documents those decisions and their rationale and shares appropriate information with the relevant internal and external stakeholders. A worksheet is provided in the appendix for documenting information, assumptions, and decisions.[10]

Step 6: Review and Adapt. Through regularly scheduled and triggered reviews, the user updates and re-executes the risk evaluation, ensures that risk management systems are working as expected, and adapts those systems in the face of new information or new conditions. Reviews may be prompted by development milestones, changes in production or use, or new hazard or exposure data. As in Step 5, the user not only documents changes, decisions, and actions but also shares appropriate information with relevant stakeholders.

Another significant private sector initiative is the Nanoparticle Benchmarking Occupational Health, Safety, and Environment Program. This initiative consists of the efforts of a consortium of companies that convened to address common analytical needs to measure airborne concentrations of nanoscale materials and particle sizes, and to assess the effectiveness of controls. Several work products are being developed: a chamber test to define aerosols and monitor aerosol behavior as a function of time; a prototypical instrument to measure particle concentration in workplace ambient air in discrete particle size range; and the ability to measure penetration of nanoparticles from an air stream through filters, gloves, or protective clothing.

A third initiative is the *Responsible NanoCode*.[11] Britain's Royal Society, the Nanotechnology Industries Association, Insight Investment, and the United Kingdom government-sponsored Nanotechnology Knowledge Transfer Network collaborated on the proposed code. The objective of this "principles-based" voluntary code of conduct is to encourage industries, retailers, universities, research institutes, and other public or privately funded bodies involved in developing, manufacturing, and selling products of nanotechnology to adhere to seven principles to demonstrate responsible governance. The seven principles are as follows:

- **Principle One**—Each organization should ensure that responsibility for guiding and managing its involvement with nanotechnologies resides with the board or governing body.
- **Principle Two**—Each organization should proactively engage with its stakeholders and be responsive to their views in its development or use of products using nanotechnologies.
- **Principle Three**—Each organization should identify and minimize sources of risk for workers handling products using

nanotechnologies, at all stages in the production process or in industrial use, to ensure high standards of occupational health and safety.

- **Principle Four**—Each organization should carry out thorough risk assessments and minimize any potential public health, safety, and environmental risks relating to its products using nanotechnologies.
- **Principle Five**—Each organization should consider and respond to any social and ethical implications and impacts in the development or sale of products using nanotechnologies.
- **Principle Six**—Each organization should adopt responsible practice in the sales and marketing or products using nanotechnologies.
- **Principle Seven**—Each organization should engage with suppliers and/or business partners to encourage and stimulate their adoption of the code and so assure its own ability to fulfill its code commitments.

Code proponents held a consultation period in the United States, which ended on November 12, 2007. On May 13, 2008, the Working Group of the Responsible Nano Code signed off on the Code.[12]

Most recently, in May 2009, the International Council on Nanotechnology (ICON) launched the GoodNanoGuide, http://goodnanoguide. org. The Guide is an Internet-based collaboration platform specifically designed to enhance the ability of experts to exchange ideas on how best to handle nanomaterials in an occupational setting. It is meant to be an interactive forum that fills the significant need for up-to-date information about current good practices for the handling of nanomaterials in an occupational setting, highlighting new practices as they develop and on a real-time basis. The GoodNanoGuide is open to everyone.

Conclusion

Because evolving legal and regulatory standards are slow in developing, voluntary initiatives and evolving stewardship standards will continue to have a significant impact on setting the bar for private sector behavior with respect to nanotechnology. These initiatives will continue to be looked to as the prevailing industry norm, regardless of what the "letter of the law" actually provides. Voluntary and stewardship initiatives, and best industry practices—for the foreseeable future, anyway—will be looked to as the best means to manage risk effectively and avoid liability.

Notes

1. *See* ISO, "TC 229: Nanotechnologies," *available at* http://www.iso.org/iso/iso_catalogue/catalogue_tc/catalogue_tc_browse.htm?commid=381983.
2. *See* ASTM, "Committee E56 on Nanotechnology," *available at* http://www.astm.org/cgi-bin/SoftCart.exe/COMMIT/COMMITTEE/E56.htm?E+mystore.
3. 73 Fed. Reg. 4861 (Jan. 28, 2008).
4. *See* 70 Fed. Reg. 24574 (May 10, 2005). EPA convened a public meeting to discuss various options in June 2005. The discussion at the public meeting yielded a consensus that a voluntary program on existing engineered nanoscale materials would have significant value. Shortly thereafter, EPA created an Interim Ad Hoc Work Group on Nanoscale Materials (Work Group) as part of the National Pollution Prevention and Toxics Advisory Committee (NPPTAC), a federal advisory group tasked with advising OPPT on TSCA and pollution prevention matters. On November 22, 2005, after the Work Group had met several times, NPPTAC submitted to the EPA Administrator its *Overview Document on Nanoscale Materials*, which outlined a framework for an EPA approach to a voluntary program for engineered nanoscale materials and a complementary approach to new chemical nanoscale requirements under TSCA and addressed various other issues pertinent to engineered nanoscale materials. NPPTAC, *Overview Document on Nanoscale Materials* (Nov. 22, 2005), *available at* http://www.epa.gov/opptintr/npptac/pubs/nanowgoverviewdocument20051125.pdf.
5. Letter from James B. Gulliford, Assistant Administrator for Prevention, Pesticides & Toxic Substances, to Stakeholders (Oct. 18, 2006), *available at* http://www.epa.gov/oppt/nano/nano-letter.pdf. According to the letter, EPA's goal is "to implement TSCA in a way that enables responsible development of nanotechnology and realizes its potential environmental benefits, while applying sound science to assess and, where appropriate, manage potential risks to human health and the environment presented by nanoscale materials."
6. *See* 72 Fed. Reg. 38079–38085 (July 12, 2007). All the notices and accompanying documents are available at http://www.epa.gov/opptintr/nano/nmspfr.htm. The first notice solicited public comment on EPA's proposed Information Collection Request under the Paperwork Reduction Act, including a draft form that NMSP participants could use to submit data to EPA; the second announced a public meeting on the NMSP; and the third solicited public comment on two draft documents: (1) the "Concept Paper for the Nanoscale Materials Stewardship Program under TSCA"; and (2) the "TSCA Inventory Status of Nanoscale Substances—General Approach."

7. EPA, *Nanoscale Materials Stewardship Program Interim Report* (Jan. 2009), *available at* http://www.epa.gov/oppt/nano/nmsp-interim-report-final.pdf.

8. OECD, *About the OECD, available at* http://www.oecd.org/pages/0,3417, en_36734052_36734103_1_1_1_1_1,00.html.

9. A complete copy of the *Framework* and other related information are available at http://nanoriskframework.com/page.cfm?tagID=1095.

10. Completed worksheets for the three DuPont demonstration projects—TiO2, CNTs, and nano-FeO—are available at http://nanoriskframework.org/page.cfm?tagID=1326.

11. Responsible NanoCode, *Background to the Responsible NanoCode, available at* http://www.responsiblenanocode.org/index.html.

12. *See The Responsible Nano Code—Update May 2008, available at* http://www.responsiblenanocode.org/documents/TheResponsibleNanoCodeUpdateAnnoucement.pdf.

CHAPTER 11

The Business of Nanotechnology: Commercial Opportunities and Risks

Executive Summary

This chapter outlines key potential commercial and business risks posed by nanotechnology. It also reviews governance and risk management mechanisms intended to address these potential risks.

Potential Liabilities and Regulatory Governance Mechanisms

Nanotech companies, large and small, face many commercial challenges and a range of potential liabilities. Assessing these liabilities is difficult given the embryonic stage of development, the lack of clear legal precedent and regulatory standards, evolving industry standards and practices, and the fast-evolving science. Nonetheless, several areas of potential liability warrant note.

Product Liability Issues

Despite the promise of new technologies, the specter of product liability casts a shadow over nanotechnology innovations just as it does with other products of technological innovation. The bad publicity following the Magic Nano product recall in Germany in 2006 has become the poster child for nanotech product liability concerns. That the product contained no nanoparticles is irrelevant. Strict liability, negligence, breach of warranty, and claims made in connection with these legal principles (e.g., design defect, manufacturer defect, and failure to warn) arguably could be asserted against manufacturers or suppliers of nano-enabled consumer

---

This chapter was prepared by Lynn L. Bergeson, Bergeson & Campbell, P.C.

215

products given the right facts. Claims for damages could include personal injury, medical monitoring, fear of future injury, deceptive trade practices (inviting treble damages), and punitive damages.

While no specific case appears to have been brought to date involving nanotechnology or a nano-enabled product per se, many believe this is expected to change sooner rather than later. Nano businesses must monitor fast-evolving science developments, evolving industry standards and "best" practices, emerging regulatory standards and disclosure practices, and developing risk management strategies in response to new information. The full range of protective measures to minimize product liability must be considered, including contractual protections with upstream suppliers and downstream customers; implementation of best management practices; contractual representations and warranties; indemnification agreements; appropriate warnings, labeling, and related disclosure strategies; and insurance coverage. Additionally, businesses need to track post-sale consumer product complaint and incident reports, analyze these data, and respond to any reports quickly and thoroughly.

Businesses also must be sensitive to the need for transparency, communication, and public relations. Workers, community residents, downstream formulators, upstream suppliers, vendors, and customers can be anticipated to want to know what a nano-enabled product contains, the health and safety implications from exposure to the product and its nano components, and related product safety information that stakeholders have come to expect under right-to-know laws and the assumptions they invite.

A related thought is the Consumer Product Safety Commission's (CPSC) soon-to-be expanded role as consumer product watchdog. Following a series of high-profile toy recalls, the Senate in early 2008 reached a compromise on a bill to overhaul and strengthen the CPSC. As of this writing, the bill, which is expected to pass, would give the CPSC greater resources to remove consumer products from the market; would raise fines for safety violations to $20 million from the current $1.8 million, would restore the CPSC to five members (from three); and would require the CPSC to create a database containing reports of injuries, illnesses, and death from consumer products based on information submitted from the public. Importantly for present purposes, the Senate version of the bill would allow state attorneys general file lawsuits to stop sales of "dangerous" products and require third-party safety certifications of children's products. If the bill is enacted, it is not much of a leap to believe nano product producers could be a bit concerned about the potential for enhanced CPSC scrutiny of nano-enabled consumer products given a newly emboldened CPSC, particularly if the November elections bring new leadership that is decidedly more cautious about potential nano risks.

Securities Law Reporting

For domestic companies, the issues of accountability and transparency raised by the Magic Nano recall serve as a reminder that nanotech businesses need to be scrupulous in complying with corporate disclosure reporting requirements and with the Sarbanes-Oxley Act of 2002, where it applies. Sarbanes-Oxley requires, among other things, that the chief executive officer (CEO) and chief financial officer (CFO) of a corporation certify the accuracy of each U.S. Securities and Exchange Commission (SEC) filing the company makes.

For publicly traded nanotech companies, three sections of Regulation S-K, which predates Sarbanes-Oxley and specifies the disclosure requirements for periodic reports filed with the SEC, require the disclosure of environmental liabilities. First, S-K 101 requires a company to disclose material effects that compliance with environmental laws will have on earnings, including on estimated material capital expenditures for environmental control facilities for the current fiscal year, the next fiscal year, and additional periods, if material. Signing off on a description of the "material effects of compliance" with environmental laws under S-K 101 is more challenging when it is uncertain if and when some of those laws will affect a nanotechnology product, or a consumer product enabled by nanotechnology.

Second, S-K 103 requires a description of "any material pending legal proceedings, other than ordinary routine litigation incidental to the business to which the registrant or any of its subsidiaries is a party"; environmental litigation is not considered "ordinary" or "routine." The impacts of environmental litigation inspired by nanotechnology, reported under S-K 103, similarly are complicated and difficult to predict in the absence of a litigation history.

Third, S-K 303 sets out a general requirement to disclose "any known trends or any known demands, commitments, events or uncertainties" that are reasonably likely to have a material effect on a company's "financial condition and results of operation"—this requires companies to assess, for example, the likely future consequences of new environmental costs or liabilities. In 1989, the SEC issued an Interpretative Release that emphasizes that this requirement applies to environmental trends and

uncertainties, including anticipated new regulations and Superfund liabilities. While not explicit in its application to nanotechnology, the scope
of this Release is sufficiently broad to include potential regulatory measures pertinent to nanotechnology.

Sections 302 and 906 are also relevant. These sections require CEOs
and CFOs to certify that a company's financial statements fairly present the company's financial status. Section 404 requires that an independent financial auditor review and attest to the adequacy of the company's
internal controls.

Related uncertainties for public and privately held companies involve
disclosure required by the Generally Accepted Accounting Principles
(GAAP).[1] In the environmental area, the most notable GAAP is Financial Accounting Standard No 5, Accounting for Loss Contingencies. A
more recent accounting standard, Financial Accounting Standard No.
143, Accounting for Asset Retirement Obligations, and the follow-on
interpretation, Financial Interpretation No. 47 (FIN 47), issued in March
2005, are also relevant. Under FIN 47, the Financial Accounting Standards
Board clarified when and how companies must estimate and recognize
costs that they expect to incur in the future when they retire fixed assets.
Before FIN 47, companies were not required to report such obligations
absent a pending or "probable" future legal action. Companies may
now be required to disclose environmental legal obligations associated
with tangible assets even without threatened or pending legal action.
The implications of FIN 47 on nanotech companies are unclear, but care
should be taken to ensure that they are carefully reviewed.

In addition to these disclosure obligations, shareholder rights activists can be expected to continue to demand enhanced transparency and
disclosure with regard to a wide array of issues, particularly environmental and product toxicity issues. On December 11, 2008, a coalition of
activists wrote then President-Elect Obama asking for the right of investors to propose and vote upon resolutions asking a company to evaluate
how specific risks may affect the company's business. Among the types
of risks, the coalition specifically identified "climate change and product
toxicity."[2] A copy of the letter is attached at Appendix A.

Similarly, the advocacy group As You Sow Foundation's Corporate
Social Responsibility Program noted in early 2009 that product safety
shareholder resolutions urging companies to disclose the presence of
nanomaterials in food and personal care products have greatly increased
in the recent past. According to the Investor Environmental Health Network, shareholders filed or refiled 46 resolutions at 28 companies for con-

sideration at shareholder meetings between 2006 and 2008. Many of these specifically requested information on nanomaterials.[3]

It is unclear whether the new administration will take up the issue of disclosure any time soon. More likely than not, however, the demand for increased transparency and disclosure will continue for the foreseeable future.

Insurance

The business uncertainties noted earlier help explain the challenges insurance coverage presents—both in terms of providing coverage (from the insurer's perspective) and obtaining it. The key issue in insuring against liabilities where nanotechnology is involved is the relative lack of certainty regarding potential environmental, health, and safety (EHS) risks. Swiss Re's much-cited report, *Small Matter, Many Unknowns,*[4] noted bluntly that in the case of nanotechnology, the uncertainties prevail since "neither the probability nor the extent of the potential losses are precisely calculable" and businesses can expect to see creative approaches by the insurance industry as it tries to address a growing need among an expanding client base reliant upon nanotechnology. One interpretation of this situation is that some risks will simply be excluded from coverage because some essential element in the risk calculus is too speculative. Alternatively, coverage may be capped at one end or the other, and insurers will either pay claims only up to a specified ceiling; or, they will pay the excess only after the insured shoulders (i.e., self-insures) a large deductible. Other types of risk-pooling and limitation—in the form of bond sales/purchases, for instance—may be employed. This is an emerging area, and no hard-and-fast rules yet apply.

In an article in *Insurance Networking News,* Dr. Robert Blaunstein notes that the position of insurers and reinsurers is best viewed along a continuum.[5] We are now in the "early study period," and potential risks and uncertainties will be addressed under existing policies and by efforts by the insurance industry to become better aware of potential risks and insurable events. The "apprehensive phase" may inspire insurers and reinsurers to become more cautious, and "nanotechnology risk may be higher than earlier estimated. Insurers and reinsurers begin to look at reducing cover, and pressure develops to contain risk transfer by the use of sub-limits and 'claims made' covers." The final phase, a number of years off, is the "mature phase" where "customized solutions" are developed and become available at reasonable rates. The business community can expect to achieve the comfort this stage offers down the road; but for the time being, a level of discomfort will prevail.[6]

Acquisitions

The duties and challenges posed by environmental licensing, permitting, and compliance issues are well known for a seller/transferor and, especially, for a prospective purchaser/transferee of a business or a commercial property. If a business uses or produces chemical substances, or if the property has been used for the manufacture, storage, treatment, and/or disposal of these substances, it becomes all the more critical to ensure the requisite level of environmental due diligence was completed thoroughly and to negotiate the appropriate contractual representations, warranties, and indemnities in the contract for the purchase, merger, or other acquisition as well as any associated lending arrangement. If the business being acquired processes, manufactures, discharges, or emits nanomaterials, the goals of the due diligence do not change; but the context adds challenging scientific, risk identification, and risk allocation wrinkles for the parties to consider in their negotiation.

No nanomaterial has been explicitly listed as "hazardous" under the Comprehensive Environmental Response, Compensation, and Liability Act or any of the other federal statutory environmental authorities, and no such listing seems to be on the near-term horizon.[7] That is not to say, however, that engineered nanoscale versions of listed hazardous substances would somehow be treated differently than their conventional-sized counterparts. Even with significant research actively under way, it likely will be some time before sufficiently robust information is available about how nanomaterials act if they are "released into the environment," a challenge enhanced by the unique properties of many such materials.

The picture as it stands today is only a snapshot of the regulatory and best practices landscape that necessarily will evolve significantly as nanomaterials are better identified, characterized, and understood from a risk assessment and risk management perspective. From a purchaser's point of view, the purchase/sales agreement could be fashioned to insulate itself against exposure to hypothetical future liabilities of this kind. In reality, a seller will likely refuse to go beyond a certain point in consenting to bear the costs of long-term contingent liabilities, particularly those as ill defined as "nano risks," in most cases drawing the line at what has occurred or what is, or should be, known as of the transaction's closing date.

Conclusion

Against this backdrop of potential liabilities, regulatory initiatives and governance mechanisms become all the more important. As EPA, other federal and state regulatory bodies, and stakeholders alike have the benefit of better information about the EHS impacts of nanoscale materials, the regulatory pathway forward will be more informed and, from a stakeholder's perspective, less obscure. While a more developed regulatory framework is still years away, businesses also need to be mindful of potential citizen action suits under federal and state laws seeking the imposition of liability for cleanup of hazardous substances and/or natural resource damages. Even if such actions are unsuccessful, their nuisance value and potential for inviting unwanted media attention should not be underestimated.

Notes

1. These are accounting rules used to prepare and report on financial statements for public and private companies.
2. Letter from Shareholder Rights Activists to President-Elect Obama (Dec. 11, 2008).
3. *See* Pat Rizzuto, *Increase Expected in Shareholder Resolutions Urging Disclosure of Nanomaterials, Policies*, 9 Env't Rep. (BNA) A-6 (Jan. 15, 2009); Investor Environmental Health Network, *Resolutions Introduction*, *available at* http://www.iehn.org/resolutions.introduction.php.
4. Swiss Re, *Nanotechnology—Small Matter, Many Unknowns* (2004) at 48, *available at* http://www.swissre.com/resources/31598080455c7a3fb154bb 80a45d76a0-Publ04_Nano_en.pdf.
5. Robert Blaunstein, Ph.D. *Unfamiliar Exposure*, 10 Insurance Networking News 4, at 13–14 (Nov. 2006), *available at* http://www.insurancenetworking .com/issues/20061101/4372-1.html.
6. For another review of emerging risk from the insurer's perspective, *see* Lloyd's *Nanotechnology: Recent Developments, Risks and Opportunities* (2007), *available at* http://www.lloyds.com/NR/rdonlyres/7C1D8222-A3E8-4781-8C80-7FFABFC3F59E/0/Nanotechnology_Report.pdf.
7. *See* Chapter 7 for a more detailed discussion of CERCLA.

APPENDIX

December 11, 2008

Dear President-Elect Obama,

Congratulations on your election. We are writing to respond to your invitation for input on the kinds of changes needed in your new administration.

As investors, investment managers and advisors, we appreciate the range of urgent challenges that your administration will face as it takes office, first and foremost to stabilize the financial markets and get the economy back on track. We believe that greater disclosure in the financial markets and strengthened shareholder rights are among the elements that can contribute to the development of a sustainable economy. All investors need better tools to assess corporate risks and more effectively participate in corporate governance, and we look to your administration and the Securities and Exchange Commission to facilitate such reforms. We are writing to urge you to work to restore one element of investor disclosure within the first hundred days of your administration, specifically the right of investors to propose and vote upon resolutions asking a company to evaluate how specific risks may affect the company's business.

From the creation of the SEC in 1934, it has been recognized that investors stand in a unique position to monitor the companies in their portfolios, and to guard against certain risks to stock price, and to society, by encouraging responsible decision-making by management. We strongly encourage you to strengthen the ability of investors to play this important role, by both increasing the obligations of public companies to disclose data on their social and environmental performance, and by strengthening the role of shareholder resolutions in addressing these issues.

In particular, we believe that restoring the ability of institutional investors to use the shareholder resolution process to probe companies on certain areas of investment risk is an important initial step. These include the kind of credit risks associated with the mortgage crisis, as well as an array of environmental and social issues which we believe may have large financial implications, e.g., climate change and product toxicity.

On October 23rd, Alan Greenspan testified before Congress on the subject of the current economic turmoil. The *Wall Street Journal* highlighted a quote from his testimony that struck many commentators as critical to understanding the situation we find ourselves in today. Mr. Greenspan stated that it had been his assumption that companies' "ability to assess risk and their self interest would protect them from excesses." This assumption has been shown to be false. As your administration addresses these challenges, it is our belief that shareholders are in a very good position to help companies evaluate risk. Unfortunately, for the last five years, the SEC has gradually been closing the door to important shareholder concerns. Shareholder proxy requests that had been allowed in previous years asking for better disclosure of financial risks to companies have been stymied.

We strongly encourage actions by your administration to reverse a pattern of recent SEC staff decisions that have been closing the door to important dialogues between shareholders and management.

The SEC has disallowed many shareholder resolutions that ask companies to disclose the financial implications of an array of environmental, community, public health, and human rights concerns and issues. The staff has categorized such issues as "*evaluation of risk*." See SEC Staff Legal Bulletin 14C. While that bulletin expressly targeted resolutions on environmental issues, the new prohibition on risk evaluation resolutions has been applied to a wide array of issues. *Within the past year the agency even struck down a proposed resolution at Washington Mutual asking the company to discuss its potential financial exposure as a result of the mortgage securities crisis.*

The adoption of this new bar on resolutions requesting "risk evaluation" represented a significant departure -- disregarding the reasonable and principled approach that had governed at the SEC for decades, and replacing it with a radical interpretation of the rules. The result has been to limit shareholder resolutions to questions about the impact that companies are having on society in general, excluding vital questions about the impact that any of these issues may have on the company's future finances.

Institutional investors, especially those that hold long-term stakes in the marketplace, have expressed interest in being able to monitor the financial impacts that various issues pose on their portfolio holdings. This necessitates various public policy responses, including the adoption of standards for reporting of environmental, social and governance issues in corporate reports. It also merits a re-examination of the manner that the SEC has applied the ordinary business exclusion, to better secure shareholders' fundamental right to submit proposals that focus on significant issues confronting their portfolio companies. To that end, we look forward to working with your administration to develop a larger policy framework to address these needs.

We recognize that in the early days of your administration you will be focused on shoring up the economy and helping to restore consumer confidence. As part of your strategy we urge that you help us to correct decisions that have undermined our ability to use the shareholder resolution process to probe these issues on a company by company basis. The existing Securities and Exchange Commission decisions block shareholders from filing certain shareholder resolutions in fulfillment of our fiduciary obligations. For instance, it has become apparent that many companies knew about the potential financial risks posed to their companies by toxic chemicals in their product lines. However the disclosure of these issues is seldom made in existing corporate financial reports. Resolutions that would have addressed this type of risk through the proxy process are the same resolutions that the Securities and Exchange Commission staff chose, arbitrarily and without justification in law, to exclude. We believe that effective disclosure of these issues through the proxy process can lead to better anticipatory action by corporations such as the control of greenhouse gases and the development of safer alternative materials.

Strong leadership from the White House as well as Congress can aid in encouraging the SEC to retract the staff-created prohibition on resolutions that ask companies to evaluate the financial impacts of identified issues. This can help to strengthen the ability of investors to play an important role in monitoring our portfolio companies and encouraging effective, socially responsible, corporate management. We urge you to ask the Securities and Exchange Commission and relevant Congressional oversight bodies to reexamine these issues within the first hundred days of your new administration.

Sincerely,

Signatory list enclosed

Cc:
Rep. Barney Frank
Sen. Christopher Dodd

Damon Silvers
Richard H. Neiman
Elizabeth Warren

Securities and Exchange Commission

SEC Division of Corporation Finance

Letter to President-Elect Obama on
Shareholder Rights to Risk Evaluation Resolutions

Signatory List

Christina M. Adams
Vice President – Finance and Administration
John E. Fetzer Institute, Inc.

Harriet Barlow
Director
HKH Foundation

Laura Berry
Executive Director
Interfaith Center on Corporate Responsibility

Connie Brookes
Executive Director
Friends Fiduciary Corporation

Charles Clements
President and CEO
Unitarian Universalist Service Committee

Kathleen Coll, SSJ
Administrator, Shareholder Advocacy
Catholic Health East

Lauren Compere
Director of Shareholder Advocacy
Boston Common Asset Management

Kristina Curtis
Senior Vice President
Green Century Capital Management, Inc.

Florence Deacon, OSF
Director, Sisters of St. Francis of Assisi

Ron DiLuigi
St. Joseph Health System

Patrick Doherty, Esq.
Director, Corporate Responsibility
Office of the Comptroller
City of New York

Amy L. Domini & Lindsey W. Parker, Trustees
The Sustainability Group at Loring, Wolcott & Coolidge

Joanne Dowdell
Senior Vice President
Director Corporate Responsibility
Sentinel Financial Services Company

Bennett Freeman
Senior Vice President
Social Research and Policy
Calvert Group, Ltd.

Rian Fried
President
Clean Yield Asset Management

Marie Gaillac
Corporate Responsibility Coordinator
JOLT

Julie Goodridge
CEO
NorthStar Asset Management, Inc.

Julie Fox Gorte, Ph.D
Senior Vice President for Sustainable Investing
PaxWorld

John C. Harrington
President/CEO
Harrington Investments, Inc.

Linda Hayes, OP
Director, Corporate Social Responsibility
Dominican Sisters of Springfield, IL

Valerie Heinonen, o.s.u.
Consultant, Corporate Social Responsibility
Dominican Sisters of Hope
Mercy Investment Program

Sisters of Mercy Regional Community of Detroit Charitable Trust
Ursuline Sisters of Tildonk, U.S. Province

Bruce T. Herbert, AIF
Chief Executive
Newground Social Investment

Sister Linda Jansen, SSND
Treasurer, School Sisters of Notre Dame, St. Louis
and
Corporate Responsibility Committee
School Sisters of Notre Dame, St. Louis

Adam M. Kanzer, Esq.
Managing Director & General Counsel
Domini Social Investments LLC

Robert D. Kellogg
Managing Principal
Highlands Strategic Advisors, LLC

Peter D. Kinder, Esq.
President
KLD Research & Analytics, Inc.

Michael Kramer, AIF
Managing Partner and Director of Social Research
Natural Investments LLC

Rev. Joseph P. La Mar, M.M.
Assistant CFO
Maryknoll Fathers and Brothers

Leslie Leslie
Grant Director
Fred Gellert Family Foundation

Sanford Lewis
Attorney

Richard Liroff
Executive Director
Investor Environmental Health Network

Tim Little
Rose Foundation for Communities and the Environment

Mindy S. Lubber
President, Ceres
and
Director, Investor Network on Climate Risk

Elizabeth E. McGeveran
Senior Vice President, Governance & Sustainable Investment
F&C Management Ltd.

James McRitchie
Publisher
Corporate Governance

Robert A.G. Monks
LENS Governance Advisors

Renee Morgan
President, Better World Investments, Inc.
Registered Representative, NPC

Roberta Mulcahy, ssj
Socially Responsible Investment Coordinator
Congregation of the Sisters of St. Joseph
Springfield, MA

Nora Nash, OSF
Director, Corporate Social Responsibility
Sisters of St. Francis of Philadelphia

My-Linh Ngo
Associate Director, SRI Research
Henderson Global Investors – the Sustainable & Responsible Investment (SRI) team

Michael Passoff
As You Sow Foundation

Sister M. Cecile Paulik
SSM International Finance, Inc.

Frank Rauscher
Senior Principal
Aquinas Associates

Sr. Claire Regan

Corporate Responsibility Coordinator
Sisters of Charity of New York

Mark A. Regier
Stewardship Investing Services Manager
MMA Praxis Mutual Funds

John Richardson
CEO
JMR Portfolio Intelligence, Inc.

Steve Schueth
President
First Affirmative Financial Network, LLC

Judith L. Seid, CFP
Founder & President
Blue Summit Financial Group, Inc.

Morgan Simon
Director
Responsible Endowments Coalition

Annette Sinagra OP
Corporate Responsibility Analyst
Portfolio Advisory Board
Adrian Dominican Sisters

Cheryl Smith
Co-Chief Executive Officer
Jonas Kron, Attorney
Senior Social Research Analyst
Trillium Asset Management Corporation

Timothy Smith
Senior Vice President
Environment, Social and Governance Group
Walden Asset Management

James Spengler
Business Manager
American Friends Service Committee

Luan Steinhilber
Miller/Howard Investments

David Todd
Magnolia Charitable Trust

Richard W. Torgerson
President
Progressive Asset Management, Inc.

Susan Vickers, RSM
VP Community Health
Catholic Healthcare West

Stephen Viederman
Finance Committee
Christopher Reynolds Foundation

Margaret Weber
Corporate Responsibility Director
Basilian Fathers of Toronto

Allen L. White
Senior Fellow
Tellus Institute

Richard Woo
CEO
The Russell Family Foundation

Additional Endorsement
after the letter was transmitted

Chris Jochnick
Director, Private Sector Department
Oxfam America

CHAPTER 12

Nanotechnology and the National Environmental Policy Act

Executive Summary

Since its passage nearly 40 years ago, the National Environmental Policy Act (NEPA), 42 U.S.C. §§ 4321–4370f, has served as a caution signal to federal agencies to fully consider the environmental consequences—including related impacts on social, cultural, and economic resources—of any significant action the agency intends to undertake or approve. In essence it is a *mandatory* reminder to agencies to "look before you leap." Although the level of environmental review varies depending on the magnitude and specific details of a given action, including the laws and regulations that govern that action, no significant action is undertaken—at least in theory—without some thought being given to the NEPA consequences, even if only to determine that enhanced NEPA review is not required.

For its part, nanotechnology—the creation, design, and manipulation of materials at the nanoscale—offers new and seemingly boundless potential benefits to human existence. From basic necessities such as health care and the food supply to industrial processes and equipment to the items of everyday living such as computers, vehicles, clothes, and appliances, there is literally no aspect of living that is not, or at least will not soon be, influenced or affected by nanotechnology through the

This chapter was prepared by David P. Ross, Crowell & Moring LLP; James H. Andreasen, Shook, Hardy & Bacon; James C. Chen, Crowell & Moring LLP; Geraldine E. Edens, McKenna Long & Aldridge; Charles Franklin, Akin Gump Strauss Hauer & Feld LLP; Derald J. Hay, Fox Rothschild LLP; George A. Kimbrell, International Center for Technology Assessment; Rachel G. Lattimore, Arent Fox LLP; William G. Malley, Perkins Coie LLP; Christopher M. Roe, Fox Rothschild LLP; Jonathan Wells, Alston & Bird LLP; and Daniel W. Wolff, Crowell & Moring LLP.

incorporation of nanomaterials into such products and devices.[1] At the nanoscale—particles a mere 1 to 100 nanometers[2] in size—materials have the potential to act very differently from their macro counterparts. While not "chemically" different, nanoscale material exhibits qualitatively different properties than the same material of much larger size. It is in these fundamentally different properties that nanomaterials offer potential benefits to all modes of life.

But as with most technological revolutions, there are undoubtedly collateral consequences to the use of nanomaterials. Enter NEPA. To the extent a federal agency is involved in a nanotechnology-related project, either as its proponent or as the agency charged with approving or regulating it, NEPA imposes a framework for reviewing the environmental consequences of that project. This chapter discusses how NEPA might be applied to such an action. It is not intended to address all facets of NEPA, or examine every conceivable agency action dealing with nanotechnology that might trigger NEPA concerns—that would be a task far beyond the scope of this chapter. Rather, it is intended to serve as a piece in the larger dialogue on how existing federal law is equipped to address this emerging technology. Based on this premise, this chapter explores how NEPA, as written 40 years ago, can be applied by the federal agencies to any nanotechnology-related actions they may undertake or otherwise approve. There are limitations in how well NEPA can be applied to such projects, but that is due largely to the scientific uncertainty that surrounds the movement of nanoparticles into and through the human and natural environment.

The Application of NEPA to Nanotechnology

The balance of this chapter provides an overview of the NEPA regulatory framework, highlighting the program requirements that would likely receive the greatest attention when applied to a nanotechnology-related project. As part of that review, it would appear that NEPA can and should be applied to analyze the potential environmental impacts of nanomaterials. Given this, the chapter discusses the likely federal actions involving nanotechnology that may be subject to NEPA review. Finally, the chapter explores several limitations in the application of NEPA to nanotechnology projects, namely, the difficulty in analyzing environmental impacts in the face of significant scientific uncertainty and making decisions based on that uncertainty, and the fact that many of the federal activities that may ultimately authorize the release of nanomaterials into the environment have already been exempted from NEPA review by Congress or the courts.

The NEPA Framework

NEPA is the United States' "basic national charter for protection of the environment."[3] The principal objective of NEPA is to ensure that federal agencies conduct adequate environmental analyses before taking "major Federal actions significantly affecting the quality of the human environment."[4] Congress enacted NEPA to make sure that federal agencies consider the environmental effects of their actions and inform the public of those deliberations.[5] In doing so, Congress hoped "to promote efforts which will prevent or eliminate damage to the environment and biosphere"[6] while recognizing the need to "fulfill the social, economic and other requirements of present and future generations of Americans."[7]

To do so, Congress requires all federal agencies to consider (1) the environmental impact of any proposed action, including whether there will be any significant adverse environmental impacts that cannot be avoided as a result of that action; (2) alternatives to the proposed action and any irreversible commitment of federal resources should the action be implemented; and (3) both the short- and long-term aspects of the proposed action with respect to how it impacts the environment.[8] This analysis must be applied before any final agency decision is made with respect to proposed legislation, rules, plans, policies, and agency procedures; before approving or financing any federal project or program; and before issuing permits, licenses, grants, or other approvals for private or nonfederal actions.[9] In essence, whenever the federal government must approve or provide funding for any particular action, it must comply with NEPA.

In undertaking a NEPA analysis, federal agencies must follow a general decisional framework established by the Council on Environmental Quality (CEQ),[10] the federal agency charged with overseeing implementation of NEPA for the federal government.[11] That framework allows agencies to conduct varying levels of NEPA analysis depending on the significance of the impacts anticipated by the federal action. In some cases, agencies can rely on predetermined "categorical exclusions" from NEPA for common types of actions that the agency determines "do not individually or cumulatively have a significant effect on the human environment . . . and for which, therefore, neither an environmental assessment nor an environmental impact statement is required."[12] Where a categorical exclusion does not exist and the agency is unsure of the level of anticipated environmental impact resulting from the proposed action, it may conduct an environmental assessment (EA) of the action to determine whether it can render a finding of no significant impact (FONSI) for the project or whether it must perform and develop a full-blown environmental impact statement (EIS).[13] If it is clear that the action will result in a significant environmental impact, an agency will likely move straight to the EIS process.[14] If an EIS is required, the agency is required to follow a number of very specific steps to show that it complied with both the letter and spirit of NEPA.[15]

Thus, if the federal government approves, implements, or provides funding for a project that results in nanomaterials being released into the environment, NEPA would necessarily apply as long as that release has the potential to significantly affect the quality of the human environment. There is, however, a threshold question about whether the science of nanotechnology has advanced to the stage where scientists can accurately predict what kind of effects nanotechnology will have on the human environment.[16] As discussed below, even with the significant scientific uncertainty surrounding nanotechnology, NEPA was drafted to specifically address technological revolutions like nanotechnology.

Technological Revolutions, Scientific Uncertainty, and NEPA

Although Congress could not have envisioned the development of nanotechnology when it enacted NEPA some 40 years ago, the law was crafted in a manner that provides a framework for federal agencies to obtain data and invite public scrutiny on the environmental impacts of their actions involving new technologies as those technologies come into existence and use. As summarized by the U.S. Court of Appeals for the District of Columbia in a landmark case involving the application of NEPA to biotechnology 20 years ago:

> In passing NEPA Congress emphasized its particular concern with the role of new technologies and their effect on the environment. The statute explicitly enumerates "new and expanding technologies" as one of the activities with the potential to threaten the environment. 42 U.S.C. § 4331(a). The legislative history reveals an underlying concern with "[a] growing technological power . . . far outstripping man's capacity to understand and ability to control its impact on the environment." S. Rep. No. 91-296, [91st Cong., 1st Sess. (1969)], at 6. One of NEPA's main functions was to bolster this capacity to understand and control the effects of new technology. *See Scientists' Institute for Public Information v. AEC*, 481 F.2d 1079, 1089–90 (D.C. Cir. 1973).

NEPA thus stands as a landmark legislation, requiring federal agencies to consider the environmental effects of major federal actions, empowering the public to scrutinize this consideration, and revealing a special concern about the environmental effects of new technology.[17]

That NEPA was created to require the consideration of environmental issues in a timeless manner is evident from the environmental policy that the law promotes. The statutory provisions do not discuss particular environmental problems or controversies that existed in 1969; rather, they speak in broad terms to the "systematic, interdisciplinary approach" necessary to ensure informed decision making by federal agencies.[18] Although the technology is in many ways novel, nanotechnology does not present any characteristics that would render NEPA's procedural and information-driven mandates obsolete. In fact, NEPA arguably may be among the best existing statutes for analyzing the use of nanotechnology precisely because federal agencies' responsibilities under NEPA do not depend on statutory definitions or jurisdictional limitations on subject matter. Indeed, Dinah Bear, a former General Counsel of CEQ, wrote in 1989 that "[i]t is impossible to think of any environmental issue of current concern—whether beaches blighted by medical wastes, alarming predictions of climate change, or decline of species and ecosystem diversity—that is not already encompassed by NEPA."[19]

Nanotechnology and its potential applications in modern society may present issues that are different than those posed by the emerging technologies of previous decades, but NEPA offers a procedural vehicle for the government to analyze and consider those issues as they arise in the federal agency decision-making process. For example, much like nanotechnology today, biotechnology and genetic engineering presented novel questions that were initially poorly understood from a regulatory point of view. Again, as summarized by the District of Columbia Court of Appeals:

> This case poses no less a formidable challenge: to ensure that the bold words and vigorous spirit of NEPA are not similarly lost or misdirected in the brisk frontiers of science.

> For this appeal presents an important question at the dawn of the genetic engineering age: what is the appropriate level of environmental review required of the National Institutes of Health (NIH) before it approves the deliberate release of genetically

engineered, recombinant-DNA-containing organisms into the open environment. . . .

. . .

Genetic engineering is an important development at the very cusp of scientific advances. . . .

Broad claims are made about both the potential benefits and the potential hazards of genetically engineered organisms. Use of recombinant DNA may lead to welcome advances in such areas as food production and disease control. At the same time, however, the environmental consequences of dispersion of genetically-engineered organisms are far from clear.[20]

Despite this uncertainty, the court required the agency to fully consider the potential environmental consequences of the dispersion of those organisms into the environment under NEPA even if those consequences were not readily understood.[21]

Nanotechnology today is similar to biotechnology 20 or 30 years ago in that it is new and not entirely understood. A growing body of scientific literature is exploring the fate and transport of various nanomaterials into and through the environment.[22] The literature is also growing with respect to potential exposure pathways and related ecological and human health effects associated with nanomaterials.[23] However, the general consensus is that much more needs to be learned before the implications of deliberately releasing nano-sized particles into the environment are fully understood.[24]

The question then is what kind of deliberation must federal agencies devote to analyzing and discussing the environmental impacts of nano-technology-related projects when so much uncertainty exists? The answer is found in CEQ's NEPA regulations. Those regulations require the agency to make clear that the information contained in its environmental analysis is incomplete or unavailable.[25] The agency must also discuss the relevance of the missing information, provide a summary of the existing credible science, and evaluate the potential impacts based upon theoretical approaches or research methods generally accepted in the scientific community.[26] In other words, the agency must make do with what it can. That, according to the courts, is enough.[27] NEPA, at the end of the day, is a procedural statute; if an agency complies with the relevant procedures, takes a "hard look" at the available information, and makes an informed decision based on that evidence, NEPA's requirements are satisfied.[28]

Major Federal Actions Involving Nanotechnology

Because it is apparent that NEPA can be applied to nanotechnology-related projects, even in the face of significant scientific uncertainty, the next threshold question is when would NEPA apply? What are the types of federal projects where the convergence of NEPA and nanotechnology might exist, at least in the near term?

As mentioned earlier, NEPA has broad applicability in administrative law: in theory, absent an applicable exemption or exclusion, its procedural requirements generally apply to all major federal actions significantly affecting the quality of the human environment.[29] Thus, whenever there is a federal agency action, including those involving nanotechnology, that is not categorically excluded from NEPA review under the agency's regulations, some level of NEPA review must be undertaken. "Major federal actions" can include "projects and programs entirely or partially financed" by federal agencies.[30] While the mere fact that federal money finds its way into a project's budget is not enough to classify a project as a federal action,[31] a project may be considered a federal action when the federal government has sufficient control, responsibility, or involvement with the project because of its financing.[32] Projects implemented by local, state, or private organizations can also be subject to NEPA review, as long as some federal approval is required. These "major federal actions" can include, for example, the building of dams,[33] correctional institutions,[34] recreational facilities,[35] and highways.[36] While the types of federal projects involving nanotechnology could eventually be innumerable, some potential NEPA "triggers" at several high-visibility agencies that will likely assess nanotechnology projects in the very near future are discussed in the following section.

NEPA Triggers

At this early stage in the nanotechnology revolution, it is impossible to provide an exhaustive list of the types of federal actions that might trigger meaningful NEPA review.[37] However, a few of the more common actions that might trigger NEPA review are discussed below.

ENVIRONMENTAL PROTECTION AGENCY

EPA is required to comply with NEPA before providing construction grants to wastewater treatment facilities pursuant to the Clean Water Act (CWA) and before issuing National Pollutant Discharge Elimination System (NPDES) permits to "new sources," as well as in connection with many of its research and development activities and other projects that are funded through annual appropriation measures. As discussed later in "NEPA Exemptions," however, many of EPA's activities are exempt from NEPA either under a statutory exclusion or court-adopted exemptions (i.e., the "functional equivalency" doctrine). Perhaps this explains why EPA failed to mention NEPA in its seminal Nanotechnology White Paper published in February 2007.[38] Regardless, many of EPA's current actions involving nanotechnology could be subject to NEPA and certainly will be subject to NEPA in the future.

Of the nonexempt actions, one area that will require frequent analysis of nanoparticle dispersion into the environment is the issuance of NPDES permits to new sources under CWA § 402. In something like the statutory version of a double negative, NPDES new source permitting is expressly carved out of an otherwise broad CWA NEPA exemption.[39] Section 402 requires EPA (or authorized states) to set and enforce limits on the concentrations of specific pollutants in effluent from new and existing point sources and to codify such restrictions in specific permits.[40] New sources are defined as facilities that come online after EPA has issued specific effluent limitation guidelines for a particular category of point sources.[41] If a new or significantly expanding facility wants to release nanoscale pollutants or particles into regulated waters for which EPA is the permitting authority, and EPA has established effluent limitation guidelines for the industry in which that new facility operates, a review of the environmental risks of using and releasing those nanomaterials must be conducted under NEPA.[42]

An example of where that might happen is in the growing field of aquaculture. EPA promulgated effluent limitation guidelines for the aquatic animal production industry in 2004.[43] Nanotechnology is currently being explored in this industry for use as growth enhancers, vaccinations, and cleaning fish ponds.[44] To the extent a new aquaculture facility seeks NPDES permitting from EPA in the future and proposes to use nanoparticles in the production and maintenance of the facility, it is likely that EPA would evaluate the use of those materials pursuant to NEPA in addition to its NPDES permitting review authorities.

Another example can be found in the oil and gas industry. Nanotechnology is receiving significant research attention for its ability to enhance oil and gas recovery by reducing the thickness of oil mixtures, injecting nanosensors into the underground oil and gas reservoirs, and a variety of other uses.[45] As these industries are subject to new source performance standards under the CWA,[46] any proposal for a new source NPDES permit that involves potential nanoparticle releases into CWA jurisdictional waters would be subject to NEPA review.

EPA is also funding significant research in the nanotechnology arena.[47] Many of these areas are specifically targeted at delivering new "green" products and technologies to the marketplace that will take advantage of the special properties of nanomaterials, including in the areas of green manufacturing and soil and groundwater remediation.[48] For example, EPA is funding research on the inclusion of nanotechnology in building materials that could be incorporated into the construction of green buildings.[49] This type of funding should be evaluated to determine whether it is subject to NEPA review (which is dependent on the specific program governing the funding and whether the funding approval has the potential to cause significant environmental effects).

In addition to reviewing its own actions under NEPA, Section 309 of the Clean Air Act authorizes EPA to comment on the environmental impacts of decisions made by other federal agencies.[50] Thus, EPA has the authority to review the environmental effects of nanotechnology-related activities at most other federal agencies. If EPA determines that a proposed action of any agency is "unsatisfactory from the standpoint of public health or welfare or environmental quality," EPA may refer the action to CEQ for review.[51]

FOOD AND DRUG ADMINISTRATION

The Food and Drug Administration (FDA) regulates a wide range of potential substances used in food, animal feed, drugs, cosmetics, and medical devices under the Federal Food, Drug, and Cosmetic Act (FFDCA). Many of the agency's final actions to approve such products or take other regulatory action may trigger NEPA compliance obligations, including

- approval of food additive petitions and color additive petitions;
- establishment of a tolerance for unavoidable poisonous or deleterious substances in food or in food packaging materials;
- approval of new drug applications;
- approval of new animal drug application;
- approval of pre-market approval applications for medical devices;
- establishment by regulation of labeling requirements, standards, or monographs; and
- the issuance and amendment of other FDA regulations.[52]

A 2007 report from an FDA Task Force on Nanotechnology has recommended that FDA take a "case-by-case approach ... to assessing NEPA requirements for products using [nanotech] materials."[53] However, according to FDA's NEPA regulations,

[t]here are no categories of agency actions that routinely significantly affect the quality of the human environment and that
therefore ordinarily require the preparation of an EIS. . . . EISs
are prepared for agency actions when evaluation of data or information in an EA or otherwise available to the agency leads to a
finding by the responsible agency official that a proposed action
may significantly affect the quality of the human environment.[54]

It remains unclear whether this default position will change as the scientific understanding of exposure pathways associated with nanotechnology evolves. For example, the scientific community is only recently
grappling with the effects that endocrine disruptors have on the aquatic
environment, including those that pass through humans—like birth control drugs and fertility treatments—and through our wastewater treatment facilities into the nation's waters.[55]

Department of Defense
The domestic, noncombat actions of the military service branches under
the Department of Defense (DOD), like civilian agencies, are presump-
tively subject to NEPA's procedural requirements.[56] Each branch of DOD
has developed its own procedures for determining the appropriate level
of NEPA analysis for specific actions.[57] Examples of actions by DOD or its
subordinate entities that might trigger NEPA review of nanotechnology
projects include

- The disposal of nuclear materials, munitions, explosives, industrial and military chemicals, and other hazardous or toxic substances that have the potential to cause significant environmental
  impact.[58]
- Actions proposed during the life cycle of a weapon system if the
  action produces a new hazardous or toxic material or results in a
  new hazardous or toxic waste.[59]
- Production of hazardous or toxic materials.[60]
- Development of an installation pesticide, fungicide, herbicide,
  insecticide, and rodenticide-use program/plan.[61]

DOD has also funded research that includes the use of nanotechnology in the manufacturing of high-surface-area fibers, detecting infrared
light below room temperature, a patterned ink-jet printer for photovoltaic
dyes, and the stabilization of waterborne toxins, among other activities.[62]
These funding decisions may require NEPA compliance if the funded

program directly leads to a release of nanomaterials into the environment in quantities sufficient to cause significant environmental effects.

DEPARTMENT OF AGRICULTURE

Pursuant to its authority under the Plant Protection Act, the U.S. Department of Agriculture (USDA) Agricultural Plant Health Inspection Service (APHIS) conducts a variety of weed and pest eradication efforts to address pests ranging from medfly infestations to noxious weeds.[63] These efforts are subject to review under NEPA.[64] Pest control is a significant market for current nanotechnology development efforts. While the registration of pesticides with EPA is exempt from NEPA review, other pesticide-related activities, such as the use of pesticides by other federal agencies in a pest control or eradication program, are likely not exempt from NEPA review.[65] APHIS also regulates another potential market where nanotechnology may ultimately be reviewed under NEPA—genetically modified organisms (GMOs). APHIS regulates the introduction (i.e., importation, interstate movement, or environmental release) of certain GMOs within the United States through both permitting and notification requirements.[66] The issuance of such permits is subject to NEPA review, as is any deregulation of genetically engineered organisms.[67] Thus, if nanotechnology and genetic engineering converge through future technological developments, those developments might be reviewed under NEPA through an APHIS permitting procedure.

Another agency under the USDA umbrella—the U.S. Forest Service—manages hundreds of millions of acres of national forest lands throughout the United States. The management of those forests necessarily involves decisions to control pests, weeds, and other noxious plants and organisms, which are activities generally subject to NEPA review.[68] Those decisions in the future will undoubtedly include options for using products that incorporate nanotechnology, subjecting those products to NEPA review before their release into the environment.

DEPARTMENT OF THE INTERIOR

The Department of the Interior (DOI) and its subordinate agencies are responsible for managing hundreds of millions of acres of public lands, including national parks managed by the National Park Service (NPS) and rangelands managed by the Bureau of Land Management (BLM). In this management capacity, the NPS and BLM—like the Forest Service—may develop and execute natural resource management plans and make pest management decisions that trigger the need for NEPA reviews. To the extent that these agencies make decisions to use pesticides, fertilizers, or other products that contain ingredients qualifying as or derived from nanotechnology, such actions would have to be reviewed as part of the NEPA process that applies to the underlying federal decision.[69]

OTHER FEDERAL AGENCIES

The foregoing list is by no means exhaustive with respect to the relevant agencies or even relevant actions within such agencies that may concern nanotechnology and trigger NEPA review. For example, the Federal Highway Administration (within the Department of Transportation) is supporting research on nanoscale modifications to asphalt to improve performance.[70] Another example lies within the Department of Energy (DOE), which has constructed and outfitted five Nanoscale Science Research Centers.[71] It appears that DOE complied with NEPA in the planning and development of those research centers and analyzed the risks of using nanomaterials in those centers.[72] As nanotechnology and its products proliferate, many other federal agencies may find that their actions raise potential nanotechnology risk issues and therefore may be subject to NEPA review.

In summary, it is clear that the federal government is making substantial investments in nanotechnology throughout its many agencies. In fact, the National Nanotechnology Initiative (NNI) is a multiagency federal program initiated in 2001 that is charged with "accelerating the discovery, development, and deployment of nanometer-scale science, engineering, and technology."[73] This effort was further codified and funded under the 21st Century Nanotechnology Research and Development Act, signed into law in December 2003.[74]

According to the annual report for NNI submitted to Congress in September 2008, there are 13 federal agencies with budgets dedicated to nanotechnology research and development in the 2009 NNI budget, involving estimated investments of $1.5 billion.[75] The eight categories of research and development investment are

1. fundamental nanoscale phenomena and processes;
2. nanomaterials;
3. nanoscale devices and systems;
4. instrumentation research, metrology, and standards for nanotechnology;
5. nanomanufacturing;
6. major research facilities and instrumentation acquisition;
7. environment, health and safety; and
8. education and societal dimensions.[76]

As the federal government continues to pursue nanotechnology as a strategic initiative, it seems almost inevitable that it will have to evaluate the release of nanomaterials into the environment pursuant to NEPA. How pervasive NEPA becomes engrained in the nanotechnology revolution, however, may depend on how many federal actions involving nanotechnology will qualify for NEPA exemptions.

NEPA Exemptions

Since NEPA's passage, Congress (through other statutes), the courts (based on principles of interpretation), and the executive branch (through policy rationales) have exempted, or (in the case of the courts) recognized the existence of exemptions for, a wide variety of agency actions from NEPA coverage. Some of these exemptions could affect whether and when federal actions raising nanotechnology concerns trigger NEPA review.

For example, Congress has exempted all federal actions under the Clean Air Act from NEPA regulation.[77] This exemption is significant, as several of the Clean Air Act's provisions might otherwise prove fertile ground to review the environmental impacts associated with the release of nanoscale pollutants and particles into the environment.[78] Similarly, the Clean Water Act exempts most federal actions from NEPA, with the exception of federal financial assistance for the purpose of assisting the construction of publicly owned treatment works and—as noted earlier—NPDES permitting actions involving new sources.[79]

For their part, the courts have also recognized exemptions "by implication" in certain statutes that are facially silent about NEPA. For example, where a "clear and unavoidable conflict" in statutory authority exists between NEPA and another statute, courts have held that "NEPA must give way."[80] Courts have applied this exemption rationale in cases where a statute's short, mandatory deadline for agency action renders compliance with NEPA's EIS requirement impossible[81] and in cases where the language of a statute eliminates any agency discretion to act.[82] If Congress were to mandate specific action to utilize, approve, or release into the environment specific products of nanotechnology using direct, nondiscretionary language and short, mandatory time frames, this exemption might provide a similar bar to NEPA review of that action.

Courts have also exempted many EPA actions under a doctrine of "functional equivalence," reasoning that

> [a]lthough NEPA says that "all agencies" must comply with its terms, most circuits have already recognized . . . that an agency need not comply with NEPA where the agency is engaged

primarily in an examination of environmental questions and where "the agency's organic legislation mandate[s] specific procedures for considering the environment that [are] functional equivalents of the impact statement process."[83]

To date, courts have applied the functional equivalence doctrine in the following contexts:

- actions by EPA to approve land disposal of PCBs under the Toxic Substances Control Act (TSCA);[84]
- actions by EPA to issue ocean dumping permits under the Ocean Dumping Act;[85]
- actions by EPA to register specific pesticides under the Federal Insecticide Fungicide and Rodenticide Act (FIFRA);[86]
- actions to grant hazardous management permits under the Resource Conservation and Recovery Act (RCRA);[87]
- actions by EPA to develop a cleanup remedy under the Comprehensive Environmental Response, Compensation, and Liability Act (CERCLA);[88]
- actions by EPA to exempt portions of aquifers from underground injection well restrictions under the Safe Drinking Water Act (SDWA);[89] and
- actions of the Federal Communication Commission to promulgate health and safety guidelines for radio frequency radiation.[90]

Courts have also held that the *functional differences* between the workings of NEPA and a second statutory regime can evince the intent of Congress to exempt certain federal actions from NEPA's procedural requirements. Most notably, in *Merrell v. Thomas*, the Ninth Circuit Court of Appeals ruled that NEPA did not apply to EPA actions to register herbicides for roadside use, holding that

> FIFRA's standard for denying registration, "unreasonable adverse effects on the environment," differs both from NEPA's standard for preparing an EIS, "significantly affecting the quality of the human environment . . ." and from NEPA's definition of the scope of the EIS, "the environmental impact of the proposed action." . . . Congress has made its choice. We must abide by it.[91]

To date, most of the court decisions applying the functional equivalence or functional difference doctrines to exempt NEPA requirements have been limited to actions by EPA.[92] Courts have been decidedly less willing to apply the functional equivalence or difference doctrines to actions involving other agencies.[93] Thus, while precedent appears to significantly reduce the scope of EPA-related actions subject to NEPA, NEPA continues to be a viable tool in ensuring careful consideration of the impacts of nanotechnology by the other federal agencies.[94]

A Note on Programmatic Environmental Impact Statements
In addition to individual actions taken by federal agencies, the CEQ regulations authorize agencies to prepare programmatic environmental impact statements (PEIS) for federal programs or initiatives that are broad in scope. "Adoption of programs, such as a group of concerted actions to implement a specific policy or plan [and] systematic and connected agency decisions allocating agency resources to implement a specific statutory program or executive directive" are "federal actions" that may require analysis under NEPA.[95]

According to the D.C. Circuit Court of Appeals, the purpose of a PEIS is to "reflect the broad environmental consequences attendant upon a wide-ranging federal program. The thesis underlying programmatic EISs is that a systematic program is likely to generate disparate yet related impacts. . . . [T]he programmatic EIS looks ahead and assimilates 'broad issues' relevant to [the program]. . . ."[96]

Although a PEIS is not required for every federal program,[97] the CEQ regulations suggest that certain broad, related actions are amenable to programmatic treatment, such as

- actions occurring in the same general location, such as a body of water, region, or metropolitan area;
- actions that have relevant similarities, such as common timing, impacts, alternatives, methods of implementation, media, or subject matter; and
- actions directed at technological development of a certain stage (including federal or federally assisted research, development, or demonstration programs).[98]

In determining whether a PEIS is appropriate, agencies are to consider whether the actions are "connected," "cumulative," or sufficiently "similar" such that a PEIS would be "the best way to assess the combined impacts of similar actions or reasonable alternatives to such actions."[99] Further, even if an agency thinks that its actions are amenable to programmatic treatment, the agency must still determine whether those actions "significantly affect[] the quality of the human environment."[100] The Supreme Court has also instructed agencies to consider issues such as "the extent of the inter-relationship among proposed actions and practical considerations of feasibility" when determining whether a PEIS is warranted.[101]

As this relates to the development of nanotechnology, federal agencies will likely need to consider whether proposed nanotechnology programs, research grant initiatives, or regulatory initiatives should be evaluated on a programmatic basis if the individual actions are connected, cumulative, or sufficiently similar—and if those actions, taken together, significantly affect the quality of the human environment. For example, Section 246 of the Bob Stump National Defense Authorization Act of 2003 established the "Defense Nanotechnology Research and Development Program" to "coordinate all nanoscale research and development within the Department of Defense."[102] To date, however, there does not appear to have been any agency that has published a PEIS specifically directed at nanotechnology programs or regulations. The closest example of a PEIS directly involving nanotechnology appears to have been a recent DOE discussion of nanotechnology applications in its PEIS for managing energy corridors on federal lands in the western United States.[103] As the use and development of nanotechnology continues to grow and expand, federal agencies may need to—and in some instances may be forced to—take a programmatic hard look at their programs to ensure compliance with NEPA.[104]

Analysis of Environmental Effects of Nanotechnology under NEPA

Once a determination has been made that a federal action may cause a release of nanomaterials into the environment, the federal agency must then determine whether that action will likely result in significant environment impacts utilizing the organization outlined earlier in "The NEPA Framework." If it will, NEPA applies.

The critical question that drives this entire analysis is what are the potential environmental effects of the proposed federal action? The importance of the question was aptly summarized by EPA in its recent *Draft Nanomaterial Research Strategy*:

> Because they are so small, nanomaterials may be readily transported through the air, water and soil, perhaps over much greater distances than conventional materials. Uncontrolled release of these materials can occur during production, through spills, casual disposal, recycling, wastewater, agricultural operations, or weathering (of paints containing nanomaterials, for

example) which may eventually lead to the presence of a large variety of nanomaterials in the environment. It may be difficult, economically unfeasible, or even impossible to remove nano-materials from some media (e.g., surface waters or drinking water), potentially resulting in exposures to large segments of the population to complex mixtures of these materials. In order to understand the implications of nanomaterials and to identify potential approaches to manage emissions/releases, it is critical to understand potential entry points of nanomaterials into the environment.[105]

To answer this question, agencies must analyze how nanomaterials might enter the environment and what they might do when they get there.

Exposure Pathways

While there is significant uncertainty about how nanomaterials behave in the natural and human environment, it is generally understood how and when they will likely get there. For example, synthetic nanomaterials may enter the environment through

- air emissions, water discharges and solid waste shipments from processes that create or utilize nanomaterials;
- spills of nanomaterials during transportation, storage or use;
- product usage (e.g., an insect repellant that contains nano-sized particles can drift during application and settle on plants or directly on the soil); and
- post-consumer discard of nanomaterials (including everything from discarding less-than-empty packages of a nano-based sunscreen to nanotech medications passing through humans, through wastewater treatment facilities, and into rivers, lakes, and oceans).[106]

As described in its *Draft Nanomaterial Research Strategy*, EPA plans to "conduct research to understand emissions/releases that can occur either during production, use, recycling, or disposal of nanomaterials."[107] As that body of evidence develops, federal agencies will be better equipped to assess their NEPA compliance requirements and more accurately study the effects of nanomaterials once they enter the environment.

Environmental Effects of Nanotechnology

Despite the increasing commercialization of nanotechnology, little is known about the likely fate, behavior, and effects of nanomaterials on the environment.[108] Their toxicology is not fully understood and there is little empirical data on ecotoxicity, bioaccumulation, or the persistence potential of nanoparticles.[109] In the absence of basic toxicological or impacts information, it is difficult to address the potential environmental risks and impacts of nanomaterials. Nonetheless, as discussed earlier in "Technological Revolutions, Scientific Uncertainty, and NEPA," NEPA requires federal agencies to at least try.

It is reasonable to assume that the unique chemical and physical properties of nanomaterials may have the potential to create environmental risks. Just as the size and chemical characteristics of engineered and manufactured nanoparticles can give them exciting properties, those same new properties—tiny size, high ratio of surface area to volume, high reactivity—also have the potential to create unique and possibly unpredictable human health and environmental risks. For example, EPA has stated that "some of the same special properties that make nanomaterials useful are also properties that may cause some nanomaterials to pose hazards to humans and the environment, under specific conditions."[110] The potential health and ecological impacts of nanomaterials could occur as a result of direct and/or new routes of exposure, the potential toxicity of the materials themselves, and synergistic effects from interactions with other compounds and the environment over time,[111] suggesting the importance of life-cycle analyses in this arena.[112] Scientists, however, have yet to determine what physicochemical properties will be most important in determining ecological and toxicological properties of nanomaterials, but the developing research does make clear that life-cycle analysis and comparative research studies will play an important role in the ongoing development of nanotechnology.[113]

Given all the unknowns about nanomaterials, researchers have begun focusing on the traits that make nanomaterials attractive for applications in industry and medicine—their ability to enter cells due to their size and their ability to transport materials along the way. Because of their tiny size, it may be possible for nanomaterials to pass through the blood-brain barrier, enter human and animal bloodstreams through the skin,[114] or be absorbed by plants in ways radically different from larger particles.[115] Once there, nanomaterials may have various unintended effects. Because of their tiny size, nanomaterials may also be highly mobile and travel farther than larger particles do in soil and water.[116] And while little is known about the biodegradation potential of nanoparticles, the "high durability and reactivity of some nanomaterials raise issues of their fate in the environment."[117] Because little is known regarding nanomaterials' effects in and on the environment, the decision makers at federal agencies dealing with or being asked to authorize nanotechnology-related projects may struggle to identify and consider environmental risks in their deliberations and thus overlook the potential for releases of nanomaterials into the environment. For this reason, the lack of specific regulatory provisions that address the unique properties or risks of nanoparticles may be a factor in a NEPA analysis. However, as will be discussed later, NEPA on balance provides an excellent framework to study the effects or use of nanotechnology in a host of applications despite this scientific uncertainty.

Consideration of Environmental Effects in the NEPA Process
Uncertainty with respect to the potential environmental impacts associated with the use of nanomaterials is inevitable because nanotechnology is an emerging technology. This uncertainty, however, does not need to hamstring a federal agency's NEPA analysis of nanotechnology-related projects, because NEPA does not require agencies to engage in crystal-ball gazing or consider worst-case situations when conducting their environmental analyses.[118] Rather, the CEQ regulations direct that the agency must make clear that information is incomplete or unavailable and include in the environmental analysis a discussion of the relevance of the missing information, a summary of the existing credible science, and an evaluation of the potential impacts based upon theoretical approaches or research methods generally accepted in the scientific community.[119] But above all else, NEPA requires federal agencies to take a "hard look" at the environmental consequences of their actions, including direct effects, indirect effects, and cumulative impacts.[120] Direct effects are those caused by the action and occur at the same time and place.[121] Indirect effects are caused by the action but are later in time or farther removed in distance from the action; nevertheless, they are reasonably foreseeable.[122] Cumulative impact analysis involves examining the incremental impact of the action when aggregated with other past, present, and reasonably foreseeable future actions regardless of which agency undertakes such other actions.[123]

Armed with the knowledge of the potential consequences of an action, and assuming an EIS is warranted, a federal agency can then develop potential mitigation measures to reduce those impacts.[124] As the Supreme Court has explained:

[T]he requirement that an EIS contain a detailed discussion of possible mitigation measures flows both from the language of the Act and, more expressly, from CEQ's implementing regulations.

Implicit in NEPA's demand that an agency prepare a detailed statement on "any adverse environmental effects which cannot be avoided should the proposal be implemented," is an understanding that the EIS will discuss the extent to which adverse effects can be avoided. . . . Without such a discussion, neither the agency nor other interested groups and individuals can properly evaluate the severity of the adverse effects.[125]

The federal agency can then make a final decision based on that information regarding whether to approve the project as proposed, select an alternative that will achieve the intended purpose of the project while minimizing the adverse environmental impacts of the project, impose mitigation measures, or in rare circumstances, reject the project. In fact, the "heart" of the NEPA process is a detailed consideration of alternatives to the proposed action.[126] CEQ's regulations require that the environmental impacts of the proposal and alternatives to it be presented in comparative form,[127] thus providing a clear basis for choice among options by the decision maker.[128] This procedural requirement is bounded by "some notion of feasibility," and consideration need be given only to reasonable, nonspeculative alternatives.[129] Thus, an environmental analysis is satisfactory if the treatment of alternatives, when judged against a "rule of reason," is sufficient to permit a reasoned choice among the various options.[130] That choice is then memorialized in a "record of decision" that describes the purpose and need for the project, the alternatives considered, and whether "all practicable means" to avoid or minimize environmental harm from the alternative selected have been adopted, and if not, why not.[131]

A federal agency faced with a decision to approve a project that could release nanomaterials into the environment with potentially significant consequences can follow this process to determine whether to approve the project as proposed, approve a modified version of the project with potential mitigation measures, or decide to forgo or discontinue the proposed project altogether. For example, if EPA was asked to issue an NPDES permit for a proposed fish farm in a state or other jurisdiction where EPA is the permitting authority, and that farm intended to use nanomaterials in the maintenance and operation of that facility, EPA may need to review the permitting action pursuant to NEPA. EPA may need to analyze the potential release of those nanomaterials outside the boundaries of the fish farm, and determine whether the native fish populations or other species in the surrounding aquatic environment could be impacted. If the risk of that were sufficiently high, an EIS may be required, and EPA may then need to consider alternatives to the nanomaterials, including traditional chemicals. If no feasible alternatives exist, EPA may need to impose additional conditions in the NPDES permit to mitigate for the potential harm.

Limitations in the Application of NEPA to Nanotechnology

There are significant limitations in relying on NEPA to analyze—and in certain respects regulate—the environmental impacts of nanotechnology. Foremost among those limitations is that NEPA does not actually guarantee a particular result; it only guarantees a process.[132] As the Supreme Court has stated: "NEPA does set forth significant substantive goals for the Nation, but its mandate to the agencies is essentially procedural."[133] Thus, NEPA "merely prohibits uninformed—rather than unwise—agency action."[134] As a result, NEPA does not require the selection of an alternative for the proposed action that has the least impact on the environment.[135] Nor does it impose any substantive requirements that mitigation measures actually be implemented.[136]

Another crucial limitation is that NEPA is not a jurisdictional statute; it does not grant any federal agency actual regulatory authority over a particular project.[137] Without an underlying federal action, there can be no NEPA review.[138] For example, it is possible that nanomaterials will be discharged to jurisdictional waters of the United States from existing wastewater treatment facilities or as by-products of the manufacturing processes. Those actions would be subject to NEPA review if EPA were still the primary permitting authority under the Clean Water Act for new source NPDES permits. However, because EPA has delegated NPDES permitting authority to nearly all but a handful of states, those permit actions will not be subject to NEPA review.[139]

Still another limitation, as discussed earlier in "NEPA Exemptions," is the extent to which most EPA actions have been exempted from NEPA. EPA is the major federal agency that oversees many of the major economic activities that release chemicals and other pollutants into the environment. As a result of the exemptions, the number of nanotechnology-related projects that could be analyzed under NEPA is greatly reduced.

Finally, until the significant scientific uncertainty surrounding the fate and transport of nanomaterials in the environment is overcome, federal agencies will be limited in the detail they can include in environmental impact analyses. The agencies can summarize what is currently known about the potential effects of nanomaterials in the environment, but the agencies do not need to crystal-ball their analyses. If an environmental effect is not known, then it cannot inform the agency's decision. However, NEPA will force both private and public actors to further study the intersection between nanotechnology and the environment if they want project-specific approvals. In that way, NEPA has the potential to greatly advance the study of nanotechnology and the environment.

Conclusion

NEPA can be a critical tool in analyzing the environmental consequences of the nanotechnology revolution. In certain circumstances, federal agencies have the authority under NEPA to review the environmental effects of any nanotechnology-related actions they may undertake or otherwise approve. There are limitations on how well NEPA can be applied to such projects; but, on balance, the statute can serve as an effective tool to analyze the movement of nanoparticles into and through the human and natural environment and the potential environmental effects that may follow.

Notes

1. *See, e.g.*, M. Mauter & M. Elimelech, *Environmental Applications of Carbon-based Nanomaterials*, 42 ENVTL. SCI. TECH. 5843–58 (2008) (noting that carbon-based nanomaterials may be used in a broad range of environmental applications, including sorbents, high-flux membranes, depth filters, antimicrobial agents, environmental sensors, renewable energy technologies, and pollution prevention strategies).
2. A nanometer is one-billionth of a meter.
3. 40 C.F.R. § 1500.1.
4. 42 U.S.C. § 4332(2)(C).
5. *See* Baltimore Gas & Elec. Co. v. Natural Res. Def. Council, 462 U.S. 87, 97 (1983).
6. 42 U.S.C. § 4321.
7. 42 U.S.C. § 4331(a).
8. 42 U.S.C. § 4332(2)(C).
9. 40 C.F.R. § 1508.18.
10. *See* 40 C.F.R. Part 1501.
11. 42 U.S.C. § 4344.
12. 40 C.F.R. § 1508.4. While such exclusions are well established at many regulatory agencies, even the most entrenched and common categorical exclusions may not apply where "a normally excluded action may have a significant environmental effect." *Id.* As such, certain regulatory

activities that would otherwise fall under a categorical exclusion might, upon consideration of the additional risks and concerns raised by the action's use of nanoscale materials, require development of a more formal environmental analysis. Courts have made such determinations regarding the field testing of genetically engineered crops, for example. *See* Ctr. for Food Safety v. Johanns, 451 F. Supp. 2d 1165, 1183–90 (D. Haw. 2006) (holding, inter alia, that USDA's application of categorical exclusions to field trials of genetically engineered, pharmaceutical producing crops violated NEPA because the agency failed to analyze whether the field tests met the exceptions to the agency's list of categorical exclusions); Int'l Ctr. for Tech. Assessment v. Johanns, 473 F. Supp. 2d 9, 28–30 (D.D.C. 2007) (challenge to USDA's application of NEPA categorical exclusion to field tests of genetically engineered creeping bentgrass; holding, inter alia, that USDA acted arbitrarily and capriciously when it did not undertake any analysis to determine whether its exceptions to the categorical exclusion applied and that there was substantial evidence in the record that the field tests may have the potential to significantly affect the quality of the human environment). In any event, agencies generally identify actions that can be categorically excluded from NEPA through their experience analyzing the potential environmental impacts associated with the same or similar actions. Thus, it will likely take time for agencies to understand the effects of specific actions involving nanomaterials and develop appropriate categorical exclusions, if any.

13.	40 C.F.R. §§ 1501.3–4. So-called significance determinations are made on a case-by-case basis considering the degree to which (1) the proposed action affects public health or safety; (2) the effects on the quality of the human environment are likely to be highly controversial; (3) the possible effects on the human environment are highly uncertain or involve unique or unknown risks; and (4) the action may establish a precedent for future actions with significant effects or represents a decision in principle about a future consideration. 40 C.F.R. § 1508.27. If the EA concludes that the impacts are not significant, the agency issues a FONSI and need not prepare an EIS. On the other hand, if the EA concludes that a proposed action will significantly affect the quality of the human environment, the more comprehensive EIS must be prepared. 40 C.F.R. § 1501.4(b)–(c).

14.	*See* 40 C.F.R. § 1501.4(a).

15.	*See* 40 C.F.R. §§ 1502.1–25.

16.	*See, e.g.,* Matthew J. Lepore, *Nanotechnology and Human Health: We Don't Know Nano,* American Bar Association, Toxic Torts and Environmental Law Committee Newsletter, at 14 (Spring 2008) (reviewing available scientific research and concluding that "[i]t is evident that our understanding of the potential human health risks associated with engineered nanoparticles remains very limited"); K. Dreher et al., *Nanotechnology Implications in Health and the Environment*, at 31, in NANOTECHNOLOGY AND THE ENVIRONMENT, Report of the National Nanotechnology Initiative Workshop (May 8–9, 2003) ("Information describing the relative health and environmental risk assessment of nanotechnology and associated nanomaterials is severely lacking.").

17. Found. on Economic Trends v. Heckler, 756 F.2d 143, 147 (D.C. Cir. 1985).

18. 42 U.S.C. § 4332(2)(A); *see generally* 42 U.S.C. § 4331.

19. Dinah Bear, *NEPA at 19: A Primer on an "Old" Law with Solutions to New Problems*, 19 Envtl. L. Rep. (Envtl. L. Inst.) 10,060, 10,061 (Feb. 1989).

20. Found. on Economic Trends, 756 F.2d at 143, 147.

21. 756 F.2d at 153–54.

22. *See, e.g.*, E. Barrera et al., *Nanotechnology Implications in Natural and Global Processes*, at 25, in NANOTECHNOLOGY AND THE ENVIRONMENT, Report of the National Nanotechnology Initiative Workshop (May 8–9, 2003) (reviewing current scientific and technological advancements).

23. *See, e.g.*, *Nanotechnology Implications in Health and the Environment*, *supra* note 16, at 31.

24. *See, e.g.*, *Nanotechnology Implications in Natural and Global Processes*, *supra* note 22, at 25 ("experts still do not know how to anticipate the fate of nanoparticles in most environmental systems (soils, groundwater, bed sediments, lakes, and other systems)"); *see also Nanotechnology Implications in Health and the Environment*, *supra* note 16, at 31; *Nanotechnology and Human Health: We Don't Know Nano*, *supra* note 16, at 14.

25. 40 C.F.R. § 1502.22.

26. 40 C.F.R. § 1502.22.

27. *See, e.g.*, Sierra Club v. Sigler, 695 F.2d 957, 973 (5th Cir. 1983) ("Uncertainty as to environmental consequences need not bar action as long as the uncertainty is forthrightly considered in the decisionmaking process and disclosed in the EIS."); Cady v. Morton, 527 F.2d 786, 796 (9th Cir. 1975) ("Neither s 102(2)(B) or (C) . . . can be read as a requirement that complete information concerning the environmental impact of a project must be obtained before action may be taken.").

28. Baltimore Gas, 462 U.S. at 97.

29. 42 U.S.C. § 4332(2)(C).

30. 40 C.F.R. § 1508.8(a).

31. Touret v. Nat'l Aeronautics & Space Admin., 485 F. Supp. 2d 38, 43 (D.R.I. 2007) (holding that federal funding amounting to 11% of the total construction costs of building a biomedical research building did not amount to a "major federal action" because the funding did not give the government sufficient control over the project).

32. Atlanta Coalition on the Transp. Crisis, Inc. v. Atlanta Reg'l Comm'n, 599 F.2d 1333, 1347 (5th Cir. 1979) (holding that "federal financial assistance is generally just one factor in the analysis of whether there is sufficient

federal control over, responsibility for, or involvement with an action to require preparation of an EIS").

33. Homeowners Emergency Life Prot. Comm. v. Lynn, 541 F.2d 814 (9th Cir. 1976).

34. Monarch Chem. Works, Inc., v. Exon, 452 F. Supp. 493 (D. Neb. 1978).

35. Smith v. City of Cookeville, 381 F. Supp. 100 (M.D. Tenn. 1974).

36. Ross v. Fed. Highway Admin., 162 F.3d 1046 (10th Cir. 1998).

37. *See, e.g.,* 40 C.F.R. §§ 1501.3–4.

38. EPA, *Nanotechnology White Paper*, EPA 100/B-07/001 (Feb. 2007), *available at* http://es.epa.gov/ncer/nano/publications/whitepaper12022005.pdf. NEPA is notably absent in the section discussing the "statutes administered by EPA," which it viewed as "a starting point for evaluating and managing risks and benefits from nanomaterials." *Id.* at 65.

39. 33 U.S.C. § 1371(c).

40. 33 U.S.C. § 1342.

41. 40 C.F.R. § 122.2.

42. *See* 40 C.F.R. § 207.5 (establishing NEPA requirements in development of new source NPDES permits for new major industrial discharges).

43. *See* 40 C.F.R. Part 451.

44. *See, e.g.,* AZoNanotechnology, *Agriculture, Fishing and Veterinary Medicine—How Nanotechnology Might Impact These Industries,* http://www.azonano.com/Details.asp?ArticleID=1331#_DNA_Nano-Vaccines_Using_Nanocapsule (last visited July 27, 2009).

45. *See, e.g., Could Nanotechnology Revolutionize Natural Gas Industry?,* Sci. Daily (Oct. 31, 2007), *available at* http://www.sciencedaily.com/releases/2007/10/071030120538.htm; *Nano-Prospecting: Energy Companies Pour Millions Into Nanotechnology for Oil and Gas Recovery,* Tech. Rev. (Jan. 25, 2008), *available at* http://www.technologyreview.com/Nanotech/20114/.

46. *See* 40 C.F.R. Part 435.

47. *See* Nanotechnology White Paper, *supra* note 38, at 18–21.

48. *See id.* at 18.

49. *See generally* EPA, *Nanotechnology: Green Manufacturing,* http://es.epa.gov/ncer/nano/research/nano_green.html (last visited July 27, 2009).

50. 42 U.S.C. § 7609.

51. 42 U.S.C. § 7609(b).

52. *See* 21 C.F.R. § 25.20.

53. *See* FDA, *Nanotechnology: A Report of the U.S. Food and Drug Administration Nanotechnology Task Force,* at 28 (July 25, 2007), http://www.fda.gov/nanotechnology/taskforce/report2007.html#act (last visited July 27, 2009).

54. 21 C.F.R. § 25.22 ("There are no categories of agency actions that routinely significantly affect the quality of the human environment and that therefore ordinarily require the preparation of an EIS. . . . EISs are

prepared for agency actions when evaluation of data or information in an EA or otherwise available to the agency leads to a finding by the responsible agency official that a proposed action may significantly affect the quality of the human environment.").

55. *See generally* EPA, *Endocrine Disruptors Research Initiative*, http://www .epa.gov/endocrine/index.html (last visited July 27, 2009).

56. *See, e.g.,* 32 C.F.R. § 641 (environmental analysis of Army actions); 32 C.F.R. § 775 (environmental analysis of Navy actions); *id.* § 989 (environmental analysis of Air Force actions).

57. 32 C.F.R. §§ 641, 775, and 989.

58. 32 C.F.R. § 641.42 (Army actions normally requiring an EIS).

59. 32 C.F.R. § 641.32 (Army actions normally requiring an EA).

60. 32 C.F.R. § 641.32.

61. 32 C.F.R. § 641.32.

62. *See* DOD, *Defense Nanotechnology Research and Development Program,* at 6 (Apr. 2007), http://nano.gov/html/res/pdf/DefenseNano2007.pdf (last visited July 27, 2009).

63. 7 U.S.C. § 7715 (governing USDA's declaration of extraordinary emergencies and resulting authorities).

64. *See* 7 C.F.R. § 372.5 (requiring an EIS for the development for "new or untried methodologies, strategies, or techniques to deal with pervasive threats to animal and plant health").

65. *See* Save Our Ecosystems v. Clark, 747 F.2d 1240, 1247–49 (9th Cir. 1984) ("The mere fact that a program involves use of substances registered under FIFRA does not exempt the program from the requirements of NEPA."); Citizens Against Toxic Sprays, Inc. v. Bergland, 428 F. Supp. 908, 927 (D. Or. 1977) (holding that the Forest Service's reliance on EPA's registration data did not satisfy the agency's NEPA requirements, because NEPA requires a case-by-case balancing and the only agency in the position to make such a judgment is the agency with the responsibility for the proposed action).

66. *See* 7 C.F.R. § 340.4.

67. 7 C.F.R. § 340.4; *see, e.g.,* Geertson Seed Farms v. Johanns, 2007 WL 518624, *12 (N.D. Cal. 2007) (requiring APHIS to prepare an EIS in support of its decision to deregulate genetically engineered, pesticide-resistant alfalfa), *affirmed* 541 F.3d 938 (9th Cir. 2008).

68. *See* Citizens Against Toxic Sprays, 428 F. Supp. at 926–27 (effects of herbicide spraying in a national forest must be thoroughly analyzed under NEPA).

69. *See* Northwest Coalition for Alternatives to Pesticides v. Lyng, 673 F. Supp. 1019, 1024 (D. Or. 1987) (upholding BLM analysis of the use of herbicides on federal lands in Oregon); Edmonds Inst. v. Babbitt, 42 F. Supp. 2d 1, 18–19 (D.D.C. 1999) (decision to allow biotechnology company to collect specimens in National Park required detailed analysis under NEPA).

70. The National Nanotechnology Initiative, *Supplement to the President's FY 2009 Budget*, at 14 (Sept. 2008), *available at* http://www.nano.gov/NNI_09Budget.pdf (hereinafter *NNI 2009 Budget*).

71. The National Nanotechnology Initiative, *Supplement to the President's FY 2008 Budget*, at 13 (July 2007), http://www.nano.gov/NNI_08Budget.pdf (last visited July 27, 2009).

72. For example, an EA was drafted for the construction of the Nanoscale Science Research Center at Lawrence Berkeley Laboratories. *See* Draft Environmental Assessment for Construction and Operation of The Molecular Foundry (Dec. 2002), *available at* http://lso.oak.doe.gov/SiteMgr/Env_Rprts/MolecFoundry/docs/EA_MolecularFoundry.pdf. The EA did not identify any environmental risks or hazards unique to the use of nanoparticles for the research in the building.

73. *NNI 2009 Budget, supra* note 70, at 3.

74. 15 U.S.C. §§ 7501–7509.

75. *NNI 2009 Budget, supra* note 70, at 7. The five agencies with the largest investments were the National Science Foundation, DOD, DOE, the National Institutes of Health, and the National Institute for Standards and Technology.

76. *Id.* at 5.

77. 15 U.S.C. § 793(c)(1) ("No action taken under the Clean Air Act . . . shall be deemed a major Federal action significantly affecting the quality of the human environment within the meaning of the National Environmental Policy Act.").

78. *See e.g.*, 15 U.S.C. § 7412 (stationary source emissions standards and permits for hazardous air pollutants); 15 U.S.C. § 7521 (emissions standards for mobile sources of air pollutants); 15 U.S.C. § 7545 (regulations governing standards for fuel and fuel additives used in mobile sources, nonroad vehicles, and nonroad engines).

79. 33 U.S.C. § 1371(c). With respect to NPDES permits for "new sources," EPA notes that "[t]he issuance of NPDES permits by an EPA-authorized state is a state, not federal, action and is, thus, not subject to NEPA. Currently, most states are authorized and, thus, the bulk of the NPDES permits issued in the United States are not subject to NEPA." 72 Fed. Reg. 53,652, 53,655 (Sept. 19, 2007).

80. City of New York v. Minetta, 262 F.3d 169, 178 (2d Cir. 2001).

81. *See, e.g.*, Flint Ridge Dev. Co. v. Scenic Rivers Ass'n of Okla., 426 U.S. 776, 788 (1976); *see also* Westlands Water Dist. v. Natural Res. Def. Council, 43 F.3d 457, 462 (9th Cir. 1994) (rejecting the applicability of NEPA to a DOI action to divert water from streams for agricultural purposes under the Central Valley Project Improvement Act where water deliveries were required "upon enactment" of the statute).

82. *See, e.g.*, City of New York v. Minetta, 262 F.3d at 178 (declining to require NEPA review of a Department of Transportation action to grant slot

exemptions to an air carrier that satisfies the conditions listed in the statute).

83. Alabama ex rel. Siegelman v. EPA, 911 F.2d 499, 504 (11th Cir. 1990).

84. Twitty v. North Carolina, 527 F. Supp. 778, 783 (E.D.N.C. 1981) ("It is not contended that the Toxic Substances Control Act requires an environmental impact statement be prepared or circulated."); *see also* Warren County v. North Carolina, 528 F. Supp. 276, 283 (E.D.N.C. 1981) (declining to extend NEPA civil action authority to TSCA decisions).

85. Maryland v. Train, 415 F. Supp. 116, 121 (D. Md. 1976), *rev'd in part and remanded in part on other grounds*, Maryland v. Train, 1977 U.S. App. LEXIS 14752 (4th Cir. 1977).

86. Wyoming v. Hathaway, 525 F.2d 66, 71–72 (10th Cir. 1975) (finding that the Administrator's order, findings, and conclusions supporting a pesticide product cancellation substantially complied with the NEPA requirement); *see also* Envtl. Def. Fund, Inc. v. EPA, 489 F.2d 1247, 1254–56 (D.C. Cir. 1973) (upholding the cancellation of DDT without NEPA review where "the functional equivalent of a NEPA investigation was provided, for all of the five core NEPA issues were carefully considered: the environmental impact of the action, possible adverse environmental effects, possible alternatives, the relationship between long- and short-term uses and goals, and any irreversible commitments of resources.").

87. *See, e.g.,* Alabama ex rel. Siegelman, 911 F.2d at 505 ("RCRA is the functional (though not the structural or literal) equivalent and more specific counterpart of NEPA. . . . The RCRA permitting procedures 'strike a workable balance between some of the advantages and disadvantages of full application of NEPA.'"). EPA has interpreted the functional equivalence doctrine as applying broadly to all EPA actions under the RCRA program. *See* 72 Fed. Reg. at 53,656.

88. *See* Frey v. EPA, 2006 U.S. Dist. LEXIS 71366, *11–12 (S.D. Ind. 2006) (exempting EPA from NEPA but denying EPA the right to waive the Remedial Investigation/Feasibility Study: "This court agrees . . . that more recent environmental legislation has produced numerous more specific 'functional equivalents' to the broad requirement of NEPA that an EIS issue. . . . However, in part, that functional equivalency here has to be the RI/FS. . . .") (internal citations omitted).

89. W. Neb. Res. Council v. EPA, 943 F.2d 867, 871–72 (8th Cir. 1991) ("EPA does not need to comply with the formal requirements of NEPA in performing its environmental protection functions under organic legislation that mandates specific procedures for considering the environment that are functional equivalents of the impact statement process. We further agree that SDWA is such legislation, and that the procedures employed and the analysis undertaken by EPA in this proceeding covered the core NEPA concerns.") (internal citations and quotations omitted).

90. Cellular Phone Taskforce v. FCC, 205 F.3d 82 (2d Cir. 2000) ("The proce-
    dures followed by the FCC in the instant rulemaking satisfy the func-
    tional compliance test. . . . Thus, no EIS was required."). The *Cellular
    Phone* case is notable because, overall, courts have been less willing to
    apply a functionality test when reviewing actions by agencies other
    than EPA.
91. Merrell v. Thomas, 807 F.2d 776, 782 (9th Cir. 1986).
92. EPA, in turn, has interpreted the functional equivalency doctrine
    broadly to exempt many, if not most regulatory actions under EPA. *See,
    e.g.,* 40 C.F.R. § 6.101 ("Subparts A through C of this part do not apply
    to EPA actions for which NEPA review is not required. EPA actions
    under the Clean Water Act, except those identified in § 6.101(a), and
    EPA actions under the Clean Air Act are statutorily exempt from NEPA.
    Additionally, the courts have determined that certain EPA actions for
    which analyses that have been conducted under another statute are
    functionally equivalent with NEPA.").
93. For example, in *Save Our Ecosystems v. Clark*, the court enjoined the
    Forest Service's application of an EPA-registered pesticide until it ful-
    filled NEPA's requirements. 747 F.2d at 1247–49. Although the Service
    argued that its reliance on EPA's registration of the pesticide it planned
    to use satisfied its NEPA obligations, the court held that FIFRA does not
    require or contemplate the same examination that the agency is required
    to undertake to satisfy NEPA. "The mere fact that a program involves
    use of substances registered under FIFRA does not exempt the program
    from the requirements of NEPA." 747 F.2d at 1248 (internal quotations
    omitted); *see also* Citizens Against Toxic Spray, 428 F. Supp. at 927.
94. Even in the context of EPA actions, there is no guarantee that courts will
    continue to apply the functional equivalence or other implied exemp-
    tion doctrines in future challenges to agency actions involving different
    facts, particularly actions that may involve unique nanotechnology risk
    issues that may not have been anticipated under EPA's organic statutes.
95. 40 C.F.R. § 1508.18(b)(3). Discussion of PEISs usually incorporates the
    concept of "tiering." 40 C.F.R. § 1508.2 provides: "'Tiering' refers to cov-
    erage of general matters in broader environmental impact statements
    (such as national program or policy statements) with subsequent nar-
    rower statements or environmental analyses. . . . Tiering is appropriate
    when the sequence of statements or analyses is . . . [f]rom a program,
    plan, or policy environmental impact statement to a program, plan or
    policy statement or analysis of lesser scope or to a site-specific statement
    or analysis." *See also* 40 C.F.R. § 1502.20.
96. Found. on Econ. Trends, 756 F.2d at 159; *see also* Nevada v. DOE, 457 F.3d
    78, 92 (D.C. Cir. 2006).
97. 40 C.F.R. § 1502.4(b) ("Environmental impacts statements may be pre-
    pared, and are sometimes required, for broad Federal actions such as

the adoption of new agency programs or regulations (§ 1508.18)."); Nevada v. DOE, 457 F.3d at 92 ("The decision whether to prepare a programmatic EIS is committed to the agency's discretion.").

98. 40 C.F.R. § 1502.4(c). For research and development programs, the CEQ regulations suggest that such a PEIS be prepared "before the program has reached a stage of investment or commitment to implementation likely to determine subsequent development or restrict later alternatives." *Id.*

99. 40 C.F.R. § 1508.25(a).

100. 42 U.S.C. § 4332(2)(C).

101. Kleppe v. Sierra Club, 427 U.S. 390, 412 (1976).

102. 10 U.S.C. § 2358, Pub. L. 107–314, Div. A, Title II, § 246; *see also* 15 U.S.C. § 7501(c)(3).

103. *See* DOE, *Programmatic Environmental Impact Statement, Designation of Energy Corridors on Federal Land in 11 Western States* (DOE/EIS-0386), Vol. II, App. G, G.1.5.3 (Nov. 2008).

104. *See* International Center for Technology Assessment, *Petition for Rulemaking Requesting EPA Regulate Nano-Silver Products as Pesticides*, at 92–96 (May 1, 2008) (requesting that EPA comply with NEPA, including, inter alia, that it prepare a PEIS before developing regulations for nano-silver pesticide regulation); International Center for Technology Assessment, *Petition Requesting FDA Amend Its Regulations for Products Composed of Engineered Nanoparticles Generally and Sunscreen Drug Products Composed of Engineered Nanoparticles Specifically*, at 33–37 (May 16, 2006) (requesting that FDA comply with NEPA, including, inter alia, that it prepare a PEIS before developing regulations addressing nanomaterials in consumer products).

105. EPA, *Draft Nanomaterial Research Strategy*, at 23 (Jan. 24, 2008), http://epa. gov/ncer/nano/publications/nano_strategy_012408.pdf (last visited July 27, 2009).

106. *Id*. at 23–24.

107. *Id*. at 23.

108. *See, e.g.*, Colvin, *The Potential Environmental Impact of Nanomaterials*, 21 NATURE BIOTECH. 1166–70 (2003).

109. Nanotechnology White Paper, *supra* note 38, at 14, 33.

110. *Id*. at 13.

111. *See Draft Nanomaterial Research Strategy*, *supra* note 105, at 2, 38.

112. *See* Vikas Khanna et al., *Carbon Nanofiber Production: Life Cycle Energy Consumption and Environmental Impact*, 12 J. INDUS. ECOLOGY 394–410 (2008) (life-cycle impacts of certain nanomaterials may be much greater than traditional materials on a per unit basis).

113. *See, e.g.*, Maynard et al., *Safe Handling of Nanotechnology*, 444 Nature 267 (Nov. 16, 2006); Oberdorster et al., *Nanotoxicology: An Emerging Discipline Evolving from Studies of Ultrafine Particles*, 113 ENVTL. HEALTH

PERSPECTIVES 823–39 (2005); Harper et al., *In Vivo Biodistribution and Toxicity Depends on Nanomaterial Composition, Size, Surface Functionalization and Route of Exposure*, 3 J. EXPERIMENTAL NANOSCIENCE 195–206 (2008).

114. *See, e.g.*, DeLouise et al., *In Vivo Skin Penetration of Quantum Dot Nanoparticles in the Murine Model: The Effect of UVR*, 8(9) NANO LETTERS 2779–87 (2008).

115. *See* Nanotechnology White Paper, *supra* note 38, at 58 (noting that "nanomaterials may affect aquatic or terrestrial organisms differently than larger particles of the same materials"). For example, available scientific literature suggests that some nanomaterials may be potentially more mobile in organisms and cells than their non-nano counterparts. *See, e.g.*, Limbach et al., *Oxide Nanoparticle Uptake in Human Lung Fibroblasts: Effects of Particle Size, Agglomeration, and Diffusion at Low Concentrations*, 39 ENVTL. SCI. TECH. 9370–76 (2005); Rothen-Rutishauser et al., *Interaction of Fine Particles and Nanoparticles with Red blood Cells Visualized with Advanced Microscopic Techniques*, 40 ENVTL. SCI. TECH. 4353–59 (2006); Geiser et al., *Ultrafine Particles Cross Cellular Membranes by Non-phagocytic Mechanisms in Lungs and in Cultured Cells*, 113 ENVTL. HEALTH PERSPECTIVES 1555–60 (2005). And recent research suggests that certain nanoparticles may have a "Trojan horse"-like toxicity mechanism that could transport metals across cell membranes. *See* Limbach et al., *Exposure of Engineered Nanoparticles to Human Lung Epithelial Cells: Influence of Chemical Composition and Catalytic Activity on Oxidative Stress*, 41 ENVTL. SCI. TECH. 4158–63 (2007); *see also* Lin et al., *Computational and Ultrastructural Toxicology of a Nanoparticle, Quantum Dot 705, in Mice*, 42 ENVTL. SCI. TECH. 6264–70 (2008) (commercially available quantum dot caused kidney damage in laboratory mice; damage potentially caused by metal leaching from quantum dot core).

116. Nanotechnology White Paper, *supra* note 38, at 34; *see also* Zhang et al., *Nanoscale Iron Particles for Environmental Remediation: An Overview*, 5 J. NANOPARTICLE RESEARCH 323–32 (2003) (comparing transport of iron particles in soil and groundwater).

117. Nanotechnology White Paper, *supra* note 38, at 14; *see also* Johansen et al., *Effects of C60 Fullerene Nanoparticles on Soil Bacteria and Protozoans*, 27 ENVTL. TOXICOLOGY & CHEMISTRY 1895–1903 (2008) (analyzing the impacts of fullerenes on soil ecosystems).

118. Robertson v. Methow Valley Citizens Council, 490 U.S. 332, 356 (1989).

119. 40 C.F.R. § 1502.22.

120. 40 C.F.R. § 1508.8; Kleppe v. Sierra Club, 427 U.S. 390, 410 n.21 (1976) ("The only role for a court is to insure that the agency has taken a "hard look" at environmental consequences. . . .").

121. 40 C.F.R. § 1508.8(a).

122. 40 C.F.R. § 1508.8(b).

123. 40 C.F.R. § 1508.7.

124. 40 C.F.R. §§ 1502.14(f), 1502.16(h). The CEQ regulations define mitigation to include "(a) avoiding the impact altogether by not taking a certain action or parts of an action; (b) minimizing impacts by limiting the degree or magnitude of the action and its implementation; (c) rectifying the impact by repairing, rehabilitating, or restoring the affected environment; (d) reducing or eliminating the impact over time by preservation and maintenance operations during the life of the action; and (e) compensating for the impact by replacing or providing substitute resources or environments." 40 C.F.R. § 1508.20.

125. Methow Valley Citizens Council, 490 U.S. at 352.

126. 40 C.F.R. § 1502.14; *see also* 42 U.S.C. § 4332(2)(C)(iii). While these provisions specifically addresses EIS requirements, CEQ also requires a consideration of alternatives in EAs as well. 40 C.F.R. § 1508.9(b).

127. 40 C.F.R. § 1502.14.

128. *See, e.g.,* N. Buckhead Civic Ass'n v. Skinner, 903 F.2d 1533, 1540 (11th Cir. 1990) ("Consideration of other realistic possibilities forces the agency to consider the environmental effects of a project and to evaluate against the effects of alternatives.").

129. *Id.*

130. *Id.*

131. 40 C.F.R. § 1505.2.

132. Stryker's Bay Neighborhood Council, Inc. v. Karlen, 444 U.S. 223, 227–28 (1980) (*per curiam*).

133. Vermont Yankee Nuclear Power Co. v. Natural Res. Def. Council, 435 U.S. 519, 558 (1978).

134. Methow Valley Citizens Council, 490 U.S. at 351.

135. *Id.* at 350–51.

136. *Id.* at 351–52.

137. *See* Borough of Morrisville v. Del. River Basin Comm'n, 382 F. Supp. 543, 545 (E.D. Pa. 1974) ("The National Environmental Policy Act of 1969 does not in itself create jurisdiction; it merely creates a cause of action for which jurisdiction must be found in another statute.").

138. *See* Macht v. Skinner, 916 F.2d 13, 18 (D.C. Cir. 1990) ("NEPA requires *federal agencies*—not states or private parties—to consider the environmental impacts of their proposed actions."); *see also* Citizens Alert Regarding the Env't v. EPA, 259 F. Supp. 2d 9, 19 n.8 (D.D.C. 2003); Bennett v. Taylor, 505 F. Supp. 800, 805 (M.D. La. 1980).

139. Citizens Alert Regarding the Env't, 259 F. Supp. 2d at 19 ("Pennsylvania's decision to grant a permit . . . was a state decision, and therefore beyond the scope of NEPA"); *see also* District of Columbia v. Schramm, 631 F.2d 854, 862 (D.C. Cir. 1980).

GLOSSARY

TSCA Terms

Category of Chemical Substances—"[A] group of chemical substances the members of which are similar in molecular structure, in physical, chemical, or biological properties, in use, or in mode of entrance into the human body or into the environment, or the members of which are in some other way suitable for classification as such for purposes of this [Act], except that such term does not mean a group of chemical substances which are grouped together solely on the basis of their being new chemical substances." TSCA § 26(c), 15 U.S.C. § 2625(c).

Chemical Substance—"[A]ny organic or inorganic substance of a particular molecular identity, including—(i) any combination of such substances occurring in whole or in part as a result of a chemical reaction or occurring in nature and (ii) any element or uncombined radical." TSCA § 3(2)(A), 15 U.S.C. § 2602(2)(A); *see also* 40 C.F.R. § 720.3(e).

DNA—"[H]owever created, is 'an organic substance of a particular molecular identity.'" 49 Fed. Reg. 50880, 50886 (Dec. 31, 1984).

Existing Chemical Substance—A chemical substance that is listed on the TSCA Inventory.

High Production Volume (HPV) Challenge Program—A program established by EPA and the Chemical Manufacturers Association (now the American Chemistry Council); encourages chemical manufacturers and importers to conduct testing of chemicals on EPA's list of HPV chemicals, as compiled under the 1990 Inventory Update Rule issued under TSCA.

Interagency Testing Committee (ITC)—A committee with membership from several federal agencies that makes recommendations to the EPA regarding chemical substances and mixtures to which EPA should give priority consideration for promulgation of a TSCA Section 4 test rule. The ITC member agencies are EPA, the Occupational Safety and Health Administration, the Council on Environmental Quality, the National Institute of Occupational Safety and Health, the National Institute of Environmental Health Services, the National Cancer Institute, the National Science Foundation, and the Department of Commerce. *See* TSCA § 4(e), 15 U.S.C. § 2603(e).

265

Inventory Update Rule—A rule issued by EPA under TSCA Section 8(a) that requires certain manufacturers and importers of certain chemical substances listed on the TSCA Inventory to report, every four years, data on production volume, plant site, and site-limited status of those chemical substances. TSCA § 8(a), 15 U.S.C. § 2607(a); 40 C.F.R. pt. 710.

Microorganism—"A living organism [which] is [a] 'combination of such substances occurring in whole or in part as a result of a chemical reaction or occurring in nature.'" 49 Fed. Reg. 50880, 50886 (Dec. 31, 1984).

Nanometer—One-billionth of a meter, or 10^{-9} m. *See* National Nanotechnology Initiative (NNI), *Frequently Asked Questions*, http://www .nano.gov/html/facts/faqs.html (last visited July 27, 2009).

Nanoscale Materials Stewardship Program (NMSP)—A voluntary program that EPA established to assemble existing data and information from manufacturers and processors of certain nanoscale materials. Under the Basic Program, participants are invited to report voluntarily available information on the engineered nanoscale materials they manufacture, import, process, or use. Under the In-Depth Program, participants are invited to work on a plan for the development of data on representative nanoscale materials over a longer time frame. *See* http://www.epa.gov/oppt/nano/stewardship.htm (last visited July 27, 2009).

Nanotechnology—The creation or use of materials or processes at a scale of approximately 1 to 100 nanometers in at least one dimension.

New Chemical Substance—"[A]ny chemical substance which is not included in the chemical substance list [TSCA Inventory] compiled and published under section 2607(b) of [TSCA]." TSCA § 3(9), 15 U.S.C. § 2602(9); *see also* 40 C.F.R. §§ 710.3, 720.3(v), 720.25(a).

Premanufacture Notification—Notification submitted to EPA that the submitter intends to manufacture or import a new chemical substance. TSCA § 5, 15 U.S.C. § 2604; 40 C.F.R. pt. 720.

Significant New Use Rule—A rule limiting the manufacture and processing of a chemical substance for a use that EPA has determined to be a significant new use. TSCA § 5(a), 15 U.S.C. § 2604(a); 40 C.F.R. pt. 721.

TSCA Inventory—"[A] list of each chemical substance which is manufactured or processed in the United States." The Inventory consists of two subsets—the Public Inventory and the Confidential Inventory. TSCA § 8(b)(1), 15 U.S.C. § 2607(b)(1).

Unreasonable Risk of Injury to Health or the Environment—A standard to be applied by EPA in determining whether to promulgate a rule or issue an order concerning a chemical substance or mixture. The unreasonable risk standard appears throughout TSCA. For example, EPA is to promulgate Section 4 test rules to develop data necessary to determine whether a chemical substance or mixture presents an unreasonable risk of injury to health or the environment. Similarly, EPA is to promulgate a Section 6 limitation or ban upon a finding that activities involving a chemical substance or mixture present or will present an unreasonable risk of injury to health or the environment. *See* TSCA §§ 2(a), 2(b), 4(a), 4(e), 4(f), 5(b), 5(e), 5(f), 5(h), 6, 9(a), 12(a)(2), 14(a)(3), 21(b)(4)(B); *see also* 15 U.S.C. §§ 2601(a), 2601(b), 2603(a), 2603(e), 2603(f), 2604(b), 2604(e), 2604(f), 2604(h), 2605, 2608(a), 2611(a)(2), 2613(a)(3), 2620(b)(4)(B).

FIFRA Terms

Active Ingredient—"[I]n the case of a pesticide other than a plant regulator, defoliant, desiccant, or nitrogen stabilizer[,] an ingredient which will prevent, destroy, repel, or mitigate any pest." FIFRA § 2(a)(1), 7 U.S.C. § 136(a)(1).

Agrochemical Delivery—Delivery of pesticides and other chemicals only when needed or for better absorption.

Bottom-Up Process—A process that creates structures from atoms and molecules. U.S. Environmental Protection Agency (EPA), *Nanotechnology White Paper* (Feb. 2007) at 7, http://www.epa.gov/osa/pdfs/nanotech/epa-nanotechnology-whitepaper-0207.pdf (last visited July 27, 2009).

Dendrimers—Nanosized polymers built at the molecular level from branched units. *Nanotechnology White Paper* (Feb. 2007) at 9, http://www.epa.gov/osa/pdfs/nanotech/epa-nanotechnology-whitepaper-0207.pdf (last visited July 27, 2009).

Experimental Use Permits—Permits that allow persons to apply an unregistered pesticide for the purpose of developing information needed to register under FIFRA Section 3 either (1) a pesticide not registered with EPA, or (2) a registered pesticide for a use not previously approved in the registration of that pesticide. 40 C.F.R. § 172.3.

Inert Ingredient—"[A]n ingredient which is not active"; or "any substance (or group of structurally similar substances if designated by the Agency), other than an active ingredient, which is intentionally included in a pesticide product"; or an ingredient that is intentionally added to a pesticide product, but that is not pesticidally active, such as a solvent, detergent, emulsifier, filler, carrier, or perfume. FIFRA § 2(m), 7 U.S.C. § 136(m); 40 C.F.R. § 152.3(m).

Nanopesticides—Pesticidal products developed using nanotechnology.

Nanosensor—Nanoscale sensors are being developed that can detect the presence of chemical substances in the environment at very low concentrations. U.S. Environmental Protection Agency (EPA), *Nanotechnology White Paper* (Feb. 2007) at 23–24, http://www.epa.gov/ osa/pdfs/nanotech/epa-nanotechnology-whitepaper-0207.pdf (last visited July 27, 2009).

Office of Pesticide Programs (OPP) Nanotechnology Workgroup— Cochaired by senior managers in OPP's Antimicrobials Division and Health Effects Division, the Workgroup includes legal, science, and policy experts from across OPP and the Office of General Counsel. The Workgroup has dual purposes: first, to help OPP develop a regulatory and technical framework (including data needs) for reviewing nanopesticides submitted for registration under FIFRA; and second, to advise OPP decision makers on technical and policy issues raised on a case-by-case basis with specific applications. *See OPP Presentation to the Pesticide Program Dialogue Committee* (Nov. 9, 2006), http:// www.epa.gov/pesticides/ppdc/2006/november06/session7-nanotec .pdf (last visited July 27, 2009).

Pesticide—"[A]ny substance or mixture of substances intended for preventing, destroying, repelling, or mitigating any pest, [and] (2) any substance or mixture of substances intended for use as a plant regulator, defoliant, or desiccant." FIFRA § 2(u), 7 U.S.C. § 136(u); *see also* 40 C.F.R. § 152.15.

Pesticide Registration Improvement Renewal Act (PRIA 2)—Requires EPA to conduct more stringent reviews of the "completeness" of registration applications and imposes financial penalties for submission of incomplete applications. Pub. L. No. 110–94 (enacted Oct. 9, 2007).

Safe—Required that EPA assess the "harm [that] will result from aggregate exposure to the pesticide residue." FFDCA § 408(b)(2)(A)(ii), 21 U.S.C. § 346a(b)(2)(A)(ii).

Stop Sale, Use, or Removal Order (SSURO)—Under FIFRA, "whenever any pesticide or device is found by the Administrator in any State and there is reason to believe on the basis of inspection or tests that such pesticide or device is in violation of any of the provisions of [FIFRA], or that such pesticide or device has been or is intended to be distributed or sold in violation of any such provisions, or when the registration of the pesticide has been canceled by a final order or has been suspended, the Administrator may issue a written or printed 'stop sale, use, or removal' order to any person who owns, controls, or has custody of such pesticide or device." After receipt of such an order, "no person shall sell, use, or remove the pesticide or device in the order except in accordance with the provisions of the order." FIFRA § 13(a), 7 U.S.C. § 136k(a).

To Distribute or Sell—"[T]o distribute, sell, offer for sale, hold for distribution, hold for sale, hold for shipment, ship, deliver for shipment, release for shipment, or receive and (having so received) deliver or offer to deliver. The term does not include the holding or application of registered pesticides or use dilutions thereof by any applicator who provides a service of controlling pests without delivering any unapplied pesticide to any person so served." FIFRA § 2(gg), 7 U.S.C. § 136(gg).

Tolerance—"[T]he amount of a pesticide residue that legally may be present in or on a raw agricultural commodity under the terms of a tolerance under FFDCA section 408 or a processed food under the terms of a food additive regulation under FFDCA section 409." 40 C.F.R. § 177.3.

Top-Down Process—A process such as milling or machining larger particles into smaller particles. U.S. Environmental Protection Agency (EPA), *Nanotechnology White Paper* (Feb. 2007) at 7, http://www.epa.gov/osa/pdfs/nanotech/epa-nanotechnology-whitepaper-0207.pdf (last visited July 27, 2009).

Unreasonable Adverse Effects on the Environment—"(1) any unreasonable risk to man or the environment, taking into account the economic, social, and environmental costs and benefits of the use of any pesticide, or (2) a human dietary risk from residues that result from a use of a pesticide in or on any food inconsistent with [certain standards]." FIFRA § 2(bb), 7 U.S.C. § 136(bb).

CAA Terms

Air Pollutant—"[A]ny air pollution agent or combination of such agents, including any physical, chemical, biological, radioactive (including source material, special nuclear material, and byproduct material) substance or matter which is emitted into or otherwise enters the ambient air. Such term includes any precursors to the formation of any air pollutant, to the extent the Administrator has identified such precursor or precursors for the particular purpose for which the term 'air pollutant' is used." CAA § 302(g), 42 U.S.C. § 7602(g).

Criteria Pollutant—The term "criteria pollutant" derives from CAA Section 108(a)(2), which requires EPA to publish air quality "criteria" for each of the listed pollutants that will "accurately reflect the latest scientific knowledge useful in indicating the kind and extent of all identifiable effects on public health or welfare that which may be expected from the presence of such pollutant in the ambient air."

Engineered Nanoparticles—Those nanoparticles manufactured through construction at the molecular level.

Extremely Hazardous Substance—Extremely hazardous substances are not limited to the list of regulated substances listed under Section 112(r), nor the extremely hazardous substances under EPCRA § 302 (40 C.F.R. Part 355, Appendices A and B). "Extremely hazardous substance" would include any agent "which may or may not be listed or otherwise identified by any Government agency which may as the result of short-term exposures associated with releases to the air cause death, injury or property damage due to its toxicity, reactivity, flammability, volatility, or corrosivity." Senate Committee on Environment and Public Works, Clean Air Act Amendments of 1989, Senate Report No. 228, 101st Congress, 1st Session (1989) at 211 (Senate Report). "The release of any substance which causes death or serious injury because of its acute toxic effect or as a result of an explosion or fire or which causes substantial property damage by blast, fire, corrosion or other reaction would create a presumption that such substance is extremely hazardous." *Id.*

Hazardous Air Pollutant—A pollutant, other than a criteria pollutant, that causes severe health and/or environmental effects. "Any air pollutant listed pursuant to subsection (b) of [CAA Section 112]." CAA § 112(a)(6), 42 U.S.C. § 7412(a)(6).

Maximum Achievable Control Technology—The technology requirement for sources of hazardous emissions. For new sources, it must at least equal the most stringent level of control achieved in practice by a similar source. For existing sources, it must be no less stringent than the average level of control achieved by the "best performing" 12 percent of sources.

Mobile Source—A movable source of emissions (e.g., a motor vehicle, aircraft, train, or vessel).

National Ambient Air Quality Standard—Standards promulgated by EPA establishing the maximum concentration of criteria pollutants in the ambient air.

National Emission Standards for Hazardous Air Pollutants—The pre-1990 program for the regulation of hazardous air emissions.

New Source Performance Standard—Standards promulgated by EPA under CAA Section 111 for new stationary sources. A New Source Performance Standard provides the floor for all other technology requirements for new sources, including Best Available Control Technology and Lowest Achievable Emission Rate.

State Implementation Plan—A plan promulgated by a state to implement the state's regulatory obligations under the CAA, such as those that relate to attainment of a NAAQS. *See* CAA § 110, 42 U.S.C. § 7410.

Volatile Organic Compound—A group of substances that act as precursors to ozone. *See* 40 C.F.R. § 51.100(s).

Welfare—"All language referring to effects on welfare includes, but is not limited to, effects on soils, water, crops, vegetation, manmade materials, animals, wildlife, weather, visibility, and climate, damage to deterioration of property, and hazards to transportation, as well as effects on economic values and on personal comfort and well-being, whether caused by transformation, conversion, or combination with other air pollutants." CAA § 302(h), 42 U.S.C. § 7602(h).

ESA Terms

Conservation—Action that permits eventual recovery of the listed species to the point that it no longer requires ESA protection. ESA § 3(3), 16 U.S.C. § 1532(3).

Conservation Plan—The plan required by ESA Section 10(a)(2)(A) that an applicant must submit when applying for an incidental take permit. Conservation plans also are known as "habitat conservation plans." 50 C.F.R. § 17.3.

Critical Habitat—"For a threatened or endangered species means—(i) the specific areas within the geographical area occupied by the species, at the time it is listed in accordance with the provisions of [ESA] section 1533 . . . , on which are found those physical or biological features (I) essential to the conservation of the species and (II) which may require special management considerations or protection; and (ii) specific areas outside the geographical area occupied by the species at the time it is listed in accordance with the provisions of [ESA] section 1533 . . . , upon a determination by the Secretary that such areas are essential for the conservation of the species. (B) Critical habitat may be established for those species now listed as threatened or endangered species for which no critical habitat has heretofore been established as set forth in subparagraph (A) of this paragraph. (C) Except in those circumstances determined by the Secretary, critical habitat shall not include the entire geographical area which can be occupied by the threatened or endangered species." ESA § 3(5), 16 U.S.C. § 1532(5).

Endangered Species—"[A]ny species which is in danger of extinction throughout all or a significant portion of its range other than a species of the Class Insecta determined by the Secretary to constitute a pest whose protection under the provisions of this chapter would present an overwhelming and overriding risk to man." ESA § 3(6), 16 U.S.C. § 1532(6).

Harm—In the definition of "take" in the ESA, "harm" refers to an act that actually kills or injures wildlife. Such act may include significant habitat modification or degradation where it actually kills or injures wildlife by significantly impairing essential behavioral patterns, including breeding, feeding, or sheltering. 50 C.F.R. § 17.3.

Incidental Take—Takings that result from, but are not the purpose of, carrying out an otherwise lawful activity conducted by the federal agency or applicant. 50 C.F.R. § 402.02.

Incidental Take Permit—A permit that exempts a permittee from the take prohibition of Section 9 of the ESA issued by the FWS or [the] NMFS pursuant to Section 10(a)(1)(B) of the ESA. *Habitat Conservation Handbook and Section 7 Consultation Handbook* at 8–4 (1996). *See also* ESA § 10(a)(1)(B), 16 U.S.C. § 1539(a)(1)(B).

Person—"[A]n individual, corporation, partnership, trust, association, or any other private entity; or any officer, employee, agent, department, or instrumentality of the Federal Government, of any State, municipality, or political subdivision of a State, or of any foreign government; any State, municipality, or political subdivision of a State; or any other entity subject to the jurisdiction of the United States." ESA § 3(13), 16 U.S.C. § 1532(13).

Species—"[I]ncludes any subspecies of fish or wildlife or plants, and any distinct population segment of any species of vertebrate fish or wildlife which interbreeds when mature." ESA § 3(16), 16 U.S.C. § 1532(16).

Take—"[T]o harass, harm, pursue, hunt, shoot, wound, kill, trap, capture, or collect, or to attempt to engage in any such conduct." ESA § 3(19), 16 U.S.C. § 1532(19).

Threatened Species—"[A]ny species which is likely to become an endangered species within the foreseeable future throughout all or a significant portion of its range." ESA § 3(20), 16 U.S.C. § 1532(20).

RCRA Terms

Conditionally Exempt Small Quantity Generator (CESQG)—CESQGs generate 100 kilograms or less per month of hazardous waste, or 1 kilogram or less per month of acutely hazardous waste. Requirements for CESQGs include

- CESQGs must identify all the hazardous waste generated.
- CESQGs may not accumulate more than 1,000 kilograms of hazardous waste at any time.
- CESQGs must ensure that hazardous waste is delivered to a person or facility who is authorized to manage it.

See EPA, *Conditionally Exempt Small Quantity Generators*, http://www .epa.gov/osw/hazard/generation/cesqg.htm (last visited July 27, 2009); *see also* 40 C.F.R. § 261.5.

Hazardous Waste—"[A] solid waste, or combination of solid wastes, which because of its quantity, concentration, or physical, chemical, or infectious characteristics may—(A) cause, or significantly contribute to an increase in mortality or an increase in serious irreversible, or incapacitating reversible, illness; or (B) pose a substantial present or potential hazard to human health or the environment when improperly treated, stored, transported, or disposed of, or otherwise managed." SWDA § 1004(5), 42 U.S.C. § 6903(5). *See also* 40 C.F.R. § 261.3.

Large Quantity Generator (LQG)—LQGs generate 1,000 kilograms per month or more of hazardous waste, or more than 1 kilogram per month of acutely hazardous waste. Requirements for LQGs include

- LQGs may only accumulate waste on-site for 90 days. Certain exceptions apply.

- LQGs do not have a limit on the amount of hazardous waste accumulated on-site.
- There must always be at least one employee available to respond to an emergency. This employee is the emergency coordinator responsible for coordinating all emergency response measures.
- LQGs must have detailed, written contingency plans for handling emergencies.
- LQGs must submit a biennial hazardous waste report.

See EPA, *Large Quantity Generators*, http://www.epa.gov/osw/hazard/generation/lqg.htm (last visited July 27, 2009).

Small Quantity Generator (SQG)—SQGs generate more than 100 kilograms, but less than 1,000 kilograms, of hazardous waste per month. Requirements for SQGs include

- SQGs may accumulate hazardous waste on-site for 180 days without a permit (or 270 days if shipping a distance greater than 200 miles).
- The quantity of hazardous on site waste must never exceed 6,000 kilograms.
- There must always be at least one employee available to respond to an emergency. This employee is the emergency coordinator responsible for coordinating all emergency response measures. SQGs are not required to have detailed, written contingency plans.

See EPA, *Small Quantity Generators*, http://www.epa.gov/osw/hazard/generation/sqg/index.htm (last visited July 27, 2009).

Solid Waste—"[A]ny garbage, refuse, sludge from a waste treatment plant, water supply treatment plant, or air pollution control facility and other discarded material, including solid, liquid, semisolid, or contained gaseous material resulting from industrial, commercial, mining, and agricultural operations, and from community activities, but does not include solid or dissolved material in domestic sewage, or solid or dissolved materials in irrigation return flows or industrial discharges which are point sources subject to permits under section 1342 of Title 33, or source, special nuclear, or byproduct material as defined by the Atomic Energy Act of 1954, as amended. . . ." SWDA § 1004(27), 42 U.S.C. § 6903(27). *See also* 40 C.F.R. § 261.2.

Totally Enclosed Treatment Facility—"[A] facility for the treatment of hazardous waste which is directly connected to an industrial production process and which is constructed and operated in a manner which prevents the release of any hazardous waste or any constituent thereof into the environment during treatment. An example is a pipe in which waste acid is neutralized." 40 C.F.R. § 260.10.

CERCLA Terms

Extremely Hazardous Substances (EHS)—According to EPA, "[t]he EHS list was first compiled by EPA, and subsequently incorporated into EPCRA, to identify chemicals that could cause serious irreversible health effects from accidental releases. EHSs are listed in 40 CFR Part 355. . . . There are currently about 360 EHSs defined under EPCRA section 302; over a third of them are also CERCLA hazardous substances. Aside from this overlap of listed substances, CERCLA and EPCRA also have closely related notification requirements when releases of CERCLA hazardous substances occur." EPA, *Reportable Quantities*, http://www.epa.gov/superfund/policy/release/rq/index.htm (last visited July 27, 2009).

Facility—"(A) any building, structure, installation, equipment, pipe or pipeline (including any pipe into a sewer or publicly owned treatment works), well, pit, pond, lagoon, impoundment, ditch, landfill, storage container, motor vehicle, rolling stock, or aircraft, or (B) any site or area where a hazardous substance has been deposited, stored, disposed of, or placed, or otherwise come to be located; but does not include any consumer product in consumer use or any vessel." CERCLA § 101(9), 42 U.S.C. § 9601(9).

Hazardous Substance—"(A) any substance designated pursuant to [CWA Section 311(b)(2)(A)], (B) any element, compound, mixture, solution, or substance designated pursuant to [CERCLA Section 102], (C) any hazardous waste having the characteristics identified under or listed pursuant to [SWDA Section 3001] . . . (but not including any waste the regulation of which under the [SWDA] . . . has been suspended by Act of Congress), (D) any toxic pollutant listed under [CWA Section 307(a)], (E) any hazardous air pollutant listed under [CAA Section 112] . . . , and (F) any imminently hazardous chemical substance or mixture with respect to which the Administrator has taken action pursuant to TSCA Section 7]. The term does not include petroleum, including crude oil or any fraction thereof which is not otherwise specifically listed or designated as a hazardous substance under subparagraphs (A) through (F) of this paragraph, and the term does not include natural gas, natural gas liquids, liquefied natural gas, or synthetic gas usable for fuel (or mixtures of natural gas and such synthetic gas)." CERCLA § 101(14), 42 U.S.C. § 9601(14).

Hazard Ranking System—"The Hazard Ranking System (HRS) is the principal mechanism EPA uses to place uncontrolled waste sites on the National Priorities List (NPL). It is a numerically based screening system that uses information from initial, limited investigations—the preliminary assessment and the site inspection—to assess the relative potential of sites to pose a threat to human health or the environment. Any person or organization can petition EPA to conduct a preliminary assessment using the Preliminary Assessment Petition." EPA, *Introduction to the Hazard Ranking System*, http://www.epa.gov/superfund/programs/npl_hrs/hrsint.htm (last visited July 27, 2009).

National Contingency Plan—"[T]he national contingency plan published under section 1321(c) of Title 33 or revised pursuant to [CERCLA Section 105]." CERCLA § 101(31), 42 U.S.C. § 9601(31).

National Priorities List—"The National Priorities List is a list of the worst hazardous waste sites that have been identified by Superfund. Sites are only put on the list after they have been scored using the Hazard Ranking System (HRS), and have been subjected to public comment. Any site on the NPL is eligible for cleanup using Superfund trust money." EPA, *Frequent Questions about Superfund Redevelopment*, http://www.epa.gov/superfund/programs/recycle/faqs/index.html (last visited July 27, 2009).

Potentially Responsible Parties—"[CERCLA] describes four classes of potentially responsible parties:

- Current owners or operators,
- Owners or operators at the time of disposal,
- Generators and parties that arrange or arranged for disposal, and
- Transporters that select or selected disposal sites.

Current owners can be liable for a site without having contributed to the release. Current operators are any parties that control current operations at the site. The key factor in establishing the liability of a former owner or operator is that disposal must have occurred while the party owned or operated the site. Such owners or operators need not have contributed to the release.

The term *generator* has come to be used as the term for anyone who arranged for disposal (the definition differs from that under RCRA). Generators are often the largest group of PRPs, sometimes including thousands of people and companies at any given site." EPA, *Superfund Frequently Asked Questions: Superfund Enforcement*, http://

www.epa.gov/compliance/resources/faqs/cleanup/superfund/
enf-faqs.html (last visited July 27, 2009).

CWA Terms

Effluent Limitation—"[A]ny restriction imposed by the Director on quantities, discharge rates, and concentrations of 'pollutants' which are 'discharged' from 'point sources' into 'waters of the United States,' the waters of the 'contiguous zone,' or the ocean." 40 C.F.R. § 122.2.

Effluent Limitation Guidelines—"[A] regulation published by the Administrator under section 304(b) of CWA to adopt or revise 'effluent limitations.'" 40 C.F.R. § 122.2.

Hazardous Substance—"[A]ny substance designated pursuant to subsection (b)(2) [of CWA Section 311]." CWA § 311(a)(14), 33 U.S.C. § 1321(a)(14); *see also* 40 C.F.R. § 122.2.

CWA Section 311(b)(2)(A) states: "The Administrator shall develop, promulgate, and revise as may be appropriate, regulations designating as hazardous substances, other than oil as defined in this section, such elements and compounds which, when discharged in any quantity into or upon the navigable waters of the United States or adjoining shorelines or the waters of the contiguous zone or in connection with activities under the Outer Continental Shelf Lands Act [43 U.S.C. 1331 *et seq.*] or the Deepwater Port Act of 1974 [33 U.S.C. 1501 *et seq.*], or which may affect natural resources belonging to, appertaining to, or under the exclusive management authority of the United States (including resources under the Magnuson-Stevens Fishery Conservation and Management Act [16 U.S.C. 1801 *et seq.*]), present an imminent and substantial danger to the public health or welfare, including, but not limited to, fish, shellfish, wildlife, shorelines, and beaches." 33 U.S.C. § 1321(b)(2)(A).

Medical Waste—"[I]solation wastes; infectious agents; human blood and blood products; pathological wastes; sharps; body parts; contaminated bedding; surgical wastes and potentially contaminated laboratory wastes; dialysis wastes; and such additional medical items as the Administrator shall prescribe by regulation." CWA § 502(20), 33 U.S.C. § 1362(20).

National Pollutant Discharge Elimination System (NPDES)—The basic features of the NPDES program are (1) the issuance of point source discharge permits with pollutant-specific numeric effluent limitations based on either technology-forcing standards or water quality protection standards; (2) the measurement of compliance against those effluent limitations by routine and frequent monitoring of effluent quality using standardized sampling and analytical methods; and (3) the routine and frequent reporting of the effluent quality measurements through discharge monitoring reports that are readily available to and understandable by the public as well as regulators. *See* CWA § 402, 33 U.S.C. § 134.

"[T]he national program for issuing, modifying, revoking and reissuing, terminating, monitoring and enforcing permits, and imposing and enforcing pretreatment requirements, under sections 307, 402, 318, and 405 of CWA. The term includes an 'approved program.'" 40 C.F.R. § 122.2.

National Pretreatment Program—"The national pretreatment program (CWA Section 307(b)) controls the indirect discharge of pollutants to POTWs by "industrial users." Facilities regulated under Section 307(b) must meet certain pretreatment standards. The goal of the pretreatment program is to protect municipal wastewater treatment plants from damage that may occur when hazardous, toxic, or other wastes are discharged into a sewer system and to protect the quality of sludge generated by these plants. Discharges to a POTW are regulated primarily by the POTW itself, rather than the state/tribe or EPA." EPA, *Clean Water Act*, http://www.epa.gov/oecaagct/lcwa.html#Nonpoint%20Source%20Pollution (last visited July 27, 2009).

Navigable Waters—"[T]he waters of the United States, including the territorial seas." CWA § 502(7), 33 U.S.C. § 1362(7).

Nonpoint Source Pollutants—"Nonpoint source (NPS) pollution, unlike pollution from industrial and sewage treatment plants, comes from many diffuse sources. NPS pollution is caused by rainfall or snowmelt moving over and through the ground. As the runoff moves, it picks up and carries away natural and human-made pollutants, finally depositing them into lakes, rivers, wetlands, coastal waters, and even underground sources of drinking water.

These pollutants include

- Excess fertilizers, herbicides, and insecticides from agricultural lands and residential areas
- Oil, grease, and toxic chemicals from urban runoff and energy production
- Sediment from improperly managed construction sites, crop and forest lands, and eroding stream banks
- Salt from irrigation practices and acid drainage from abandoned mines

- Bacteria and nutrients from livestock, pet wastes, and faulty septic systems
- Pollutants resulting from atmospheric deposition and hydro-modification."

EPA, *Clean Water Act*, http://www.epa.gov/oecaagct/lcwa.html# Nonpoint%20Source%20Pollution (last visited July 27, 2009).

Point Source—"[A]ny discernible, confined and discrete conveyance, including but not limited to any pipe, ditch, channel, tunnel, conduit, well, discrete fissure, container, rolling stock, concentrated animal feeding operation, or vessel or other floating craft, from which pollutants are or may be discharged. This term does not include agricultural stormwater discharges and return flows from irrigated agriculture." CWA § 502(14), 33 U.S.C. § 1362(14); 40 C.F.R. § 122.2.

Pollutant—"[D]redged spoil, solid waste, incinerator residue, sewage, garbage, sewage sludge, munitions, chemical wastes, biological materials, radioactive materials, heat, wrecked or discarded equipment, rock, sand, cellar dirt and industrial, municipal, and agricultural waste discharged into water. This term does not mean (A) 'sewage from vessels or a discharge incidental to the normal operation of a vessel of the Armed Forces' within the meaning of section 1322 of this title; or (B) water, gas, or other material which is injected into a well to facilitate production of oil or gas, or water derived in association with oil or gas production and disposed of in a well, if the well used either to facilitate production or for disposal purposes is approved by authority of the State in which the well is located, and if such State determines that such injection or disposal will not result in the degradation of ground or surface water resources." CWA § 502(6), 33 U.S.C. § 1362(6); 40 C.F.R. § 122.2.

Publicly Owned Treatment Work (POTW)—"[A] treatment works as defined by section 212 of the Act, which is owned by a State or municipality (as defined by section 502(4) of the Act). This definition includes any devices and systems used in the storage, treatment, recycling and reclamation of municipal sewage or industrial wastes of a liquid nature. It also includes sewers, pipes and other conveyances only if they convey wastewater to a POTW Treatment Plant. The term also means the municipality as defined in section 502(4) of the Act, which has jurisdiction over the Indirect Discharges to and the discharges from such a treatment works." 40 C.F.R. § 403.3(q).

Standard of Performance—"'[S]tandard of performance' means a standard for the control of the discharge of pollutants which reflect the greatest degree of effluent reduction which the Administrator determines to be achievable through application of the best available demonstrated control technology, processes, operating methods, or other alternatives, including, where practicable, a standard permitting no discharge of pollutants." CWA § 306, 33 U.S.C. § 1316.

Total Maximum Daily Load—According to EPA's Clean Water Act website, "[s]ome waters in the nation still do not meet the Clean Water Act national goal of 'fishable, swimmable' despite the fact that nationally required levels of pollution control technology have been implemented by many pollution sources. Clean Water Act Section 1313 addresses these waters that are not 'fishable, swimmable' by requiring states to identify the waters and to develop total maximum daily loads (TMDLs) for them, with oversight from the U.S. Environmental Protection Agency. As such, TMDLs can play a key role in watershed management. . . . Each state must identify waters at risk and establish Total Daily Maximum Loads (TMDLs) to protect those waters. This includes identification of needed load reductions within a watershed from agricultural producers and other nonpoint sources. These load reductions are to be achieved through nonpoint source programs established under Clean Water Act Section 319 and Coastal Zone Act Reauthorization Amendment (CZARA) section 6217." EPA, *Clean Water Act*, http://www.epa.gov/oecaagct/lcwa.html#Nonpoint%20 Source%20Pollution (last visited July 27, 2009).

Toxic Pollutant—"[T]hose pollutants, or combinations of pollutants, including disease-causing agents, which after discharge and upon exposure, ingestion, inhalation or assimilation into any organism, either directly from the environment or indirectly by ingestion through food chains, will, on the basis of information available to the Administrator, cause death, disease, behavioral abnormalities, cancer, genetic mutations, physiological malfunctions (including malfunctions in reproduction) or physical deformations, in such organisms or their offspring." CWA § 502(13), 33 U.S.C. § 1362(13); *see also* 40 C.F.R. § 122.2.

Governance Terms

Active Nanostructures—The International Risk Governance Council (IRGC) recognizes four generations of nanotechnologies. Second-generation *active nanostructures* have properties that are expected to change during operation, so behavior is variable and potentially unstable. These nanostructures are beginning to emerge. IRGC, *White*

Paper on Nanotechnology Risk Governance (June 2006) at 14; IRGC, *Policy Brief, Nanotechnology Risk Governance: Recommendations for a Global Coordinated Approach to the Governance of Potential Risks* (2007) at 7.

Heterogeneous Molecular Nanosystems—The IRGC recognizes four generations of nanotechnologies. Fourth-generation *heterogeneous molecular nanosystems* allow engineered nanosystems and architectures to be created from individual molecules or supramolecular components, each of which have a specific structure and are designed to play a particular role. Fundamentally new functions and processes begin to emerge with the behavior of applications being based on that of biological systems and could include nanoscale genetic therapies. Heterogeneous systems are anticipated after 2015. IRGC, *White Paper on Nanotechnology Risk Governance* (June 2006) at 14; IRGC, *Policy Brief, Nanotechnology Risk Governance: Recommendations for a Global Coordinated Approach to the Governance of Potential Risks* (2007) at 7.

Integrated Nanosystems—The IRGC recognizes four generations of nanotechnologies. Third-generation *integrated nanosystems* are systems in which passive or active nanostructures are integrated into systems using nanoscale synthesis and assembling techniques. These systems will develop based on the convergence of nanotechnology, biotechnology, information technology, and the cognitive sciences and could include artificial organs. Nanosystems are expected to be in use after 2010. IRGC, *White Paper on Nanotechnology Risk Governance* (June 2006) at 14; IRGC, *Policy Brief, Nanotechnology Risk Governance: Recommendations for a Global Coordinated Approach to the Governance of Potential Risks* (2007) at 7.

Passive Nanostructures—The IRGC recognizes four generations of nanotechnologies. First-generation *passive nanostructures* have stable behavior and quasi-consistent properties during their use and include intermediary system components such as particles, wires and nanotubes. These nanostructures have been in existence since about the year 2000. IRGC, *White Paper on Nanotechnology Risk Governance* (June 2006) at 14; IRGC, *Policy Brief, Nanotechnology Risk Governance: Recommendations for a Global Coordinated Approach to the Governance of Potential Risks* (2007) at 7.

NEPA Terms

Environmental Assessment—"(a) Means a concise public document for which a Federal agency is responsible that serves to: (1) Briefly provide sufficient evidence and analysis for determining whether to prepare an environmental impact statement or a finding of no significant impact. (2) Aid an agency's compliance with the Act when no environmental impact statement is necessary. (3) Facilitate preparation of a statement when one is necessary. (b) Shall include brief discussions of the need for the proposal, of alternatives as required by section 102(2)(E), of the environmental impacts of the proposed action and alternatives, and a listing of agencies and persons consulted." 40 C.F.R. § 1508.9.

Environmental Impact Statement—"[A] detailed written statement as required by section 102(2)(C) of the Act." 40 C.F.R. § 1508.11.

Finding of No Significant Impact—"[A] document by a Federal agency briefly presenting the reasons why an action, not otherwise excluded (Sec. 1508.4), will not have a significant effect on the human environment and for which an environmental impact statement therefore will not be prepared. It shall include the environmental assessment or a summary of it and shall note any other environmental documents related to it (Sec. 1501.7(a)(5)). If the assessment is included, the finding need not repeat any of the discussion in the assessment but may incorporate it by reference." 40 C.F.R. § 1508.13.

Major Federal Actions—"[I]ncludes actions with effects that may be major and which are potentially subject to Federal control and responsibility. Major reinforces but does not have a meaning independent of significantly (Sec. 1508.27). Actions include the circumstance where the responsible officials fail to act and that failure to act is reviewable by courts or administrative tribunals under the Administrative Procedure Act or other applicable law as agency action. (a) Actions include new and continuing activities, including projects and programs entirely or partly financed, assisted, conducted, regulated, or approved by federal agencies; new or revised agency rules, regulations, plans, policies, or procedures; and legislative proposals (Sec. 1506.8, 1508.17). Actions do not include funding assistance solely in the form of general revenue sharing funds, distributed under the State and Local Fiscal Assistance Act of 1972, 31 U.S.C. 1221 *et seq.*, with no Federal agency control over the subsequent use of such funds. Actions do not include bringing judicial or administrative civil or criminal enforcement actions. (b) Federal actions tend to fall within one of the following categories: (1) Adoption of official policy, such as rules, regulations, and interpretations adopted pursuant to the Administrative Procedure Act, 5 U.S.C. 551 *et seq.*; treaties and international conventions or agreements; formal documents establishing an agency's policies which will result in or substantially alter agency programs. (2) Adoption of formal plans, such as official documents prepared or approved by federal agencies which guide or prescribe alternative uses of Federal resources, upon which future agency actions will be based. (3) Adoption of programs, such as a group of concerted actions to implement a specific policy or plan; systematic and connected agency decisions allocating agency resources to implement a specific statutory program or executive directive. (4) Approval of specific projects, such as construction or management activities located in a defined geographic area. Projects include actions approved by permit or other regulatory decision as well as federal and federally assisted activities." 40 C.F.R. § 1508.18.

Nanometer—One-billionth of a meter.

Nanoscale—Particles a mere 1 to 100 nanometers in size.

Nanotechnology—The creation, design, and manipulation of materials at the nanoscale.

National Nanotechnology Initiative—"The National Nanotechnology Initiative (NNI) is the program established in fiscal year 2001 to coordinate Federal nanotechnology research and development.

The NNI provides a vision of the long-term opportunities and benefits of nanotechnology. By serving as a central locus for communication, cooperation, and collaboration for all Federal agencies that wish to participate, the NNI brings together the expertise needed to guide and support the advancement of this broad and complex field.

The NNI creates a framework for a comprehensive nanotechnology R&D program by establishing shared goals, priorities, and strategies, and it provides avenues for each individual agency to leverage the resources of all participating agencies.

Today the NNI consists of the individual and cooperative nanotechnology-related activities of 25 Federal agencies with a range of research and regulatory roles and responsibilities. Thirteen of the participating agencies have R&D budgets that relate to nanotechnology, with the reported NNI budget representing the collective sum of these. The NNI as a program does not fund research; however, it informs and influences the Federal budget and planning processes through its member agencies." NNI, *About the NNI—Home*, http://www.nano.gov/html/about/home_about.html (last visited July 27, 2009).

Tiering—"Tiering refers to the coverage of general matters in broader environmental impact statements (such as national program or policy statements) with subsequent narrower statements or environmental analyses (such as regional or basinwide program statements or ultimately site-specific statements) incorporating by reference the general discussions and concentrating solely on the issues specific to the statement subsequently prepared. Tiering is appropriate when the sequence of statements or analyses is: (a) From a program, plan, or policy environmental impact statement to a program, plan, or policy statement or analysis of lesser scope or to a site-specific statement or analysis. (b) From an environmental impact statement on a specific action at an early stage (such as need and site selection) to a supplement (which is preferred) or a subsequent statement or analysis at a later stage (such as environmental mitigation). Tiering in such cases is appropriate when it helps the lead agency to focus on the issues which are ripe for decision and exclude from consideration issues already decided or not yet ripe." 40 C.F.R. § 1508.28.

INDEX

A

ACC (American Chemistry Council), 196
accidental release of extremely hazardous substances, 106–108
accountability
   flexible permitting and, 188–189
   government regulation and, 187–188
   liability and, 195–196
   life-cycle analysis and, 186
   need for, 186
   public involvement and, 189–193
   self-regulation and, 196–198
   system, 198–199
   voluntary programs for, 193–195
acid deposition control, 112
active nanostructures, 180
Administrative Procedure Act, 22–23
Agency for Toxic Substances and Disease Registry (ATSDR), 152
air filters, 101–103
air pollutant emissions measurement, 97–99
air pollutant emissions modeling, 99–100

air pollutants, hazardous, 105–108
air pollution control technology, 100–102
air quality
   criteria for, 100–103
   emissions measurement in, 97–99
   emissions modeling in, 99–100
   hazardous pollutants, 105–106
   new source performance standards, 104
   pollution control and, 100–103
   stack heights and, 108
American Chemistry Council (ACC), 196
ATSDR (Agency for Toxic Substances and Disease Registry), 152

B

Babbitt v. Sweet Home, 118, 124–125
BGH (bovine growth hormone), 183
biological opinion (BiOp), 123
bovine growth hormone (BGH), 183
buckyballs, 165

C

CAA. *See* Clean Air Act (CAA)
capsules, for nanopesticides, 89